CRE▲TIVE
HOMEOWNER®

BUILD A KIDS' PLAY YARD

By Jeff Beneke

CREATIVE HOMEOWNER®, Upper Saddle River, New Jersey

Editorial Director: Timothy O. Bakke
Art Director: Annie Jeon

Editors: David Schiff, Neil Soderstrom
Copy Editor: Margaret Gallos
Editorial Assistant: Albert Huang

Graphic Designer: Melisa DelSordo

Project Editor/Illustrator: Paul M. Schumm

Illustrators: Craig Franklin
             Vincent Alessi

Cover Design: Annie Jeon
Book Design Concept: Michael James Allegra
Cover Photo: Freeze Frame Studio
Inside photos by: Freeze Frame Studio
                  Paul M. Schumm
                  Neil Soderstrom

Site Construction: Brian Tobin

Children in Photos: Kealan Bakke, Douglas Garvey,
   Jamie White Goode, Kelly Hommen, Clara Jeon,
   David Jeon, Dena Lagomarsino, Peter Lagomarsino,
   Bret Logan, Christiana Pulice, Daniel Teitell,
   Erin Tobin, Mathew Tobin, Michael Tobin

Manufactured in the United States of America

Current Printing (last digit)
10 9 8 7 6 5

Build a Kids' Play Yard
Library of Congress Catalog Card Number:
  97–075271
ISBN: 1-58011-001-0

CREATIVE HOMEOWNER®
A Division of Federal Marketing Corp.
24 Park Way, Upper Saddle River, NJ 07458
Web site: **www.creativehomeowner.com**

Safety First

Though all the designs and methods in this book have been reviewed for safety, it is not possible to overstate the importance of using the safest construction methods possible. What follows are reminders—some do's and don'ts of basic carpentry. They are not substitutes for your own common sense.

▲ *Always* use caution, care, and good judgment when following the procedures described in this book.

▲ *Always* be sure that the electrical setup is safe; be sure that no circuit is overloaded, and that all power tools and electrical outlets are properly grounded. Do not use power tools in wet locations.

▲ *Always* read container labels on paints, solvents, and other products; provide ventilation, and observe all other warnings.

▲ *Always* read the tool manufacturer's instructions for using a tool, especially the warnings.

▲ *Always* remove the key from any drill chuck (portable or press) before starting the drill.

▲ *Always* know the limitations of your tools. Do not try to force them to do what they were not designed to do.

▲ *Always* make sure that any adjustment is locked before proceeding.

▲ *Always* wear the appropriate rubber or work gloves when handling chemicals, doing heavy construction, or sanding.

▲ *Always* wear a disposable face mask when working around odors, dust, or mist. Use a special filtering respirator when working with toxic substances.

▲ *Always* wear eye protection, especially when using power tools or striking metal on metal or concrete;

▲ *Always* keep your hands away from the business ends of blades, cutters, and bits.

▲ *Always* check your local building codes when planning new construction. The codes are intended to protect public safety.

▲ *Never* work with power tools when you are tired or under the influence of alcohol or drugs.

▲ *Never* cut very small pieces of wood or pipe. Whenever possible, cut small pieces off larger pieces.

▲ *Never* change a blade or a bit unless the power cord is unplugged.

▲ *Never* work while wearing loose clothing, hanging hair, open cuffs, or jewelry

▲ *Never* use a power tool on a workpiece that is not firmly supported or clamped.

▲ *Never* support a workpiece from underneath with your leg or other part of your body when sawing.

▲ *Never* carry sharp or pointed tools, such as utility knives, awls, or chisels, in your pocket. If you want to carry tools, use a special-purpose tool belt with leather pockets and holders.

Contents

Introduction 4

Part One: Materials & Methods 7

   1. Planning & Design 8

   2. Tools 19

   3. Materials 28

   4. Techniques 41

   5. Finishing & Maintenance 58

Part Two: Kids' Playland 63

   6. Central Tower 66

   7. Swing Frame 83

   8. Monkey Bar 92

Part Three: Stand-Alone Projects 99

   9. Playhouse 101

   10. Sandboxes 114

   11. Balance Beam 123

   12. Picnic Table 127

   13. Teeter-Totter 132

Glossary 139

Index 140

Introduction

The Rewards of Play Structures. Few sights are more pleasant than children at play—running, jumping, climbing, and swinging as though life had no other purpose. Although play is usually carefree, it is much more than a mere release of energy.

Like the classroom and library, the play yard can be a center for learning and other vital development. In fact, play is an important component of a lifelong process of learning. Play, in its many forms, greatly contributes to a child's physical, cognitive, and social development.

The most obvious benefit of a play yard is physical exercise. Here a child can improve coordination, motor skills, strength, agility, balance, and endurance.

The play yard also stimulates a child's imagination and requires problem solving. And during group play, children learn verbal and other socialization skills, such as cooperating, sharing, and group decision making. These experiences help a child outgrow the self-centeredness of infancy and become more considerate.

Besides benefiting children, a play structure rewards its builder. Your "labor of love" can provide immense personal satisfaction. And because play structures will be used and appreciated for years, they will continue to reward you.

All projects in this book were designed for durability, safety, and enjoyment. A durable structure withstands the elements, as well as the punishment of active children. A safe structure minimizes potential for injuries and includes impact-reducing materials, such as wood chips or pea gravel, to cushion falls and landings. As to enjoyment, the projects have proven "kid appeal."

The Kids' Playland, with its Central Tower, Swing Beam, and Monkey Bar, allows you to customize the layout to available space and to the ages and interests of your kids. It also gives you options for building in stages—one module at a time.

Other projects include the Playhouse, the Picnic Table, the Teeter-Totter, and relatively simple sandboxes and balance beams. If you want to begin gradually, perhaps to build confidence in your abilities, begin with one of the simpler projects.

Project Difficulties and Tools Required.
Beginning with Chapter 6, each chapter opens with an illustration of the completed project and an illustration with an information box that indicates difficulty level and tools required. The difficulty level is represented by one, two, or three hammers, as shown here.

🔨 Easy, even for beginners

🔨🔨 Moderately difficult, but can be done by beginners who have the patience and willingness to learn.

🔨🔨🔨 Difficult. Can be done by a do-it-yourselfer, but requires a serious investment in time, patience, and specialty tools. Consider hiring a carpenter for some or all of the tasks.

You will often have the option of using either hand or power tools. For example, you may prefer to use hand drills, rather than an electric drill, for easier projects. So the information box may simply indicate "drilling tools," rather than indicate a preference. Illustrations throughout each project chapter and in Chapter 4, on techniques, show virtually all tool options. In Chapter 4, you'll also find safety tips and consumer guidance.

Part 1

Materials & Methods

This part of the book explains how to plan and design your play yard, and then how to choose and use tools and materials. Here you'll also find complete guidance on selecting projects. This includes optional configurations for the Kids' Playland, which has modules consisting of a Central Tower with slide, a Swing Beam, and a Monkey Bar.

We heartily recommend that even preschoolers be involved in planning and design, but we don't recommend that they participate in the construction itself, especially in procedures that involve edged tools and power tools. During construction, ensure that such tools stay out of reach of youngsters.

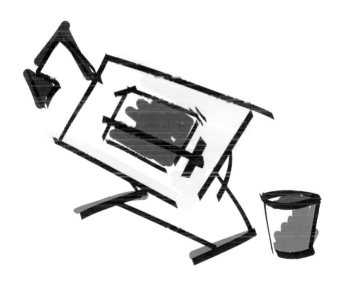

1 **Planning & Design**   **8**

2 **Tools**   **19**

3 **Materials**   **28**

4 **Techniques**   **41**

5 **Finishing & Maintenance**   **58**

1

Planning & Design

The end result may be play. But the process of planning and designing a play structure should not be taken lightly.

A play structure will make significant changes in the appearance and function of your yard, and you may need to live with them for years. A play structure will also require a significant investment of money and time. So you will want a finished project that looks good, functions properly, and lasts. The best way to achieve these objectives is to plan carefully.

Consider the kind of structure you want and can afford, as well as the best location in your yard. Then decide how much of the work you would feel comfortable doing yourself and how the final structure would affect your view and that of your neighbors. Even a modest play structure can affect a property's attractiveness and function.

Planning Ahead

Kids have a seemingly inexhaustible need for play. Even toddlers, with notoriously short attention spans, can remain content for long periods on a playground that offers a variety of appropriate diversions and challenges. Of course, as the children age and require less and less direct supervision, they develop preferences for new types of playground activities. But their need for play doesn't diminish.

Therefore, one of the design challenges is to find ways to incorporate a range of activities that can interest the youngest and oldest kids alike. Preschoolers have different physical and cognitive abilities from school kids. To ensure long-term use, the structures must "mature" in their offerings along with your children. To achieve this objective, there are two options: You could build a big, multi-functional Kids' Playland now, containing all of the components you anticipate needing in years to come.

Or you could go modular by building only what your kids would like now, with the intention of adapting and adding components later.

This book is organized to allow for either of the above two options. For example, you could build an elevated Central Tower with a slide now. Later, you could add the Swing Frame. As your kids become old enough, you might want to tack on the Monkey Bar or build it and the Swing Frame to stand alone. Or you may want to start with one of the other projects.

Kids' Playland and Other Projects

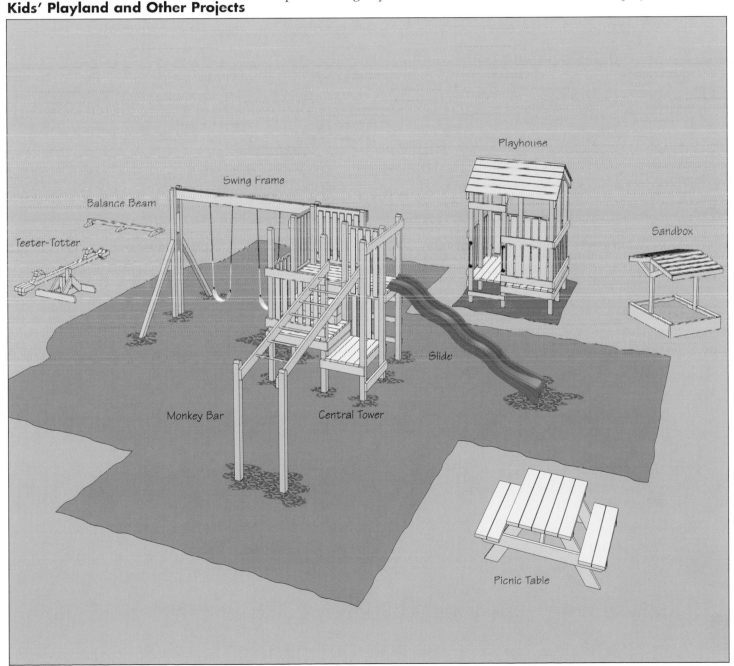

If you have doubts about what to build first, take your kids to a busy public playground and just watch. Also, study kids of various ages. See what they enjoy most, also what they are capable of or have difficulty with. One thing you will notice is that kids don't generally play with one component or in one spot for long periods. Rather, they move from one component to another. There is an important lesson in this. If given only one activity, kids will get bored. It's important to give them lots of choices.

Choosing the Site

For many families, there aren't many site options for a play structure. Your biggest challenge may be fitting your planned project into a small area. The site should be relatively level and, ideally, shouldn't interfere much with the other uses for your yard, such as picnics, games, pet runs, and relaxation. Although the backyard is usually the best location for most structures, don't automatically rule out the front yard or a side yard location that is visible from the street, if local codes allow it.

Creating Safe Spacing. Even if your siting choices are limited, it is still important to allow plenty of space for each structure, as well as "elbow room" for safe play, without overlooking the other functions of the yard. If your space is tight, you would probably be wiser to build just the Central Tower with enough free space around it than to attempt to squeeze more modules in.

Keep play structures well away from roads, sidewalks, and any other natural pathways that are likely to have people on them. This is especially important with regard to the Swing Frame: Don't let the path of swing intersect a pathway. On newer public playgrounds, you will probably notice

that the swings are isolated from the other parts of the playground. This improves playground safety by keeping the swingers away from other activities. Even if you've got little room in your yard, be sure to consider safety zoning. Likewise, position the exit chute of a slide to minimize the chance of sliding into traffic.

If you are building for preschoolers, remember that they need to be

supervised or at least watched within calling distance. You may also want to choose a spot that allows a parent or other supervisor to sit comfortably, out of the sun.

Considering Sun and Wind.
Environmental and physical factors that affect the amount and type of light, the velocity and direction of wind, and the effect of rain and snowfall may determine your siting.

Midday summer sun casts little shadow.

Afternoon winter sun covers the north and east sides in shadow.

Wind

Wind

House Windbreak

Tree Windbreak

Considering Sun and Wind. In positioning the Kids' Playland, take account of sun, shade, and wind through the seasons.

When you have a rough idea of the style of play structure you like, you need to decide which way it will face. For this, consider the effects of sun and shade.

A play structure in an unshaded location may become quite a hot spot in summer. For example, if you plan to install a metal slide, you may want to situate it on a northerly side to minimize its heating in the sun. At the same time, you probably won't want the structure entirely in the shade. So try to find a site that provides a good balance of sun and shade. Remember, the location and angle of the sun will change through the seasons. Although the low-angle winter sun may cast longer shadows in your yard, the high-angle summer sun may strike more of the play structure, unless trees protect it.

If your yard is subject to strong winds, consider possibilities for wind protection. For example, try to find a site that is downwind of a line of trees, or even your house. At the very least, if wind is a problem, create some relatively wind-free sanctuaries within the structure.

Footprint with Safety Zones. The full space requirement for the Kid's Playland includes the footprint of the components themselves, plus the safety zones extending from each. The illustrations below and on the next page show possible configurations and footprints.

Ideally, all of the zones should be filled with impact-reducing material, such as wood mulch or pea gravel, to depths recommended in the table "Impact-Reducing Materials" on page 35. The illustration below shows that the Playland, with safety zones, needs a large footprint. Following this recommendation, you ensure that impact-reducing material would soften the landing of a child falling or jumping from any part of the play structure, including extended swing arcs.

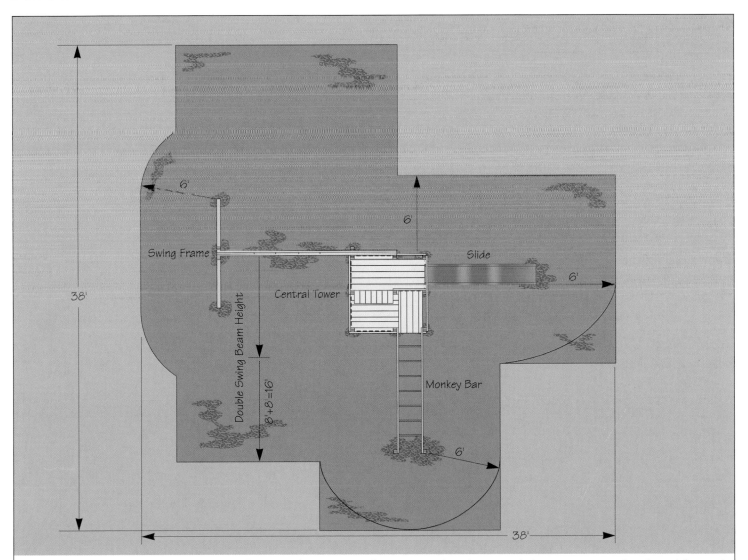

Footprint with Safety Zones. For safety, extend an impact-reducing material, such as wood chips or pea gravel, at least 6 feet out from all parts of the structure and at least double the farthest reach of the arc of the swings.

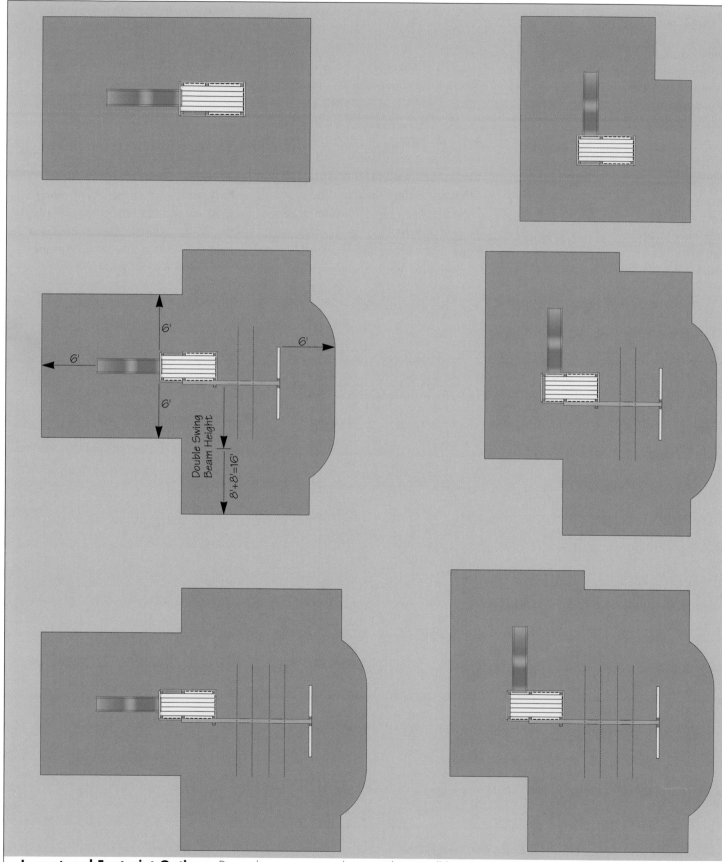

Layout and Footprint Options. Depending on your yard space, the overall layout can take many shapes with components located in separate parts of the yard. As shown, the components can be assembled to provide different footprints. Extend impact-reducing material 6 feet from structural parts and double the height of the swing beam.

Preparing a Site Plan

Once you have a rough idea of the type structure you want, the best way to visualize how much yard it will occupy is to make a scaled drawing, called a site plan. For this you can use a copy of your property's official survey map, or you can use graph paper or just plain paper and an architect's rule.

Incidentally, this is a great stage to involve your kids, if they are old enough. Just head out into the yard with paper, measuring tools, and pencil.

If you use graph paper, also called quadrille paper, use large 11x17-inch sheets or tape two 8½x11-inch pages together so that grids on their adjoining edges line up. Let each square on the paper equal 12 inches. Begin by drawing your property lines on the paper. Measure from your property lines to your house on all sides, and transfer those measurements to the graph paper. Then draw the house outline on the paper. Proceed in this fashion until you have included all important features of your yard on the graph paper.

Note: Also indicate obstacles and utilities, such as trees, phone and electric lines, septic system, well, and water pipes. Because you will be digging holes and setting posts, you need to avoid these obstacles. For example, you wouldn't want your Central Tower reaching near electrical wires. Also, be sure to consider the layout's relationships to entries to the house and other toy-storage buildings.

Now that you can see how much yard space is available for the play structure and its safety zones, you can begin sketching layout options.

Using an Architect's Rule

An architect's rule is designed for use with either plain paper or graph paper. It's a bit more complicated to use than a tape measure and graph paper, but it is more versatile. As shown, the architect's rule has three faces, which architects use to create scale versions of buildings and sites. A typical rule has 11 scales, ranging from 3/32 inch to 1 inch, that allow you to quickly translate 1-foot units on the ground into smaller units on the scale. Thus, if you use the 1/8-inch scale, each 1/8 inch on paper should equal 1 foot on your yard. For most accurate results, use the largest scale that your paper size allows. Once you decide which scale to use, make a note of it on your drawing, such as "Scale 1/8." That will remind you which scale to use when you return to the drawing. For an average-size yard, you will probably want to use 11x17-inch paper and either the 1/8-inch or the 1/4-inch scale.

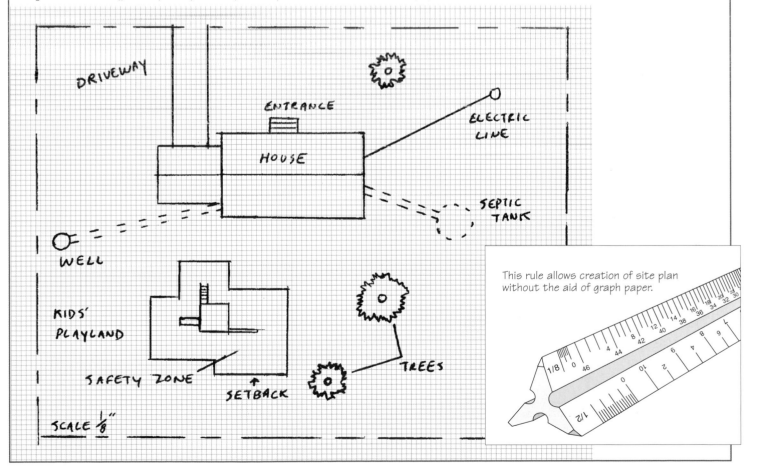

DRIVEWAY

ENTRANCE

ELECTRIC LINE

HOUSE

SEPTIC TANK

WELL

KIDS' PLAYLAND

SAFETY ZONE

SETBACK

TREES

SCALE 1/8"

This rule allows creation of site plan without the aid of graph paper.

The next step is to mark proposed outlines in the yard itself, using string and stakes.

Reducing Hazards

Wherever kids are playing, accidents and injuries will occur. While you cannot build a perfectly safe play structure, you can build one that minimizes the chances of serious injury without interfering with fun. This section highlights some of the principal safety issues for residential play structures.

Reducing Fall Hazards. According to the U.S. Consumer Product Safety Commission, about 60 percent of all playground injuries result from falls. And this percentage is even higher for serious injuries. Consequently, preventing falls—and minimizing their impact when they occur—should be your primary safety concern. Perhaps the best approach is to assume that children will fall off the highest point, as well as the highest point of the arc of a swing, and plan accordingly. The more resilient the surface that children land on, the less chance of injury.

Untrampled backyard grass can be a whole lot softer than schoolyard asphalt. But when kids start compacting a yard's ground surface, it can become nearly as hard as asphalt. If a child falls head first onto a grass surface from just a couple of feet, a serious injury could result. That same fall onto a surface of wood chips or pea gravel would be far less likely to cause serious injury.

To minimize danger from falls, three strategies are most useful. First, keep heights to a minimum. A high platform may be necessary to accommodate a slide or to help anchor a swing (as with the Central Tower for the Kids' Playland). But height is not needed for the Playhouse, where just a little elevation and some enclosure from a guardrail create all the sense of privacy and adventure that most children will need. Second, on high platforms, provide guardrails to prevent falls. Guardrails must be anchored solidly to the framing and high enough to discourage being used as a seat. Third, provide impact-reducing material where falls might occur. Chapter 3 discusses the various materials you can use.

Why Build It Yourself?

There are dozens of commercial play structures, especially swing sets, available in a wide range of prices. Some are inexpensive, four-legged metal swing sets that can be assembled with a few nuts and bolts in an hour or two. Others are expensive, heavy-duty wood kits that may take several weekends to assemble. With so much choice, you are certain to ask, "Why should I take the trouble to shop for assorted materials and build my own?"

There are several reasons. First, building your own play structures, like many home do-it-yourself projects, may save lots of money. Sure, you need to buy the materials, and maybe a few new tools, but the process of measuring, cutting, drilling, and assembling involve your own free labor ("sweat equity"), not someone else's.

Second, by designing and building your own structures, you will get exactly what you want. Rather than having to settle for a play set from a catalog or from store stock, you can equip your play structures with just the accessories that your kids will use and enjoy.

Third, you can build safer structures that are less likely to lead to accidents or injuries. Many people are aware that the U.S. Consumer Product Safety Commission has adopted safety standards for public playgrounds. What they may not know is that manufacturers of residential play sets are not required to comply with those standards. Recently, when a leading consumer magazine tested backyard swing sets, it found that most of them had major and minor violations of government safety recommendations. What's more, many public playgrounds are dangerous, first because many are built with little concern for safety, and second because maintenance and repairs are neglected. By following the safety guidelines and construction directions in this book, you will ensure that your structures meet or exceed safety standards for public playgrounds.

Lastly, with a little forethought, you can turn the process of designing your play structures into a family project that is both enjoyable and educational. Far from remaining passive, your kids can become active planners of a relatively large-scale, real-world activity.

Caution: *We recommend that kids of most ages participate in planning and design, but we don't recommend that young kids participate in the construction itself, especially in procedures involving edged tools and power tools. Also, be sure to safeguard other construction-site hazards; this includes covering open postholes and stacking materials so they won't invite injury.*

Minimizing Chances of Collisions.

Collisions are a potential hazard in any area where children move at high speed. By far, swings are the greatest hazard. You can reduce the arc, and thereby slow the velocity, of a swing by keeping its swing beam relatively low to the ground. Yet children are not likely to enjoy a "baby swing" beyond infancy.

Try to isolate the swing as much as possible from the other activities. The best strategy is to place the swing away from the rest of the play structure, but that is usually not possible on small residential lots. The Kids' Playland offers a compromise, with the swing a structural part of the larger unit but isolated enough to reduce chances that children will run or fall into the path of someone swinging.

Avoid placing swings too close to each other. Manufactured swing sets often space hangers of separate swings only 8 inches apart. Such tight spacing greatly heightens collision hazard. By building your own set, you can follow the much safer standards for public playgrounds, which suggest that the swings be at least 24 inches apart at about 48 inches above the level of the impact-reducing surface and be at least 30 inches from the side frame. Also, by spacing the hangers for the swing wider than the seat itself, you minimize the amount of side-to-side motion possible, further reducing the chances for collision.

If possible, place the Swing Frame next to bushes or a fence that discourages foot traffic nearby. Alternatively, you could erect a small fence that directs traffic safely around the swing. Or you could design a pathway around the swing and train the kids to use it.

The danger of a collision involving a swing is not just that the swinger's feet will kick a passing child. Even more serious are collisions with hard swing seats. Wood, metal, or rigid plastic seats are more likely to cause a serious injury than soft plastic or rubber seats. Soft, flexible seats are also more comfortable, and anyway are usually more popular with children. They also discourage the dangerous practice of standing on the swing. For very young children, buy a commercial infant swing that provides support on all sides. Follow installation instructions carefully.

If you decide to build swing seats from wood, make them only large enough to accommodate one child. Keep any protrusions from hardware on the bottom of the seat to a minimum. A long bolt protruding from the bottom of a seat could cause serious injury if it struck a child.

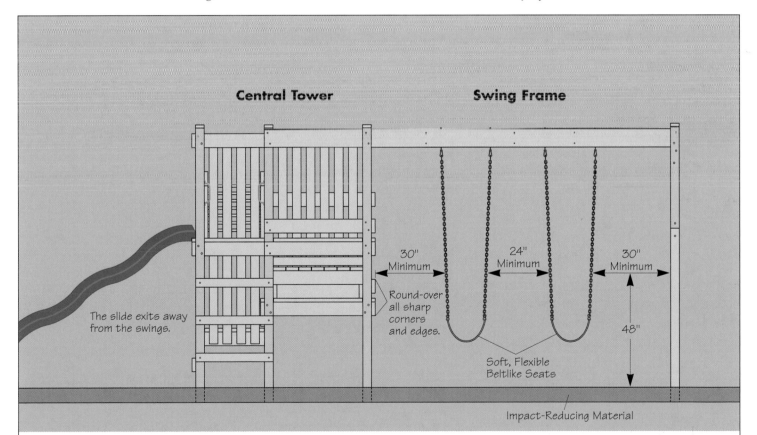

Central Tower   **Swing Frame**

The slide exits away from the swings.

30" Minimum

Round-over all sharp corners and edges.

24" Minimum

30" Minimum

48"

Soft, Flexible Beltlike Seats

Impact-Reducing Material

Minimizing Chances of Collision. Keep the slide exit far from the swings, and keep swings a safe distance from posts and other swings. Never suspend a tire swing (which swings in all directions) next to other swings. For school-age children, use soft, flexible swing seats, as shown. For toddlers and preschoolers, see the seat options on page 39.

Preventing Head Entrapment.

Wherever they find an opening, kids may try to squeeze through. An entrapped head can lead to serious injury, including strangulation. This is especially a hazard when ladders and guardrails are poorly designed. You can prevent head entrapment by keeping openings either too small for a head to fit through (that is, under 3½ inches), or too large for a head to get caught if it can pass through (that is, greater than 9 inches). If the rungs on a ladder or the risers on a stair are between 3½ and 9 inches, you should seal them up with a filler board.

Avoiding Edges, Protrusions, and Pinch Points.

Corners of wood should be rounded or "softened." Also, protruding bolts can give nasty cuts and bruises, and they can snag clothing, causing falls. Avoid bolt hazards altogether by countersinking the nut end in a recess drilled in the wood, as shown below. All moving parts should be designed to eliminate pinch points. This is a particular hazard with some manufactured swing-set accessories.

Throughout this book, we've advised rounding sharp edges and eliminating protrusions and pinch points. If you make modifications that introduce related hazards, be sure to eliminate them or find a means of keeping them out of reach.

Ensuring Safer Sliding.

It is possible to build a decent slide from wood and sheet metal, but we don't recommend it. Building a safe slide takes a lot of time and, in the end, won't save you any money. Today, a wide array of reasonably priced plastic slides are available. You can choose straight, wavy or curving slides, and slides with tubes that are safe, fun, and very easy to install. Chapter 3 discusses in more depth the choices available.

If you build or buy a metal slide, try to face it north so it won't be under

Space should be less than 3½".

Or spaces should be more than 9"

Preventing Head Entrapment. A child's head shouldn't fit into smaller gaps on the structure and should be comfortably smaller than the larger gaps.

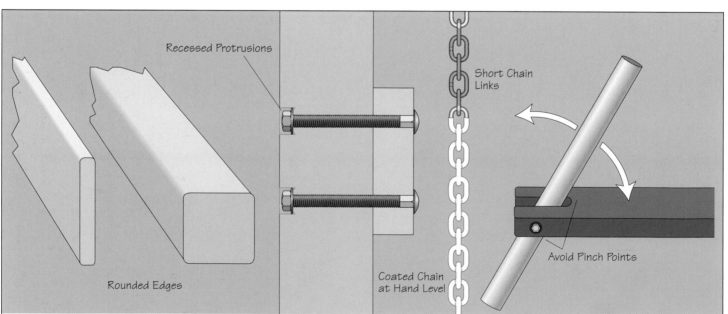

Recessed Protrusions

Short Chain Links

Rounded Edges

Coated Chain at Hand Level

Avoid Pinch Points

Avoiding Sharp Edges, Protrusion, and Pinch Points. Round-over sharp edges. Either cut off protruding bolts or recess bolts and nuts. Use chain with short links and a rubberlike plastic coating so that small fingers can't get pinched or stuck inside. Avoid commercial playground accessories, such as shown at right, with pivoting components that can pinch fingers.

direct sunlight for long periods. Otherwise, the slide may become too hot for comfort.

For any slide, you can reduce the hazard of falls by providing hand-holds at the entrance to support kids as they switch from standing to sitting. The slide must have continuous side rails that are 5 to 6 inches high, with top edges rounded to function as splinter-free handrails. The side rails should be integral to the chute, with no gaps between slide and rails. Slides should not descend straight to the ground. Instead, they should have a nearly horizontal exit chute that arrests the descent. A good plastic slide will meet or exceed these recommendations.

There is no ideal slide height for children of all ages. Younger children tend to be intimidated by slides more than 48 inches high, while most older children are happier with slides twice that height. A good compromise height is 60 to 72 inches. Regardless of the height, the recommended incline is about 30 degrees. Be sure to incorporate a platform at the top of the slide that allows kids to sit down before working their way onto the slide.

Likewise, the ideal drop from the exit chute to the ground varies with the size of the child. A drop of 3 to 8 inches is best for preschoolers on a short slide, while 10 to 14 inches is ideal for older children. Also, avoid any protrusions or projections at the top of the slide that could catch clothing, hands, and arms.

Careful Construction and Maintenance. Your play structures must be stable and secure. All posts should be buried in concrete to below the frost line. The top of the concrete itself should always remain below the impact-reducing material. All connections should be made with appropriate hardware, fastened securely, as shown in the construction instructions in later chapters. All parts and materials must be suitable for outdoor construction.

To be safe, a play yard needs more than just good design and construction. It also needs regular safety inspections and maintenance. Inspect all connections and surfaces on a routine basis. Tighten, fix, and replace materials and connections as needed. Replace or renew the surface of impact-reducing material when it becomes too compacted or shallow.

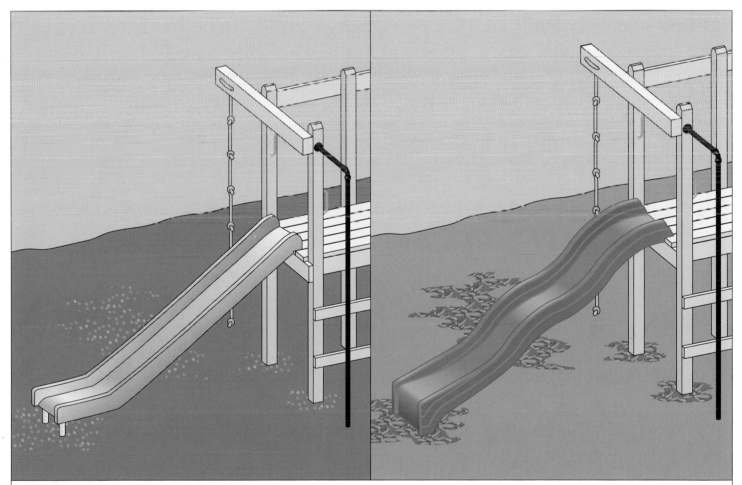

Ensuring Safer Sliding. Slides should not descend straight to the ground; instead they should have landings parallel with ground level. Also ensure that no projections could catch clothing or hands. Place a metal slide so that little sun hits it.

Building Codes and Permits

In some jurisdictions, you will need a building permit before you begin work on an in-ground structure, such as the Kids' Playland. This permit is a license from local authorities to build. States and localities follow a variety of codes. Some follow one of the major national codes, and others write their own. Thus, don't assume you will be allowed to dig footings and build without a permit.

Building codes may cover height, support, materials, safety, and area covered by the structure. As part of the permit process, inspectors may need to approve construction stages, such as holes for footings as well as the finished structure. A structure found to be in violation of code can be ordered removed.

Also check your property deed before building. Your deed should show if there are easements on your property or restrictive covenants. An easement is a right-of-way granted to a utility company or other property owner that must not be blocked or otherwise restricted. A covenant can be a restriction agreed among property owners that can be enforced in court. And it's smart to check with your home insurer

Utilities

As mentioned earlier, in instructions on preparing your site plan, know the location of all utility lines, both underground and overheard. Water, gas, sewer, electric, or telephone lines may affect your site options.

To locate these lines, check with the customer service departments of your local utility companies. Most will help you determine the location of their service installations on your property. They might even be able to suggest ways of building over or around the service. If your house was recently built, your building inspector will probably have a copy of your hookup locations. Keep this information in your files for future reference. Most often, utility lines will be well below the excavations you will make for impact-reducing materials. But they may not be deep enough to avoid damage when you dig and install posts. Again, avoid placing your play structure under telephone and electrical lines.

If local building officials require that you obtain a construction permit, they may ask that you post it prominently. Passing inspection usually earns you a Certificate of Occupancy, often called a "C.O."

2

Tools

Building the Kids' Playland may have several long term benefits. Of course, your kids and their friends will enjoy years of outdoor fun. Yet beyond that are the knowledge and confidence you will acquire in carpentry. And with the experience you gain on this project, you may perhaps consider building a deck, which involves many of the same steps. So your intentions about future projects should influence the kinds and quality of tools you purchase.

Remember, you don't need a garage full of high-priced power tools to build a play structure. In fact, you could do the entire project with few, if any, power tools. For example, postholes can be dug with an inexpensive posthole digger. A hand saw can cut all lumber, and a hand brace and a hand drill can handle all drilling tasks. Throw in a few measuring and marking tools, combined with a "Don't rush it" attitude, and you can achieve completely satisfactory results.

On the other hand, you may have future ambitions for your carpentry. If so, you can choose projects with the intention of adding skills and tools to your arsenal. That way, it's less likely that the tools you buy will gather dust once your play structures are finished. This chapter will also help you choose the best tools for the money.

Measuring and Marking Tools

For the larger projects in this book, the tape measure, the chalkline, the plumb bob, and plenty of pencils are almost essential.

Tape Measure. For the Kids' Playland, you'll find a 25- or 30-foot tape the most useful for both long and short measurements. Good tape measures have the first foot divided into $\frac{1}{32}$-inch increments for really precise work. Tapes with a 1-inch-wide blade are a little bulkier than $\frac{3}{4}$-inch blades, but 1-inch blades are much more rigid and can be extended farther without buckling. This feature is especially handy when you are working alone. When shopping for a tape, a good method for comparing options is to extend them a few inches at a time to see how far they extend before buckling. Look for a tape with a metal belt clip on the back and an easy-to-use locking mechanism.

Chalkline. Designed for marking long straight lines, a chalkline is just a roll of string inside a container filled with powdered chalk. The device allows you to mark a line between two points in a few seconds. The procedure is called "snapping a line." Here's how: Stretch the line against the flat surface you want to mark. Then lift the line away from the surface and let it "snap" back. When the line hits the flat surface, chalk powder flies off, producing a straight, chalked line. Although red chalk may be easier to see, blue is a better choice because red is permanent and will stain both wood and your hands.

Plumb Bob. This heavy, pointed bob suspended from a string enables you to drop a perfectly vertical line from a given mark. For play structures, it is especially useful for aligning posts accurately. Some chalklines can also

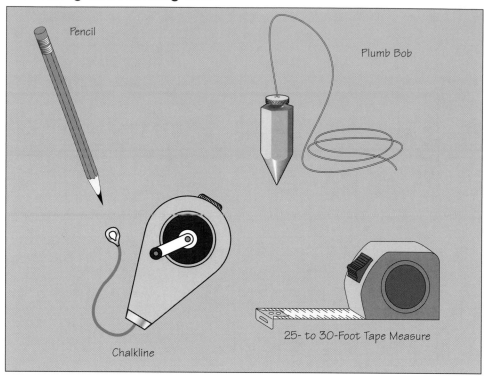

Pencil

Plumb Bob

Chalkline

25- to 30-Foot Tape Measure

be used as plumb bobs. Professional finish carpenters may prefer top-of-the-line plumb bobs, but for most projects a basic bob is quite adequate.

Pencils. For most marking, you will need pencils. You don't need specially manufactured wide, flat carpenter's pencils. Just have a plentiful supply of standard "lead" pencils on hand. If you later discover pencil lines you'd like to remove, sandpaper removes them quicker than an eraser.

Tools for Digging Postholes

You'll need a shovel to remove dirt that you will replace with impact-reducing material, such as wood chips, pea gravel, or sand. You will also need a tool for digging postholes.

Posthole Digger. If you decide on projects requiring few posts or if you have time and enjoy exercise, you can dig holes by hand with a posthole digger. This double-handled tool is designed to cut deep, narrow holes

and lift out dirt between its clamshell-like blades. A long, steel digging bar is helpful in loosening the dirt and prying out rocks.

Power Auger. For quicker digging, especially requiring six or more holes, you may prefer a power auger. Powered by a gasoline engine, the power auger works like a giant drill. A hydraulic model is easier to use by one person because the engine is separate from the auger itself. Two-person units are available, with the engine mounted directly over the auger. Even if you use a power auger, you will still need a manual posthole digger to clean out the holes.

Contracting for Postholes. If you are planning to construct the entire Kids' Playland and maybe need some other holes dug too, consider hiring someone with a truck-mounted auger. Although this is the most expensive option, it can save many hours, if not days, of fairly arduous work. Check with local fence builders and landscapers for referrals.

Tools for Digging Postholes

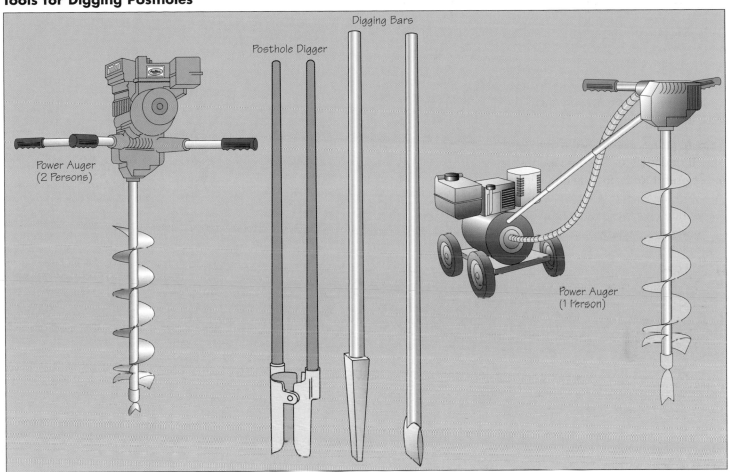

Tools for Leveling

Tool choices for leveling are determined by distances spanned and the degree of accuracy required.

Carpenter's Level. A must on any construction site, this tool helps you level beams and ensure that posts are plumb. Levels are available in 24- and 48-inch lengths. You don't need to spend a lot of money to get a pro-fessional-grade level, but you do need to take special care of it. One hard drop can render any level inaccurate. One way to test your level's accuracy is to set it on a level surface. The bubble or bubbles should be in the center. Next, turn the level around. The bubble or bubbles should still be in the center. On some levels the vials are adjustable, allowing you to correct an out-of-whack alignment.

Note: To find level over longer spans, hold the level on a long, straight board. If necessary, secure it with tape. Using this technique, you can turn a 24-inch level into a much larger level in seconds. Spans longer than 8 feet may require the use of a water level or a line level.

Water Level. The simplest water level is a length of ⅜- or ⁵⁄₁₆-inch clear plastic tubing filled with water. You can buy the tubing by the foot at hardware stores and home centers. For the Kids' Playland, you'll need about 26 feet of

Tools for Leveling

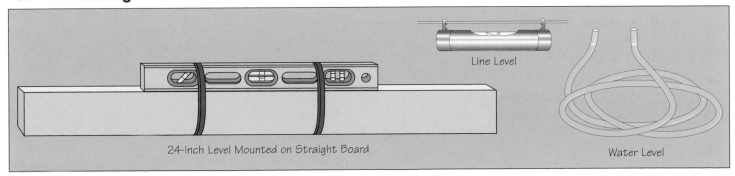

tubing. With a few minutes of practice—and a helper—you'll be able to transfer level lines from one post to another accurately. For instructions, see "Using a Water Level," page 57.

Line Level. A small, inexpensive device with a single vial, a line level is designed to be hooked under a taut string to determine level over long spans. A line level isn't good for exact leveling, but for projects in this book, it is good enough. For maximum accuracy, the string needs to be taut.

Tools for Squaring and Finding Angles

Although angles for most carpentry projects can be marked, measured, and transferred with just the framing square, smaller tools can be handier in many situations, especially for distances under 8 inches or so.

Framing Square. Sometimes called a carpenter's square or steel square, the framing square is perhaps the most commonly used marking, measuring, and squaring tool in carpentry. Its large size makes it good for marking cut lines on large boards and checking the square of lumber being joined. Made of either aluminum or steel, it usually has scales and tables that allow a variety of measurements and markings, ranging from layout of roof rafters and stair stringers to octagons.

Combination Square. The body contains both 90- and 45-degree faces and can slide up and down the blade after you unlock the thumbscrew. The movable body makes this tool ideal for transferring depth measurements or running a line along a board. Bargain-basement combination squares usually aren't worth the money. They can't be trusted to form a consistently square angle, and the dimension markings on the blade may be less than exact.

Angle Square. A thick, strong, triangular casting of either aluminum or plastic makes this square tough enough to withstand the rigors of general construction without losing its accuracy. The angle square's triangular shape enables you to lay out a 45-degree angle as quickly as a 90-degree angle. Using markings on the body, you can lay out angles other than 90 degrees, as when laying out rafters. The edges of the square can also serve when setting 90- and 45-degree blade angles on a circular saw.

Bevel Gauge. Probably the best tool for gauging and transferring angles other than 45 and 90 degrees is a sliding bevel gauge, also known as a T-bevel. This device has a flat sliding metal blade that can be locked into the handle at any angle. A bevel gauge is great for transferring an existing angle on the actual project. It can also be used along with a protractor to record and transfer a specific angle.

Wood-Cutting Tools

Most people rank cutting and joining among the most enjoyable aspects of carpentry. This results, at least in part, from the feeling of accomplishment that accompanies working with wood and making it fit the intended design. And enjoyment can be enhanced if you have the proper tools. More important, having the right tool for a specific job and knowing how to use it are the best ways to avoid wasting material and preventing injuries.

Circular Saw. On our play structures, a circular saw is perfectly adequate for cutting lumber. For most do-it-yourselfers, the circular saw has replaced the hand saw in almost every situation. That's because a circular saw is capable of crosscutting, ripping, and beveling boards or sheets of plywood quickly and cleanly. This multipurpose saw can also be used to create a variety of joints, such as miters, laps, and dadoes.

Tools for Squaring and Finding Angles

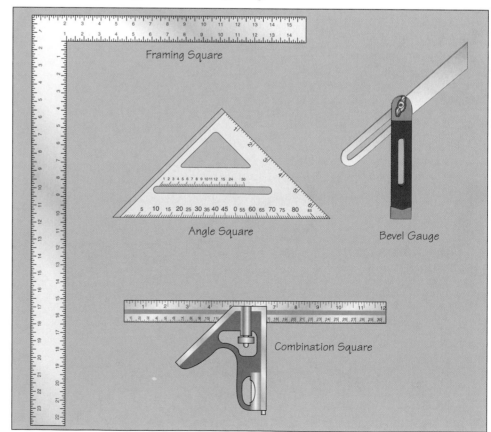

Framing Square

Angle Square

Bevel Gauge

Combination Square

The circular saws most popular with carpenters and do-it-yourselfers alike are models that take a blade of 7¼-inch diameter. This blade size allows cuts to a maximum depth of about 2½ inches at 90 degrees. This saw also allows you to cut off 4x4 posts, simply by making two cuts, one each on opposing sides.

▲ *Choosing a Circular Saw.* Several features distinguish circular saws. Perhaps the most important is power. One of the best gauges of a saw's potential performance is the amount of amperage its motor draws, not merely the saw's horsepower. Low-cost saws may have only 9- to 11-amp motors with drive shafts and arbors running on rollers or sleeve bearings. A contractor-grade saw is rated at 12 to 15 amps and is made with ball bearings. The extra power and the bear-

ings enable the saw to withstand wear better, especially when cutting tough, pressure-treated lumber. Top-of-the-line models are intended for heavy, daily use by professional carpenters. Midrange saws lack some of the power and durability of the best saws, but they still cut easier and cleaner (and thus more safely) than low-cost saws.

Plastic housings are no longer the mark of an inferior saw, but a thin, stamped-metal base is. A thicker base, extruded or cast, will stay flatter longer.

Your saw should be double insulated to minimize any chance of electric shock. Some saws have an additional safety switch that must be depressed before the trigger will work. Another feature to look for is an arbor lock. The lock secures the arbor nut and

prevents the blade from turning while you are changing the blade. A blade brake is a highly desirable safety feature. The brake stops the blade from spinning almost the moment you release the trigger. Note: A saw with a special port for dust-collection can be useful indoors.

▲ *Choosing Circular-Saw Blades.* For general use, carbide-tipped blades are the best for achieving smooth, precise cuts. Carbide blades cost more than blades made from high-speed steel, but they can also cut much longer before needing to be sharpened.

Saw-blade manufacturers offer a wide variety of blades. You can choose blades specifically made to cut plywood, two-by framing lumber, pressure-treated lumber, or one-by pine.

Wood Cutting Tools

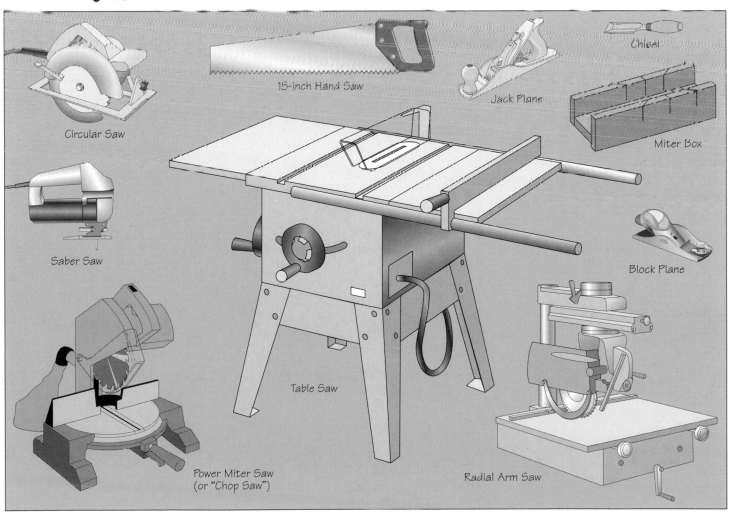

Circular Saw

15-inch Hand Saw

Jack Plane

Chisel

Miter Box

Saber Saw

Table Saw

Block Plane

Power Miter Saw
(or "Chop Saw")

Radial Arm Saw

A blade with fewer than 30 teeth will cut quicker but leave a rougher surface, while a 40- to 60-tooth blade is better for smooth cuts, especially when crosscutting (cutting across the grain). Blades are also made especially for ripping with the grain.

The key to choosing the right blade is knowing what kind of cutting you will do. A good choice for the do-it-yourselfer who wants to buy only one blade is a combination, or general-purpose, blade. This blade will do an adequate job crosscutting and ripping most wood products. But if you plan to use the blade primarily to crosscut lumber, you might be happier with a blade made especially for crosscutting. It's easy to change a blade in a circular saw, and blades aren't very expensive. So don't be afraid to buy several special-purpose blades and change them as needed.

A good blade collection would include a ripping, a combination, and a finishing blade. Newer generation thin-kerf blades keep improving. They cut faster and place less stress on the saw motor and gearing. You can also buy blades designed to cut masonry, metal, and ceramics, though you won't need them for any of the play structures.

Larger Saws. For quicker and more accurate cuts than you can get with a circular saw, you might consider a table saw, a radial arm saw, or a power miter saw (commonly referred to as a chop saw). Each can quickly and accurately crosscut lumber and can also cut dadoes, bevels and miters. The table saw is the most versatile for ripping, especially sheet material such as plywood. For mitering small pieces of wood, a simple miter box and hand saw are perfectly adequate.

Saber Saw. Also called a jigsaw or bayonet saw, a saber saw is a good tool for cutting curves, cutouts, or other elaborate shapes. Shop for a saber saw with variable speed, a

thick baseplate, and at least a 3½-amp motor. Bimetal blades provide the best service and last the longest.

Hand Saw. For some cuts, no power saw can completely replace a good hand saw. In fact, a hand saw is often quicker when you have just a couple of cuts to make, or for tough-to-reach spots. A 15-inch saw with 10 to 12 teeth per inch (tpi) will cut well and still fit into a toolbox.

Plane. A properly set plane will quickly trim a board for a better fit. You can also use it to chamfer, or "soften," the edges on a board.

Chisels. A set of three or four chisels, from ¼ to 1½ inches wide, will also be useful for close paring. To work safely and smoothly, the blades must be kept sharp.

Drilling Tools

For these projects, a drill is absolutely indispensable.

Hand Drill and Hand Brace. For holes up to ¼ inch in diameter and up to 1 or 2 inches in depth, you could get by with a hand drill and bits. Besides,

a smaller manual drill and bits allow you to drill pilot holes for screws. A hand brace and a few large-diameter bits would be sufficient for bolt holes.

Power Drill. For quicker results, you will need an electric drill. The best choice for most do-it-yourselfers is a drill with a ⅜-inch chuck, a variable speed control, and a reversing switch. A keyless chuck is a great convenience. If you're willing to spend a little more money, you should seriously consider buying a cordless drill. The quality of cordless drills has improved dramatically, and the selection is huge. For do-it-yourselfers, a drill powered by a 9.6 or 12-volt battery will suffice. A cordless drill equipped with an adjustable clutch allows you to drive screws safely, without burying the heads deeper than you intended. On many models, the battery will recharge in just 10 to 15 minutes.

Drill Bits. Standard drill-bit sets are available in sizes from ¹⁄₁₆ to ¼ inch, and a set of wood-boring (spade) bits allow you drill holes up to 1 inch or more. Other accessories allow you to convert your power drill into a grinder, sander, or paint stirrer.

Drilling Tools

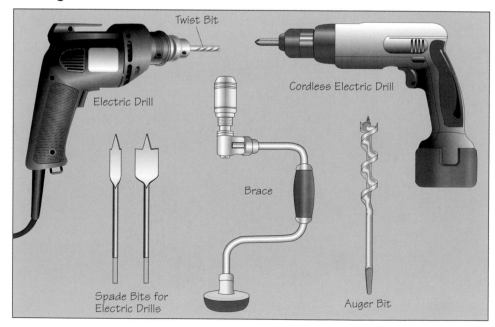

Twist Bit

Electric Drill

Cordless Electric Drill

Brace

Spade Bits for Electric Drills

Auger Bit

Safety Equipment

Many thousands of do-it-yourselfers are injured every year while using hand and power tools, often because they failed to use basic safety equipment, especially eye and ear protection.

Eye Protectors. Wear safety goggles and plastic glasses whenever you are working with power tools. Also wear goggles whenever working with chemicals. Make sure that your eye protection conforms with American National Standards Institute (ANSI) or Canadian Standards Association (CSA) requirements. Considering the cost of a visit to the emergency room and possible permanent injury, safety gear is a small investment. And it doesn't hurt to have an extra pair of eye or hearing protectors for the times when a neighbor volunteers to help or if your first pair becomes misplaced.

Hearing Protectors. The U.S. Occupational Safety and Health Administration (OSHA) recommends that hearing protection be worn when the noise level equals or exceeds an 8-hour average of 85 decibels (db). Since many power tools emit more than 85 db when operated, it's best to err on the side of caution. Hearing protectors are available as muffs and as earplugs. Whichever style you choose, look for a noise reduction rating (NRR) of at least 20 db.

Dust Masks. Your construction project will create a lot of sawdust. If you are sensitive to dust, and especially if you are working with pressure-treated wood, it's important to wear a dust mask approved for protection from dust by the National Institute for Occupational Safety and Health and the Mine Safety and Health Administration (NIOSH/MSHA). Replace the dust mask with a new one regularly.

Hand Protectors. Work gloves help avoid injury to the hands—catching a splinter off a board or developing a blister when digging postholes can spoil a workday.

Foot Protectors. Heavy-duty work boots will help protect your feet. Steel toes will prevent injuries from dropped boards or tools. Flexible steel soles will protect your feet from puncture by a rogue nail.

Clothing and Grooming. At a construction site, attire and grooming can greatly determine safety. Avoid loose clothing and jewelry that can catch on boards, tools, and hardware. Also, tie back long hair.

Shock Protector. Power tools should be plugged into a receptacle equipped with a ground-fault circuit interrupter (GFCI). A GFCI helps prevent electric shocks from faulty tools or extension cords. In other words, it can save a life. If a GFCI receptacle isn't available, use a GFCI-equipped extension cord. And before operating any power tool, check the cord and plug carefully. If either is damaged, have it replaced by a qualified service center or get a new GFCI.

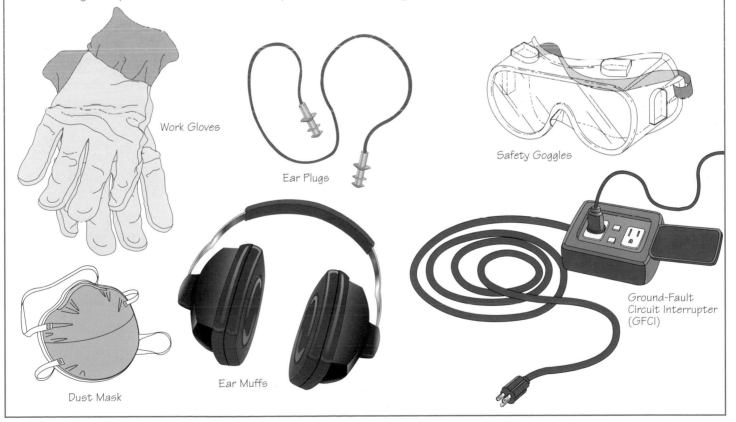

Work Gloves

Ear Plugs

Safety Goggles

Dust Mask

Ear Muffs

Ground-Fault Circuit Interrupter (GFCI)

Sanding Tools

Hand Sanders. For play-yard projects, you can get by with a plentiful supply of sandpaper and a good sanding block. Coarse- to medium-grit sandpaper (40 to 80 grit) will handle most of the work. Also, a rasp-cut file or surface-forming tool is handy for quickly smoothing rough edges.

Power Sander. A belt sander would be the best power sander for projects here because it can round-over edges and smooth boards with just a couple of quick passes.

Note: Belt sanders can remove a lot of wood very quickly, so they can be tricky to operate well. Read the owner's manual carefully and practice on scrap lumber before tackling the real thing.

The Router

You won't need a router and bits just to build a play structure. But if you've been planning to buy a router anyway, it will be handy for rounding edges on the structure.

Most veteran woodworkers feel their router is about the most important and versatile tool in their shop. A router can shape edges, cut grooves, and shape molding. A router with a fixed base will be adequate for occasional and uncomplicated use. But a good-quality plunge router is much more versatile. The motor on a plunge router is attached to two rods that allow it to slide up and down in relation to the base. This feature allows you to plunge the bit into the middle of a workpiece, which can't be done with a fixed-base router. This also allows you to adjust depth stops in order to make a deep cut in a series of successively deeper passes.

When choosing a router, you must also decide on the size of collet, which is the small part that holds the bit. Routers with ¼-inch collets are less expensive and can be satisfactory for small tasks and infrequent use. But a model with a ½-inch collet will hold larger bits and perform tougher work.

Router bits are available in dozens of shapes. On this project, a chamfer and a roundover bit will come in handy for "softening" the edges. Like saw blades, router bits with a carbide-tipped edges will stay sharp longer, though high-speed steel will cost less.

Sanding Tools

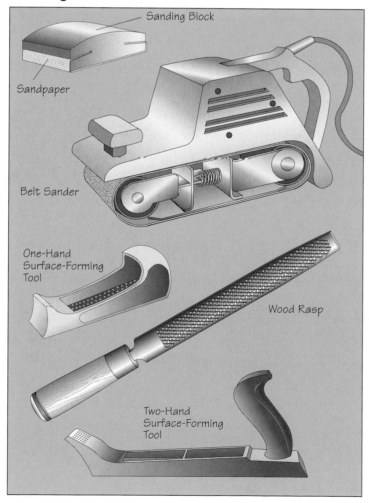

Sanding Block

Sandpaper

Belt Sander

One-Hand Surface-Forming Tool

Wood Rasp

Two-Hand Surface-Forming Tool

The Router

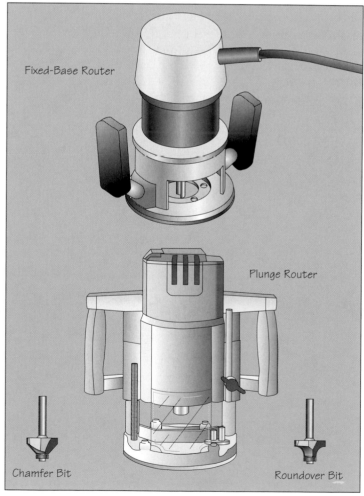

Fixed-Base Router

Plunge Router

Chamfer Bit

Roundover Bit

Other Tools

This category covers the range of tools that any do-it-yourselfer should have in the toolbox.

Turn Fasteners. It's nearly mandatory to have a full complement of screwdrivers, wrenches, and pliers. A ⅜-inch socket wrench and a set of sockets will allow you to quickly tighten nuts and drive lag screws.

Hammers. You should have a standard curved-claw hammer weighing at least 16 ounces. A lighter hammer may be helpful for fastening small pieces and driving small nails. If you'll be driving a lot of 12d or 16d nails, you will quickly learn to appreciate the greater ease and driving power of a 20- or 22-ounce framing hammer. (In most cases, we've instead recommended deck screws as the prime fasteners. They're easier to drive, using a cordless electric drill driver, and far easier to remove during disassembly.)

Nail Sets. These complement a hammer. A nail set is a punch-shaped shaft designed to countersink finishing nails or to drive them flush with the wood surface without marring the wood with unsightly hammer "dings." The points of nail sets come in various diameters approximating nail head sizes. The point may even be cupped to secure the nailhead during driving. For best results, use a point about the size of the nailhead. Countersunk holes can be filled with wood putty to produce a finish that looks nail free.

Clamps. Several large C-clamps, bar clamps, or hand-squeezed spring clamps will help hold boards and posts together while you drill bolt holes.

Bolt-Cutting Tools. You may also need a hacksaw or bolt cutter to shorten bolts so you can recess them. This will avoid protrusions that can become hazards.

Utility Knife. Well named, this knife can be used for a wide range of tasks—from sharpening pencils to marking lines, from opening boxes to shaving wood. For general use, invest in a fairly heavy-duty model that has a large retractable blade. As with all cutting tools, sharp blades are safest because they provide the most control with the least amount of effort. Replacement blades are inexpensive, yet they can also be sharpened quickly with a few passes on a whetstone.

Tool Holders. Unless you enjoy hunting for misplaced tools, a tool belt or work apron is a must. A good tool belt will have holders for a hammer, tape measure, chalkline, pencil, and other commonly used tools, as well as pouches for generous supplies of nails or screws.

Work Surface. At the very least, you will need a couple of sawhorses. A workbench may also come in handy. You can create a temporary, and portable, workbench by laying a sheet of ¾-inch plywood onto two sawhorses. Cut the plywood to the size that suits you.

Other Tools

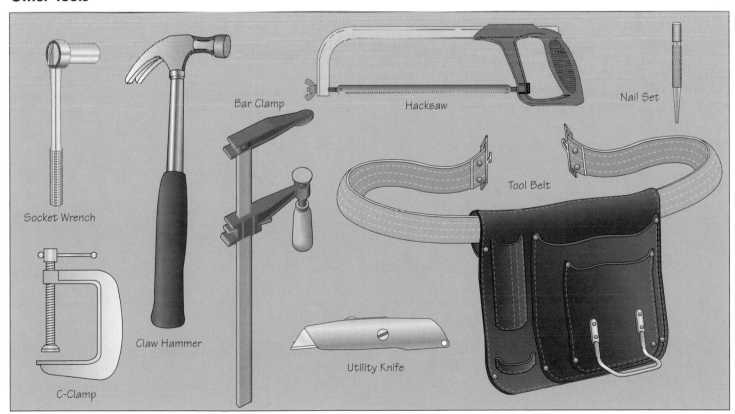

Socket Wrench

Claw Hammer

C-Clamp

Bar Clamp

Hacksaw

Nail Set

Tool Belt

Utility Knife

3

Materials

Your choice of materials will be affected by relative durabilities, appearances, costs, and safety. This book addresses options, mindful that reduced cost is acceptable only if it doesn't reduce safety.

For example, if you intend to keep the play structures for only a few years before disassembly, you may be able to save some dollars on the choice of wood without reducing structural integrity. As to appearance, a well-selected wood stain can mask the greenish cast of pressure-treated posts, helping them blend with other wood on the structure.

Play structures can be built with these categories of materials:

▲ Wood
▲ Concrete
▲ Impact-reducing materials, such as wood chips and pea gravel, to cushion falls and landings
▲ Hardware
▲ Manufactured play accessories

Wood

The wood in a play structure must fulfill these requirements: It must survive years of exposure without losing its strength or stability. It must also resist the combined effects of sun, rain, mold, and wood-boring insects. In addition, the wood should be easy to work, attractive, and affordable.

Finding appropriate wood isn't difficult. Lumber is divided into two main categories: softwoods and hardwoods. Softwoods come from coniferous trees, often called evergreens. And hardwoods come from broadleaved deciduous trees that lose their leaves in the winter. While most hardwoods are harder than most softwoods, there are exceptions. For example, southern yellow pine, a softwood, is harder than poplar, a hardwood.

Today, nearly all outdoor construction is done with softwoods because they are more readily available than hardwoods, easier to work, and generally less expensive. Softwoods are the woods used for pressure treating with preservatives. Of the softwoods redwood, cedar, and cypress are considered the most desirable for outdoor building because of their beauty and natural resistance to decay. These woods are used on decks, gazebos, and siding, and for shingles and shakes. But because these woods are in limited supply, they are the most expensive softwoods, and they may not be available in all regions of North America.

You don't need to use high-priced redwood or cedar to create an attractive play structure. Besides, in the event your play structure will be temporary, the more expensive softwoods may be more than you need. Other softwoods—including pine, fir, spruce, and larch—are widely available and more affordable. While these woods require additional weather protection, they can give many years of service, and they look good.

Wood is prized for its durability and structural capabilities. It has high resistance to impact and high strength in compression relative to its weight. And it can easily be formed into many shapes without seriously altering its structural characteristics. However, wood often has natural defects that can weaken it, such as knots, splits, and checks. It can also suffer shrinkage, decay, and warping. And different species of wood may have quite different characteristics.

The availability of particular wood species depends to some extent on geographical location, and prices can vary over time and from region to region. Wood officially becomes lumber after it has been sawn and planed to standard sizes and graded by characteristics guaranteed by the manufacturer. This guarantee of size, strength, and other characteristics assures you that the wood will behave in a predictable manner.

As to price and availability, the best advice is to shop around and ask questions. Most home centers and

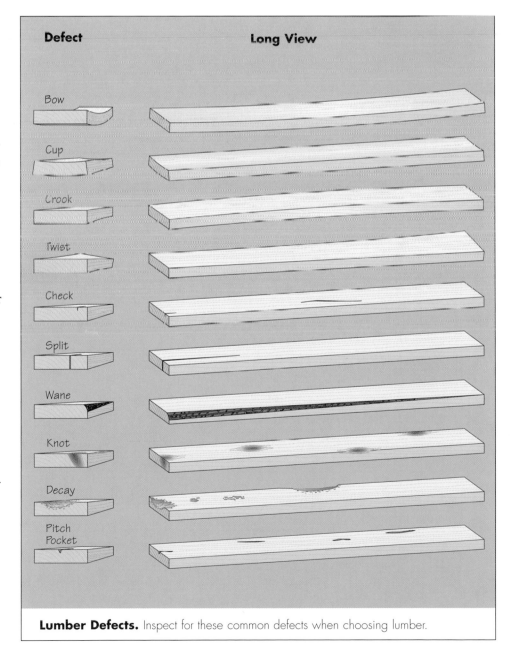

Defect	Long View
Bow	
Cup	
Crook	
Twist	
Check	
Split	
Wane	
Knot	
Decay	
Pitch Pocket	

Lumber Defects. Inspect for these common defects when choosing lumber.

lumberyards have a least a few sales-people with building experience or who otherwise have good knowledge of building supplies.

Redwood. The redwood trees of the Pacific Northwest are legendary for their size and lumber quality. Redwood's beautiful straight grain, natural glowing color, and weather resistance have traditionally made it the premier wood for outdoor building. Unfortunately, overharvesting has reduced redwood availability and driven up its price.

As in all logs, the redwood's younger, outer portion is called sapwood. The older, denser center is called heartwood. Sapwood is lighter in color and less weather resistant than heartwood. Redwood heartwood is extremely stable and can be milled to produce very smooth surfaces. When sawn, the reddish heartwood produces a wonderful fragrance by releasing the same chemicals that discourage wood-boring insects. If you like, you can let redwood age naturally to a light gray patina. Yet it will readily accept paint or stain.

There are several grades of redwood. The two grades preferred for outdoor construction, because they

consist entirely of heartwood, are Clear All Heart and Construction Heart. Of the two, Clear All Heart is more expensive because it is knot free. On a play structure, the high price of Clear All Heart tends to limit its use to railings, if used at all. In comparison, Construction Heart (Con-Heart) contains minor imperfections but is ideal for almost every other element of a play structure. Although they contain some sapwood, Clear, B Grade, Construction Common, Deck Common, and Merchantable grades of redwood are all suitable for smaller accessories in your play structure.

Although it is weather and rot resistant, redwood in contact with the ground does not last as long as pressure-treated lumber, nor would it be as strong in stress if used as posts for the Swing Beam. For these reasons, if you want to use mostly redwood, we recommend substituting pressure-treated lumber for the posts and parts of any other projects in contact with the ground.

Cedar. The heartwood of all types of cedar has better-than-average resistance to decay. Like redwood, western red cedar is a fragrant,

dark-colored wood that is extremely stable and rot resistant. It can be left to age to a gray patina, or it can be stained or painted. Cedar does have drawbacks. Because it is softer and weaker than other species, cedar is not recommended for the framing members. And its price is high because its popularity for cedar shingles, clapboards, and shakes limits its availability.

Cypress. Baldcypress, often called "cypress," is the South's answer to redwood. Native to the swamps and lowland areas throughout the Southeast, cypress is extremely resistant to decay and insect attack. Cypress is similar to redwood in hardness and strength, although it's not as stable. In the southern United States, local sawmills can be economical sources of cypress. Although cypress isn't usually stocked outside its native region, you may be able to order it if you live elsewhere.

Other Decay-Resistant Woods. Depending on where you live, you may have access to local wood species with heartwood that is quite resistant to rot. Osage orange, black locust, and white oak are all potentially good choices for outdoor projects. Because most of these species will not be readily available through home centers, you'll need to inquire with local sawmills and conduct your own surfacing and drying.

Grades of Redwood

Grades with Only Heartwood	Grades with Some Sapwood	Characteristics
Clear All Heart	Clear	Essentially knot-free
B Heart	B Grade	Limited knots
Construction Heart	Construction Common	Knottier than B
Deck Heart	Deck Common	Graded specifically for strength; similar to Construction grades
Merchantable Heart	Merchantable	Larger knots and knotholes

Source: California Redwood Association

Life Expectancy of Wood in Contact with the Ground

Southern yellow pine		
Treated		42 years
Untreated		3-12 years
Western red cedar		8-24 years
Redwood		20 years

Source: U.S. Forest Products Laboratory

Pressure-Treated Lumber

Pressure-treated lumber is wood that, in addition to being graded, has been factory treated with chemicals to repel rot, insects, and other causes of decay. The most widely used product for this treatment is chromated copper arsenate (CCA). CCA-treated Southern yellow pine is the principle pressure-treated wood sold in the United States, especially in the eastern half. Some western woods, such as Douglas fir, are treated with a slightly different formulation of preservatives.

Pressure treatment is the most effective method of applying preservative because, unlike brushing or other surface treatments, it forces the chemical deep into wood fibers. The chemical injection process gives CCA-treated wood its characteristic greenish tint. Pressure-treated wood will fade to a mellow gray if left to weather naturally. Alternatively, it can be treated with water repellents, stains, and paint.

Most pressure-treated wood in home centers and lumberyards has a fairly high moisture content. If you plan to paint or want to take extra steps to ensure the stability of the lumber or minimize chance of skin contact, consider buying lumber that has been kiln-dried after treatment. (This is known as KDAT).

The retention level achieved during pressure treatment determines the recommended uses for CCA-treated wood. Wood treated to a retention level of 0.25 pounds of preservative per cubic foot is often adequate for outdoor use above ground level. Posts and other lumber that will be in regular ground contact should have a rating of 0.40. The standards for retention levels are established by the American Wood Preservers Association, and enforcement of the standard is overseen by several independent organizations. When buying pressure-treated lumber, look for a tag or mark indicating the retention level.

Although many people dislike the greenish tint on pressure-treated wood, the tint does offer an important benefit. By studying the extent to which the green has penetrated the wood, you can determine if it has received proper treatment. By industry standards, at least 85 percent of the sapwood of lumber up to 5 inches thick should contain the preservative. Since the heartwood of the most commonly treated species does not absorb the preservatives, heartwood becomes the weak link. Because posts are often cut from tree cores, posts often contain a high percentage of heartwood. The higher the percentage of heartwood in a post, the smaller the percentage of that post that will be treated. Consequently, when shopping for critical pieces of lumber (especially posts), try to reject those with a high percentage of heartwood.

Treated wood should be cut as little as possible, but before you make crosscuts, study the inner core of the board to determine how thoroughly it has absorbed preservatives. If you find a high rate of incompletely treated lumber, consider returning it to the dealer.

Some manufacturers sell a premium line of treated lumber injected with waterproofing sealer as well as the standard preservatives. You will pay more for this lumber, but you will also be able to skip sealing it with waterproofing yourself after the structure has been constructed. In fact, you'll probably need to wait as long as six months before the surface weathers sufficiently to allow the wood to be painted or stained. That's because wood that has been waterproofed has been sealed with paraffin. If you are planning to paint or stain, you'll save money by buying just standard pressure-treated lumber.

Working with Pressure-Treated Wood. CCA is an arsenic compound that chemically bonds with the wood. Properly treated, the chemicals will not

Heartwood vs. Sapwood in Pressure-Treated Posts.
Heartwood begins at the center of a tree's annual growth rings. It is denser than sapwood rings, which are nearer the bark. After pressure treatment, the heartwood becomes the more vulnerable to rot because chemical preservatives don't penetrate into it. So try to avoid pressure-treated posts with much heartwood, as shown on the right.

Issues of Health and Environment

Many people worry about using pressure-treated lumber because it contains toxic chemicals. This concern is particularly acute for projects that will be used by children. Many studies have been conducted on the possible hazards posed by pressure-treated lumber, and studies continue. The results thus far support the argument that chemicals from properly treated lumber will not leach into the ground or rub onto skin that comes in contact with it. The U.S. Consumer Product Safety Commission has concluded that pressure-treated lumber does not pose a risk to children when used on play structures.

Regarding durability, the principal alternatives to pressure-treated lumber are redwood and western red cedar. But they pose a different but also important dilemma. The best grades of the biggest boards of both species come from centuries-old trees in native forests and are irreplaceable, and many people feel they should be protected.

As with many other choices faced by consumers, there can be consequences involved in buying lumber. If you have concerns about these consequences, you owe it to yourself to study the issues.

---

leach from the wood. For this reason, the wood has been judged safe for all types of outdoor building projects. For special projects like playground equipment and picnic tables, with surfaces that will contact food, be particularly careful to choose wood with a surface that is visibly clean, with no chemical residue left behind. To be extra safe, use wood that has been treated under the American Wood Preservers Association standard C17-88, "Playground Equipment Treated with Inorganic Preservatives." You can also reduce chances that the preservative will contact food and skin by applying a water repellent, oil-based stain, or paint.

A large number of studies confirm that working with CCA-treated wood is relatively safe. True, many builders who regularly work with pressure-treated lumber report rashes, watery eyes, itching, sneezing, and other irritations. These reactions may be caused by breathing the CCA-saturated sawdust or by being exposed to trace amounts of the chemicals released when cutting. In fact, such reactions are not uncommon to sawdust from many species of wood that have not been treated. For example, many people suffer allergy-like symptoms when exposed to cedar sawdust.

Here are precautions to take when working with pressure-treated lumber:

▲ Wear a long-sleeved shirt and long pants.

▲ Wear gloves, except when using power tools.

▲ When cutting or drilling, always wear a dust mask and eye and ear protection.

▲ Always work outdoors.

▲ Avoid sanding, as much as possible.

▲ Wash your hands thoroughly before eating.

▲ Never burn pressure-treated wood, even in a wood stove, because the smoke will carry the toxic emissions. Treated wood should be disposed of through normal trash collection.

Buying Lumber

Dimension softwood is sold by the linear foot in lengths that can range from 6 to 24 feet. The projects in this book can be built with standard sizes of lumber in their most widely available lengths—8 feet, 10 feet, and 12 feet. The more care you take in choosing lengths, the less waste you will have when you're done.

You cannot always count on the lumber dealer's providing square ends on each board, especially on lower grades of lumber. Examine the ends of any lumber of critical length to ensure that it is not slanted or damaged. Take a measuring tape with you to ensure that the boards measure their specified lengths. If you need to square-cut boards yourself, plan on losing ½ to 1 inch on both ends.

If ends are out of square, another option is to move up to the next available length and trim it. Not all suppliers stock every lumber grade in every possible length, so you might need to shop around or make some adjustments. Especially ensure that the critical support members (posts, beams, joists) will have solid end pieces.

Nominal vs. Actual Dimensions. When a 2x4 is sawn from the log, it really does measure 2 by 4 inches. But when that piece of wood is surfaced to make it flat and smooth lumber, and then dried, its actual dimensions are reduced. By the time that 2x4 gets to you, it will actually measure 1½ by 3½ inches. Fortunately, these dimensions are industry standard. See the illustration "Nominal vs. Actual Dimensions" to help in your planning.

Lumber Grades. Lumber is sorted and marked at the mill with a stamp that identifies the moisture content, grade name, mill name, species, and grading agency. Grade is determined by

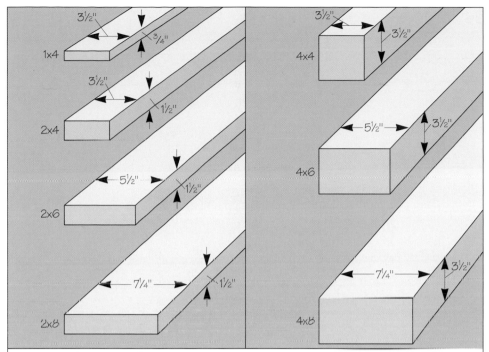

Nominal vs. Actual Dimensions. Nominal, common names for lumber sometimes mislead beginners. Lumber is sold by whole-number designations, such as 2x4 and 2x6, when each board is cut. But you actually receive lumber at industry-standard dimensions after surfacing. Be sure to account for actual sizes when measuring and marking.

natural growth characteristics (such as knots), defects that result from milling errors, and manufacturing techniques used for drying and preserving the wood. All of these factors can affect the strength, durability, and appearance of the wood.

As long as you buy from a reputable dealer, you shouldn't need to worry about which grades to buy. Dimensional lumber is used to build houses, after all, and your play yard is unlikely to carry the structural loads of a house. Just make sure that any posts, beams, and joists come from the grade abbreviated as SEL STR, which stands for Select Structural.

Your biggest challenge may be finding lumber that is reasonably straight. As most pros will tell you, the quality of construction lumber has declined markedly in recent years. If your dealer won't let you pick through piles to find the lumber you want, consider finding another source. The illustration "Lumber Defects" will give you an idea of common defects you should try to avoid. See page 29.

Plywood

You will need little, if any, plywood to build the projects in this book. The plans in Chapter 9 for the Playhouse offer the option of using plywood to create a solid, fully enclosed guardrail. You can also use plywood on the roof, either by itself or as a base for more conventional roofing materials.

Regardless of the use, choose only exterior-grade plywood for outdoor use. The principal difference between interior and exterior grades is the adhesive used to bond the layers (plies) together. Exterior-grade glues are formulated to function under exposure to temperature and moisture extremes, while interior-grade glues would quickly fail under such conditions.

If you want to use plywood for the guardrail and roofing, consider the options among the textured and patterned panels designed to serve as siding for houses, garages, and sheds. You can choose from a variety of patterns, and then select your own stain or paint.

For roof sheathing, ⅜- or ½-inch CDX is the common choice. The C and D refer to the grades of the two sides, while the X indicates that it is suitable for exterior use. But since the bottom side of the sheathing would be exposed on the Playhouse, a better choice would be ACX plywood. The "A" side would have a smooth and blemish-free appearance.

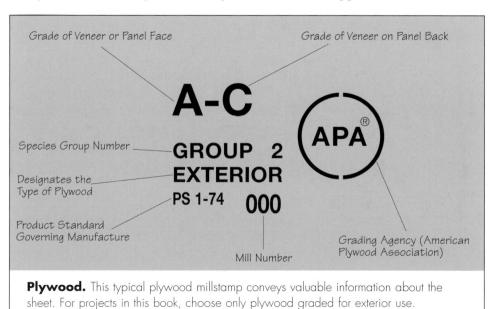

Plywood. This typical plywood millstamp conveys valuable information about the sheet. For projects in this book, choose only plywood graded for exterior use.

Wood Delivery

If you don't have access to a truck, you'll need to arrange for delivery of your lumber. Inquire if there will be a delivery charge. And make sure the supplier will deliver the lumber when you need it.

It's also important to establish policy with the dealer regarding return of unusable material. You should not need to pay for boards that are cracked, warped, or otherwise too defective to be used. For this reason, it's a good idea to be on hand when the delivery arrives so that you'll be able to give the wood a quick inspection before the truck leaves. You should be able to refuse delivery of any bad lumber.

Storing and Drying Wood. At least some of the wood you order, especially wet pressure-treated lumber, will still be fairly saturated with water when you take delivery or pick it up. Wet wood can be difficult to work with; it dulls saw blades and is much heavier than dry stock. Even worse, wet wood will continue to shrink until its moisture content matches that of its environment. You'll be happier with the results if you let the bulk of the shrinking occur before you begin building.

If you spent extra to get kiln-dried lumber, your money will be wasted if you let the wood sit outside without protection. If you need to store the wood for more than a few days, you should stack it in a well-ventilated location and cover it. Stack wood a few inches off the ground so that the boards won't wick up ground moisture. Be sure to stack the boards neatly on top of each other to help keep the lower boards straight. Stones, concrete blocks, or other weights can be placed on top of the waterproof cover to stabilize it.

If you need to store plywood, stack it flat and well off the ground.

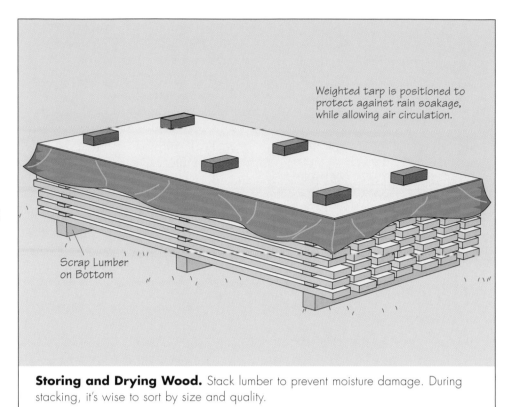

Weighted tarp is positioned to protect against rain soakage, while allowing air circulation.

Scrap Lumber on Bottom

Storing and Drying Wood. Stack lumber to prevent moisture damage. During stacking, it's wise to sort by size and quality.

Concrete

Concrete is a mixture of cement, sand, gravel, and water. When mixed in the right proportions, the concrete undergoes a chemical reaction known as "hydration." Once "cured," concrete is strong, solid, and uniform. To build the play structures in this book, the only use you will have for concrete is to form piers, which are the foundation that holds the structure safely in place.

To obtain concrete, you can take one of two approaches. You can buy bags of premixed concrete, which you mix with water, or you can order from a "ready-mix" concrete supplier. Ready-mix will be delivered in one of those "cement trucks" all mixed and ready to pour. Yet for this play structure, ready-mix would be worth investigating only if you had a large number or relatively deep holes to fill or if your neighbor also had need for some concrete.

For most home play-yard projects, you can either mix the concrete by hand in a wheelbarrow, or borrow or rent a power mixer.

Reducing Fall Impacts

Some people may question the extra effort and expense of installation of an impact-reducing material, such as wood mulch or pea gravel. Yet most playground injuries result from falls. There are really only two ways to reduce the chance for a fall-related injury: (1) build a play structure entirely free of components more than a couple of feet off the ground, or (2) install an impact-reducing material wherever a fall might occur to reduce the chance for injury.

With the first option, your choices for play components would be narrowed to sandboxes and low platform structures, such as the Playhouse. But around swings, slides, and higher platforms, you should install an impact-reducing material.

Why Not Grass? Grass is not an adequate impact-reducing material at heights above 20 inches for preschoolers or 30 inches for school-age children. Studies suggest that a child can sustain a concussion from a fall of

Impact-Reducing Materials (Minimum depth, uncompressed)		
Material	**8½-ft. Swing**	**5-ft. Tower Platform**
Wood mulch	9"	6"
Wood chips	11"	9"
Sand	12"	11"
Pea gravel	11"	9"

Source: *Public Playground Handbook for Safety*, U.S. Consumer Product Safety Commission, U.S. Government Printing Office

only 24 inches onto packed earth. A lawn will compact over time, resulting in a ground surface that can be almost as hard as asphalt. Then too, some lawns do not drain well, which could limit the time that the play structure could be used. And grass will wear away over time, leaving you with mud after a rain.

A safe play yard should have borders. And an impact-reducing surface provides a demarcation perimeter, within which you can lay down safety rules.

Choosing an Impact-Reducing Material

A number of factors can affect the cushioning ability of the various materials: degree of compaction; wetness (especially with wood products); type of material (there are different sands, gravels, and mulches); height of fall; and size of child. The U.S. Consumer Product Safety Commission has conducted tests that simulate the impact of a child's head falling onto various materials of different depths and from different heights. Their conclusions are interpreted in the table "Impact-Reducing Materials."

In the table, the greater minimum depths under "swing" assumes a fall from 8½ feet—the assumed maximum attainable angle of 90 degrees from the "at rest" position. The minimum depths under the Central Tower assume that the highest platform is 5 feet above the surface and is protected by guardrails that discourage climbing. Again, these figures are only guidelines, intended to minimize the chance of injury. The table does not include foam and rubber mat materials. Mats tend to be quite expensive and are primarily intended for public facilities. Yet because they provide the best protection, mats would be good choices for cushioning a small area, such as under a ladder or swing. For mat sources, check with your local school officials.

Wood Mulch and Chips. Mulch is composed of wood chips, twigs, and leaves of various sizes that are created by wood chippers. Aged mulch for gardens tends to be more expensive. Wood chips, sold separately, are small pieces of wood, of relatively uniform size. Both mulch and chips are available by the truckload and in 3-cubic-foot bags. Wood mulch and chips are light and easy to install, and are less abrasive to skin than sand and less likely to attract cats and dogs.

Sand. Buy only washed sand. River sand or seaside sand is comparatively inexpensive. Although fine sand provides excellent cushioning, it is more likely to blow about in the wind. Masonry sand has particles of uniform size and is less likely to compact. Chief drawbacks of sand are that it can blow around and get into clothing and thus be tracked indoors.

Pea Gravel. Washed gravel contains rounded particles about ⅜ inch or less in diameter. It doesn't compact as much as sand and is less likely to attract cats and dogs. Avoid crushed rock, sometimes sold as pea gravel; it has sharp edges that will cause skin injuries when kids fall on it.

General Guidelines. All impact-reducing materials should be contained in

Choosing an Impact-Reducing Material (Shown Actual Size)

Wood Chips

Aged Wood Mulch

Pea Gravel

Sand

a border, such as wood timbers, with good drainage beneath. Wood mulch and chips need occasional replacement, because weather causes them to decompose and compact. Also, wood should be raked now and then to level it and remove debris. In some localities, recycling centers and landfills offer wood mulch for free. Otherwise, good sources include landscapers, garden centers, tree service contractors, and nurseries.

Sand and gravel should be raked regularly, especially if cats treat it as a giant litter box. Washed sand and gravel are usually available from the same suppliers. Check the Yellow Pages under "Sand and Gravel." Rather than trying to haul your own, have a truckload delivered.

Hardware

One of the biggest mistakes of do-it-yourselfers, and some pros, is to add fasteners to a project without enough thought. For example, too many nails can do more damage than good. Keep in mind that fasteners are designed to perform specific functions. As a general rule, know why and how you are using a fastener for a particular joint. Use only what you need.

Every piece of metal on your play structure must be suitable for exterior use. That means that the metal should be hot-dipped galvanized steel, stainless steel, or aluminum. If you are concerned about vandalism, theft, or abusive use, consider using specialized hardware from manufacturers of public playground equipment. Check for sources with local school officials.

Nails. The most basic metal fastener is the nail. Nail sizes are expressed with the term penny, which is abbreviated as d. The larger the number that precedes the d, the larger the nail. Nails are typically sold by the pound.

There are dozens of types of nails, but for play yards, there are only a few types you need to consider. The most important thing to remember is that all nails for outdoor use must be rust-resistant. Under most circumstances, the best choice is hot-dipped galvanized steel nails.

Galvanized steel fasteners are coated with a rust-resistant layer of zinc or cadmium, or both. There are several methods for applying this coating, but the most trustworthy is hot-dipping. Hot-dipped galvanization involves dropping the steel into molten zinc. This process applies the thickest coating and therefore offers the best chance for long-term survival.

Don't confuse hot-dipped nails with hot-galvanized nails. The latter process is not as effective in coating the nails. Electroplated galvanized nails look nice and shiny, but they don't hold up well on exterior applications. If you have any doubts, check the box labeling; it should say "HD" for hot dipped, while "HG" will be hot galvanized.

Stainless-steel and aluminum nails are also suited for exterior use. In regions where corrosion is a problem, such as along an ocean coast, these nails can be the best investment. Aluminum nails are softer and tend to bend more easily than steel nails. Stainless-steel nails are recommended for use with redwood and western red cedar, because they are prone to staining from galvanized nails. Avoid using aluminum nails with pressure-treated lumber, because the copper in the wood preservative will cause corrosion.

As to nail design, "common" nails are preferred for general construction because they have an extra-thick shank and a broad head. You can also purchase common nails that have been coated to increase their holding power. For most connections between framing lumber (2x4s and 2x6s), 16d common nails are recommended. If splitting

is a problem, you might switch to 16d box nails, which are the same length, with the same size head, but are slimmer and thus less prone to cause splitting. As a general rule, follow the nailing schedules shown on page 54.

When you don't want nailheads to show, or when attaching thin pieces of trim, use finishing nails designed for exterior use. Finishing nails have a thin shank and a small head. The head can easily be sunk below the wood surface by means of a hammer and nail set. You can fill the hole with wood putty.

For decking over joists, use good-quality screw-shank or ring-shank nails. Their grooved sides make them less likely to work loose under duress, including that from frolicking children and changes in weather—hot and cold, wet and dry. In fact, these nails are a good choice for all critical connections, such as deck framing, stairs, and handrails. One drawback is that they are tough to pull out. So if you plan to take your play structure apart some day, and would prefer not to destroy the lumber in the process, these nails aren't the best choice.

Screws. For most general framing, it's hard to beat the speed and affordability of nails. But for some applications, screws are worth considering. Screws offer much better holding power than nails, and they can be removed quickly to replace a board or disassemble a play structure. Screws create a clean, finished appearance by eliminating the possibility of hammer dents and scuffs; and, unlike nails, screws will not "pop" loose over time.

There is a variety of corrosion-resistant screws on the market. Hot-dipped galvanized and stainless steel are the most common, but you may want to check with your supplier to see what else is available. Most hardware stores and home centers carry a generically named "decking screw." Woodworking supply

Nails

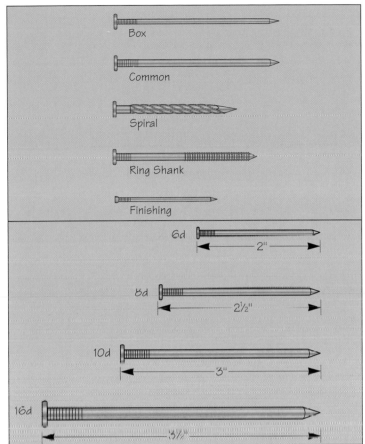

Box
Common
Spiral
Ring Shank
Finishing

6d — 2"
8d — 2½"
10d — 3"
16d — 3½"

Bolts

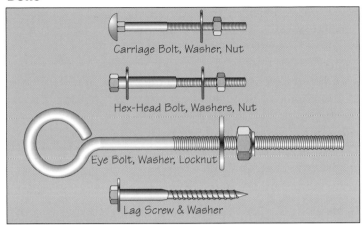

Carriage Bolt, Washer, Nut
Hex-Head Bolt, Washers, Nut

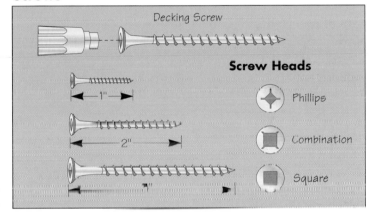

Eye Bolt, Washer, Locknut
Lag Screw & Washer

Screws

Decking Screw

1"
2"
1"

Screw Heads

Phillips
Combination
Square

catalogs are another good source for a variety of screw types. It's definitely worth a little extra expense to buy self-tapping screws, which eliminate the need to drill pilot holes first.

Caution: *Don't use all-purpose drywall screws, which look like decking screws. Most all-purpose screws are not intended for exterior use, and they are too brittle and weak for joining wood, especially load-bearing, structural members.*

Although Phillips-head screws are commonly used with drill-drivers, square-head screws and bits are highly recommended because the bits don't slip out of the screwhead as easily. Screws are also available with a combination head, allowing the use of either a square or Phillips bit.

For most outdoor construction projects, plan to use #10 screws (10-gauge screws). Gauge is a mea-sure of diameter. As a general rule, choose screws of lengths that allow them to enter two-thirds of the way into the second piece, the piece to which you are fastening. Be sure to use properly sized bits.

Bolts. Bolts are used for connections that require maximum strength. Carriage bolts and hex-head bolts both require washers and nuts. With its smooth, curved head, the carriage bolt is best for any connection that might be bumped or scraped by a child. However, hex-head bolts may be preferred high out of reach on the swing frame to join the beam to the posts. A carriage bolt requires a washer only on the nut end, while a hex-head bolt requires washers on both ends.

Eye bolts are designed for attaching chain or rope. They can be used to hang swings and other accessories from a beam. Since these bolts will be subject to a lot of stress, attach them with locknuts, which have a small nylon insert in them that helps lock the nut to the bolt threads. Check eye bolts frequently to ensure the lock nuts are doing their job.

Often called bolts because they are large and have a boltlike head, lag screws are essentially oversized wood screws. They must be driven with either an adjustable wrench or a socket wrench. Because lag screws don't fasten as strongly as carriage or hex-head bolts, use them only when the back side is inaccessible. To install most bolts, you must first drill a hole with a bit that is the same diameter as the unthreaded shank of the bolt. However, lag screws require a hole of smaller diameter than the threaded front to ensure that the threads bite in. (Drilling procedures are discussed in "Concealing Bolts" and "Installing Lag Bolts" on pages 55-56.)

Rungs. For the rungs on the Monkey Bar, you can use either metal or wood. Wood rungs can be cut from large-diameter hardwood dowels. Playground equipment manufacturers offer sets of precut, pressure-treated 1⅛-inch dowels, but you can make your own from untreated hardwood dowels. One safety concern: Dowels should be checked for splinters from time to time. Use sandpaper to smooth any questionable surfaces, and treat the rungs regularly with a good water-repellent wood preservative.

Suitable metal rungs are either 1-inch galvanized-steel water pipe or 1-inch heavy-wall (or rigid) electrical conduit; don't use thin-wall conduit. Both galvanized water pipe and heavy-wall conduit are strong and hold up well outdoors. And they can be cut with a hacksaw. An advantage of threaded galvanized pipe is that it can be joined with flanges, elbows, and other fittings to create handgrips, railings, and sliding poles. The biggest disadvantage of metal rungs is that they get cold in cold weather.

Chain. Playground stores sell rubber-like coated swing chain, which reduces chances that little fingers will get pinched or caught. If you instead buy uncoated chain, choose ³⁄₁₆-inch or ¼-inch chain for normal duty, and ⁵⁄₁₆-inch for heavy-duty use, such as for a tire swing used by older kids. Small links are preferred, because they are less likely to pinch fingers. Inspect the chain carefully for sharp edges; if you find any, file them down. Chain with sharp points can be covered with garden hose or plastic tubing to reduce the possibility of pinching or cutting.

Short-link chain is a specialized safety chain designed for use on children's playgrounds. The very small links prevent children from getting their fingers caught or pinched in the chain. In several countries in Europe, short-link chain is required on playground equipment.

Rungs and Chain

Safety-Coated Chain

Clips and Hooks

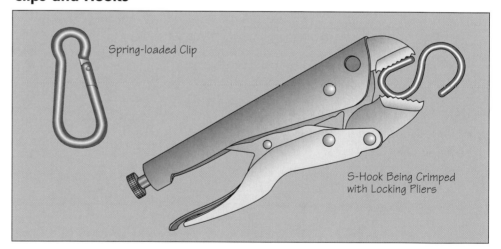

Spring-loaded Clip

S-Hook Being Crimped with Locking Pliers

Clips and Hooks. S-hooks are used to connect chain with swing seats and hangers. For most purposes, ¼-inch galvanized S-hooks will be sufficient.

Caution: *Before use, S-hooks need to be crimped with a pliers, locking pliers, or a hammer to make them secure.*

Spring-loaded connector clips allow you to connect the chain to the hanger without pliers. They are particularly useful if you need to change the height of a swing regularly for different children or to replace the swing with another accessory. Spring-loaded clips should not be used where they could be reached by children, because they are easy to remove. Also, avoid them if you are concerned about theft.

Rope

Chain is a better choice than rope for suspending swings primarily because it can be used with durable and safe fittings. Rope must be tied to beams and seats, with weaker and less durable connections. Yet rope is good for climbing. Simply loop a few knots along its length to provide hand holds and suspend it from a beam.

When buying rope, you can choose between natural fiber and synthetics. High-grade manila hemp (abaca) is good for play structures, especially for climbing. It's strong and less abrasive on hands than other types, and not nearly as slippery. Because it is popular with boaters, boatyards can be a source.

Synthetic rope is strong, but slippery. It is better for supporting swings than for climbing. Avoid polypropylene because it does not hold up well to the sun and cold. Of the synthetic ropes, polyethylene rope is probably the best choice, although nylon is nearly as good.

Be sure to check the rope manufacturer's label for the maximum load that the rope is intended to support. One-half inch nylon or polyethylene is plenty strong for our Swing Frame. If you use polypropylene, which is much weaker, you will need to at least double the thickness to support the same amount of weight.

Play Accessories

You can choose from among many dozens of manufactured accessories. This allows you to customize your project to meet your needs, and it offers the opportunity to add new accessories as your children tire of or outgrow the original activities.

To find the broadest selection, be prepared to shop around. Toy and department stores may offer a small selection, home centers a little more. Also check with playground experts at local schools and parks, and consult telephone Yellow Pages under playground-related headings. Some of the largest selections may be available through mail order. The following section surveys some of the options.

Swings. Swing seats for babies and infants are usually bucket style, made of rigid plastic or wood. They should either be fully enclosed, making it impossible for the child to slip out or climb out, or be equipped with a child-proof safety strap. In addition to design features, safe use requires constant adult presence.

Adult-supervised toddlers are comfortable in soft-rubber or molded plastic half bucket seats that provide support to the lower back and may also include a safety strap.

For older kids, the choices are more numerous. Most older kids are happy with a flexible belt-style seat, which may be made of soft rubber, canvas, or plastic. You can also choose flat, rigid seats made from wood, rubber, or plastic. As mentioned earlier, hard seats increase the hazard of injury in the event the seat strikes another child.

Some swings, especially those for the youngest children, are sold with rope or chain already attached. You should be able to find swing seats in a variety of colors.

Slides. The most commonly available slides are 8 and 10 feet long, made of molded polyethylene, in a choice of colors. You can choose straight or wavy models (the latter will slide a bit slower). These slides can be attached to a platform deck in a matter of minutes with just a couple of screws. Heavy-duty models are thicker and may be reinforced with side rails.

Most kids seem to love tube slides, which can be straight or twisting. But tube slides have disadvantages. They cost considerably more than standard slides, and they are more complicated to install. Also, from standpoints of safety and parental supervision, tubes conceal children inside and somewhat obscure the view behind them. In addition, twisting tubes may prevent the second

Swing Seats

Full bucket is safest for toddlers.

Half bucket is good for preschoolers.

Safety-Coated Swing Chain

Belt seat is one of the safest for school-age kids.

Rigid seat could encourage unsafe standing and is hard upon impact.

Slides

Wave Slide of Molded Polyethylene

Tire-Swing Connection Options

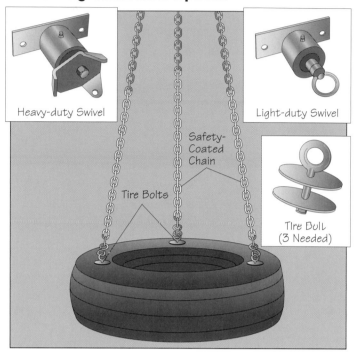

Heavy-duty Swivel

Light-duty Swivel

Safety-Coated Chain

Tire Bolts

Tire Bolt (3 Needed)

Gymnastic Equipment

Trapeze Rings

Trapeze Bar

child's ability to see when a previous child has cleared the tube and stepped safely away from the landing.

All slides are manufactured to be installed on decks of a specified height, usually 48 to 60 inches. It's vital to match your slide to deck height.

Gymnastic Equipment. In place of a permanent or temporary swing, you may want to hang a trapeze bar, with or without a set of rings attached. Spring-loaded connector clips allow you to switch gymnastic accessories in a couple of minutes. Also, instead of the Monkey Bar we've designed for the Kids' Playland, your kids might prefer trapeze rings.

Other Swings. Tire swings are popular, especially because they can be used by two or three children at once. Tire swings can be hung from the main swing beam. But avoid installing a tire swing near another swing. Because it swings in all directions, a tire swing would be likely to collide with nearby swings. You can buy tire swings complete or buy special hardware that allows you to convert your own spare tire into a swing. Tire swings should be installed with tire-swivel hardware, following the manufacturer's instructions. Also, several variations on the tire swing offer a similar type of swinging movement, but for only one child at a time.

Caution: *Don't use steel-belted radial tires because exposed belting on worn tires can be sharp.*

Other possibilities include swing discs and ball swings, often preferred by older children because they provide a free-swinging motion.

Swing Hardware. As mentioned, you'll need tire swivels to install a tire swing. Manufacturers also offer specialized swing hangers, at modest cost, that can speed installation. Hangers are available with a threaded screw or machine thread that requires a nut and washer. However, assemblies with only one threaded screw lack heavy-duty strength.

4

Techniques

Every carpenter develops unique approaches to construction projects. Yet if you were to watch a group of pros, you would notice similarities in the ways they perform many tasks. Of course, you can learn by trial and error in the School of Hard Knocks, but you don't need to learn everything that way.

This chapter provides a foundation of basic techniques. And it will help you build play structures correctly on the first try, with a minimum of wasted time and materials. As a bonus, you'll find that most of the skills transfer to other projects, particularly other outdoor structures, such as fences and decks. Although there are tricks of the trade, good building skills are basically common sense

applied to shapes, materials, tools, and techniques. With practice, these skills become second nature.

Let the following few principles guide all of your work: Take your time, work safely, and never forget the carpenter's creed: "Measure twice, cut once."

Setting Up the Work Site

Good carpenters heed the Shaker motto "a place for everything and everything in its place." If you've done some building, you may recall having wasted time looking for misplaced tools, climbing over stacked lumber, moving materials about, misplacing tools, and making extra trips to purchase forgotten items. If you've known such inefficiencies, you'll better appreciate how even a small project can devour an entire weekend. This book will help you plan better. Besides, a well-planned work site is a lot safer.

Often a quick sketch of the work site helps you visualize how the work should flow. In your sketch, try to include all the major construction elements: where the wood will be delivered, how the car or truck will reach delivery points with minimal damage to lawn or garden, where electrical cords will run, where you will perform most of the cutting, and so on. Try to imagine how these factors will relate. Then plan the work site accordingly. For example, if you will deliver lumber yourself, unload near enough to the proposed play structure to minimize wood toting but distant enough to keep materials out of your way when you begin work. If you plan to have a bulldozer remove the sod or a truck-mounted auger drill the postholes, sketch paths for the vehicles. It's also wise to have most power tools in one general location. This helps minimize the moving of sawhorses, for example, and it isolates the tripping hazard of power cords.

Besides your time in this project, your biggest investment will be in the wood. To avoid unnecessary damage to the wood and injury to yourself, use a little forethought before you stack the wood. For example, the weight from a properly stacked pile will prevent boards from cupping and warping. Also decide how and where you will pile wood scraps so they don't get in the way. Upon delivery of the lumber, begin sorting it by best and worst pieces; that way you'll know which piles or portions of piles to use for visible and hidden portions of the project. If the lumber will be outdoors, apply a rain cover that first day.

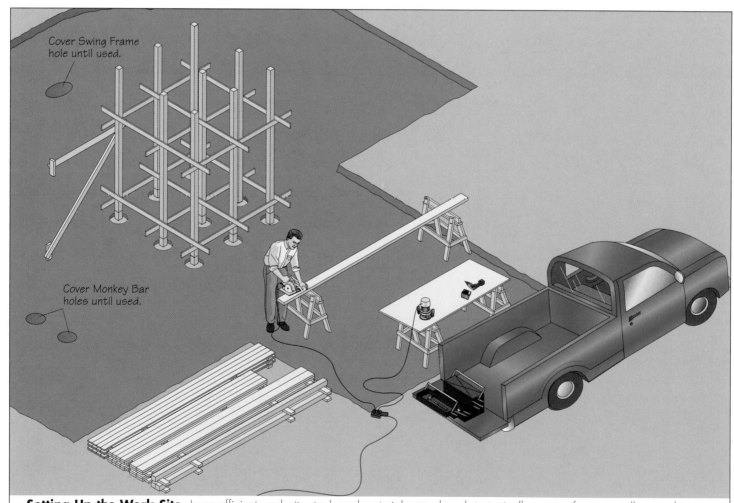

Cover Swing Frame hole until used.

Cover Monkey Bar holes until used.

Setting Up the Work Site. In an efficient work site, tools and materials are placed strategically to save footsteps, allow working room, and promote safety. Note that the lumber is stacked to allow convenient end-of-stack removal.

Preparing the Site

Site preparation involves some of the most important decisions on the project. What kind of impact-reducing material will you use? How deep do you want it? Will the surface be at grade (ground level) or above grade? Your answers will be affected by desired appearance, as well as costs in time and dollars. Here are several options:

An Above-Grade Surface. The simplest approach is to place the surface above grade. This allows you to build on top of the lawn, without the hassle of first removing sod and topsoil before adding a border and filling in with impact-reducing material. Note that the border should be high enough to hold the depth of material required. See the table "Impact-Reducing Materials" on page 35.

Since this border will be a step up from grade, it must be strong and solid. For this, you can use pressure-treated 4x6s or landscape timbers. The top edges of the timbers should be smooth and rounded. (Landscape timbers are normally sold with two rounded edges.) To hold the border in place, drill holes through the timbers about every 48 inches. Then use a sledgehammer to drive 18- to 20-inch lengths of steel reinforcing bar, called rebar, through the holes into the ground. Be sure to drive the rebar below the top surface of the timber so that it doesn't protrude.

To ensure that grass and weeds won't grow through the edge materials, underlay them with landscape fabric. This special landscape fabric is preferable to polyethylene sheeting because it allows water to drain through. Finally, fill the enclosure with at least 6 inches of wood mulch or wood chips, or with the appropriate depth of sand or pea gravel.

Sawhorses

On a work site, few devices are more useful than a pair of good sawhorses. First, they offer a sturdy, safe surface on which to measure, mark, and cut lumber. Second, they become part of a workbench when you lay a sheet of plywood over them.

Some carpenters build elaborate sawhorses, which they pamper and carry from job to job. Others see sawhorses as temporary supports, best built in minutes from scrap lumber on site and then torn apart when the job is done. The choice is yours.

The sawhorse shown without bracing can be built in about ten minutes and requires only three materials: 2x4s, 1x6s, and either 10d nails or 3-inch screws. Begin by cutting an 8-foot 2x4 in half to serve as the top of the horse. Then fasten the two pieces in an inverted T, as shown. Cut legs from the 1x6 to the length you prefer; 30 to 36 inches suits most people. Then attach each leg to each 2x4 with either nails or screws. If the sawhorses will support heavy loads, such as a long 4x6 beam, add 1x4 bracing to the legs. When you finish your play structures, you can either store the sawhorses or tear them apart.

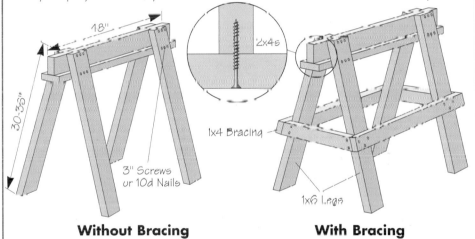

Without Bracing   **With Bracing**

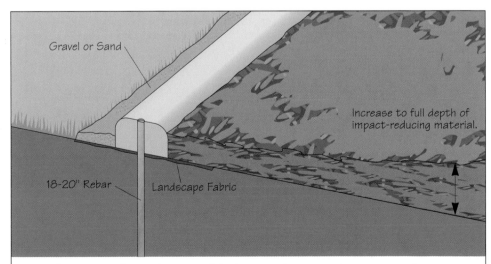

An Above-Grade Surface. Install lumber or timbers to enclose impact-reducing materials. Round-over edges and corners of timbers.

An At-Grade Surface. An at-grade sur-face blends with the yard better than an above-grade surface. But it involves considerably more work. To set the surface at grade, you will need to excavate to the depth your surface material will fill (6 to 10 inches). While you could excavate by hand, you may be better off hiring a con-tractor with a bulldozer. If you decide to do your own digging, consider renting a rototiller to loosen the soil. A heavy-duty tiller will reach down as far as 12 inches, making digging and removal much easier. But first, you might want to carefully dig up the sod and install it elsewhere in your yard. Or dig it up before rototill-ing and mix it with your compost.

With the hole dug, you can line the edges with landscape fabric, available at garden suppliers. After building the play structure, fill the excavated area with the impact-reducing materi-al of your choice.

Hybrid Grade Option. You could borrow a little from each of the two grade approaches above by building a slightly raised border. For example, you could use 3x5 landscape timbers; then remove only the sod and perhaps a couple of inches of topsoil. This hybrid approach allows you to reach a depth of at least 6 inches, the minimum for safety, with-out needing to do extensive excavation.

Laying Out the Site

Site layout establishes precise loca-tions for the posts. Once set, the posts become reference points for all remaining construction.

In this book, you'll find many optional layouts for the play structure. And although the dimensions between posts in the drawing are suggested, you may wish to alter them. Either way, it's important to understand the principles of layout described here.

The main tools of layout are a tape measure, batter boards, string, and a plumb bob. To make square corners, it's helpful to understand mathemati-cal relationships expressed in the Pythagorean theorem, but not absolutely necessary. The theorem states that the squares (side x itself) of the lengths of the two short sides of a right triangle will always equal the square of the length of the long side ($a^2 + b^2 = c^2$). On the work site, it may be easier just to remember and apply the theorem as the 3-4-5 rule, as shown in accompanying illustra-tions. That is, the intersections of the string lines (which will become the corners of the structure) will be per-

An At-Grade Surface. This requires more work than an above-grade surface but reduces tripping hazards along the border and helps make the play areas look better integrated.

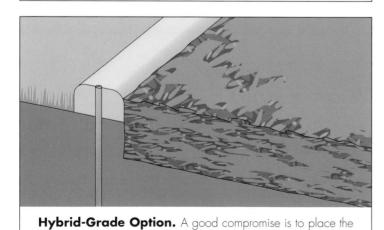

Hybrid-Grade Option. A good compromise is to place the impact-reducing material partly above and partly below grade.

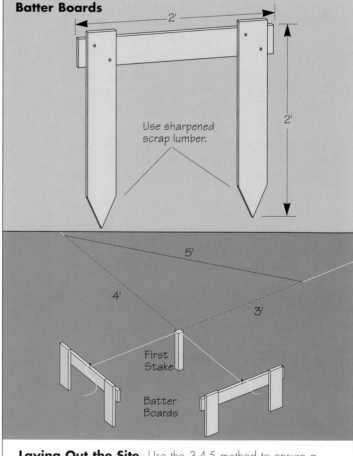

Batter Boards

2'

2'

Use sharpened scrap lumber.

5'

4'

3'

First Stake

Batter Boards

Laying Out the Site. Use the 3-4-5 method to ensure a perfectly square layout.

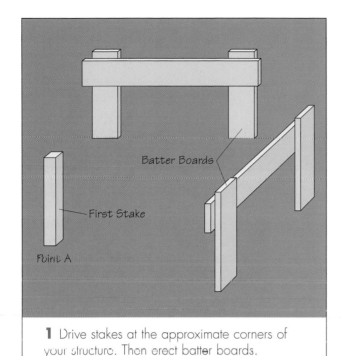

1 Drive stakes at the approximate corners of your structure. Then erect batter boards.

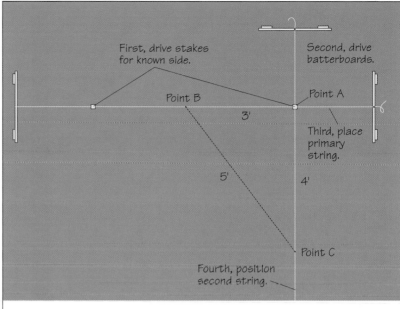

2 After driving the two stakes and batter boards for the known side of the structure, use intersecting strings to determine post positions.

fectly square when the diagonal distance from the 3-foot location on one line and the 4-foot location on the other equals 5 feet. That is because 3' (or 9) + 4' (or 16) = 5² (or 25). This principle also holds true for any multiple of 3-4-5, such as 6-8-10 or 9-12-15.

1 Find Rough Dimensions. Decide where you want one side of the play structure to be (usually the side nearest the house). Drive two small stakes where you would like its corner posts. Placement of these two stakes is important, because they become the two corner references for the entire layout.

Erect batter boards at approximate right angles to each other about 2 feet outside the stake at Point A. Erect a second batter board outside the second stake as shown. (Note: Each batter board is composed of two sharpened stakes and one horizontal brace, and can be made from scrap 1x4s or 2x4s cut to about 24-inch lengths. Rather than driving stakes and attaching braces, it's often more efficient to assemble each batter board before driving each approximately level with the other.

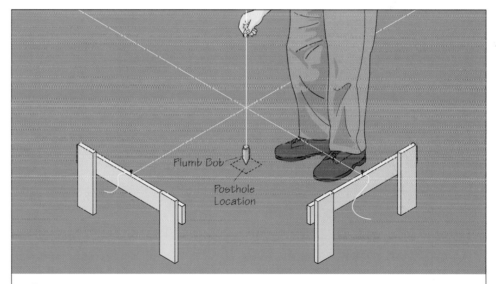

3 Mark posthole locations. Use a plumb bob to transfer string line intersections to the posthole locations on the ground.

2 String the Lines. Stretch a level string line directly over the first two stakes and tie it to opposing batter boards, as shown.

To establish the first square corner, use the 3-4-5 rule. Measure from Point A on the first corner stake along the line 3 feet and mark Point B on that string. Next, run a second line perpendicular to the first by stretching the second line over Point A and marking Point C directly on the second string 4 feet

from Point A. Then adjust line AC at the far batter board until distance BC becomes exactly 5 feet. With measurements of 3-4-5 on the sides of the imaginary triangle, angle BAC is now square—your first square corner.

3 Mark Posthole Locations. Moving to the second corner stake, install its second batter board and create the second square corner as you did the first one. In this way, proceed around to all corners.

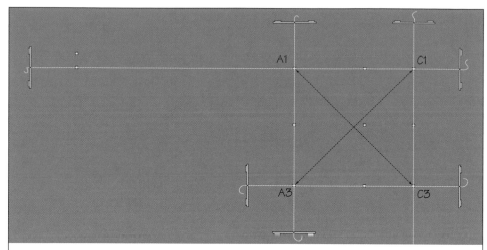

4 Check for Square. When the layout is square, the diagonal distances A1–C3 and A3–C1 will be equal.

Setting Posts

The posts should be centered in the holes. Postholes must be dug below frost line, which is the depth to which the ground in your locality will freeze during a cold winter. This requirement helps ensure that no ice forms below the posts, heaving them upward and thereby stressing joints in your structure or even throwing the structure out of alignment. Local building authorities can tell you how deep to dig and, in fact, may insist on inspecting the depth of your holes before allowing you to set the posts in concrete. If you live in a frost-free climate, the posts should be buried at least 36 inches.

Use a plumb bob, as shown, to transfer line intersections to the ground. Then drive small stakes to mark the intended holes.

4 **Check for Square.** In the event the final string line doesn't align directly over the first driven stake, your earlier string lines may not be

positioned accurately enough. In that case, return to the first stake, the second, and so on, double-checking the 3-4-5 rule at each stake and correcting line positions accordingly. In your confirming check, the distances between opposite diagonal corners of the Central Tower layout (points A1–C3 and A3–C1) should be equal.

As a general rule, postholes should be about three times the diameter of the posts. Thus, for individual 4x4 posts, you should dig 12-inch-diameter holes. For the double post on the freestanding end of the swing, the hole should measure about 12x20 inches at the top.

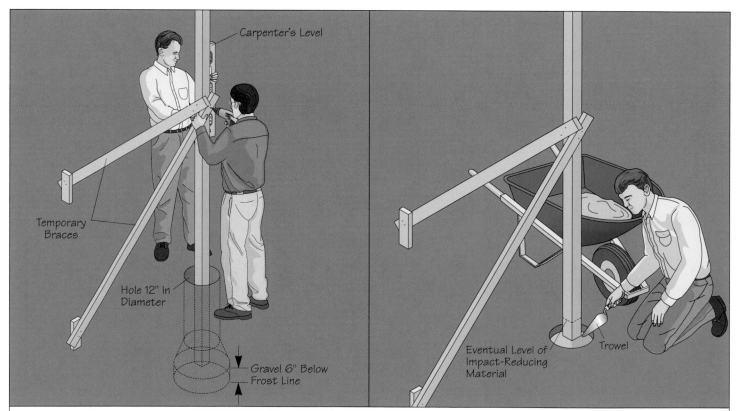

Setting Posts. Center the first post in its hole. When the post is plumb on two adjacent sides, fasten it with bracing. Pour the concrete and use a trowel to slope the wet concrete away from the post, keeping all concrete below ground level.

Keep the top surface of the concrete below ground level. This helps prevent injury to any child that might fall there. Furthermore, with the concrete buried, the eventual job of dismantling the play structure will be much easier. Rather than pulling the buried posts and concrete, you can simply cut the posts flush with the concrete, and then cover with dirt and grass.

When buying posts, calculate both aboveground and below-ground length. And buy posts a little longer than needed. Then cut post tops to their finished height after you complete the framing.

1 Dig the Holes. Dig postholes at least 6 inches below the frost line. For this task, you can use a manual posthole digger, but a power auger will speed the process considerably. You can rent one- or two-person power augers and a bit of length and diameter to suit your needs. Before using a power auger, be sure to get a thorough lesson in its operation from the rental store, and follow the manufacturer's instructions. The holes should have relatively smooth sides, with a slight flaring undercut at the bottom, as shown on page 46.

2 Add the Gravel. Shovel about 6 inches of gravel into the bottom of each posthole and tamp the gravel firmly, using the post bottom. The gravel allows water to drain away from the post.

3 Install the Posts. Set the post (or posts) on top of the gravel. While a helper holds the post steady and uses a carpenter's level to ensure that it is plumb on two adjacent sides, attach temporary bracing.

4 Pour the Concrete Piers. Mix an appropriate amount of concrete. (See the upcoming section "Working with Concrete," for estimating quantities.) Shovel wet concrete into the hole to within three inches of ground level. Again, to prevent injury to children who

might otherwise fall upon it, keep the concrete surface below ground level. Use a trowel to slope the top of the concrete away from the post and pier; this helps drain water away from the wood. Recheck the post for plumb, adjusting braces if necessary. Then leave the braces in place for about a day, allowing the pier to cure sufficiently.

Working with Concrete

Concrete is a proportioned mixture of cement, sand, gravel, and water.

To mix the concrete yourself, you have the choice of mixing by hand in a wheelbarrow or a mixing tub, or using a power mixer. The dry ingredients come in premixed bags weighing 60 to 90 pounds. Be sure to read the instructions on the bag to determine how much concrete can be made from each bag after mixing the contents with water.

But before you decide whether to mix your own concrete, consider ready-mix delivered by truck. Ready-mix will cost more but may save many hours of

Power Mixing

Using a power mixer, start by adding about half the amount of water indicated in the instructions. Then turn on the mixer. Gradually add the dry ingredients and then the rest of the water. Let the mixer run for as long as it takes for all of the ingredients to be fully mixed. Immediately empty the contents of the mixer into a wheelbarrow or buckets. When you are done mixing, unplug the mixer and thoroughly rinse it out with a hose, scraping stubborn concrete free. Otherwise, the concrete will harden there.

Electric Concrete Mixer

work. Most ready-mix companies require a minimum order, which you may be able to satisfy if you are building the full Kids' Playland and live in a cold climate requiring deep piers.

1 Estimate Your Concrete Needs. Before buying concrete mix, try to estimate how much you will need. To do this, first determine the amount needed for one hole. Then multiply the result by the number of holes you've dug.

Here's how to establish the amount of concrete needed per hole. First, calculate the total volume of the hole. Then subtract the amount of space in the hole occupied by the post. Since each hole will be cylindrical, you can use the formula for finding the volume of a cylinder. This is 3.14 (π or pi) x radius squared (r²) x height (h). Here the radius equals one-half the diameter, and the height should be the total depth of concrete needed (about three inches less than the total depth of the hole). The illustrations show calculations for determining the amount of concrete needed for a hole 42 inches deep, with a 4x4 post.

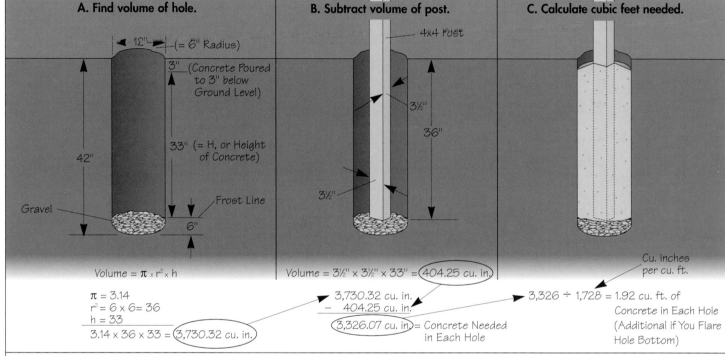

A. Find volume of hole.

12" (= 6" Radius)

3" (Concrete Poured to 3" below Ground Level)

33" (= H, or Height of Concrete)

42"

Gravel

Frost Line

6"

Volume = π x r² x h

π = 3.14
r² = 6 x 6 = 36
h = 33

3.14 x 36 x 33 = 3,730.32 cu. in.

B. Subtract volume of post.

4x4 Post

3½"

36"

3½"

Volume = 3½" x 3½" x 33" = 404.25 cu. in.

3,730.32 cu. in.
− 404.25 cu. in.

3,326.07 cu. in. = Concrete Needed in Each Hole

C. Calculate cubic feet needed.

Cu. inches per cu. ft.

3,326 ÷ 1,728 = 1.92 cu. ft. of Concrete in Each Hole (Additional if You Flare Hole Bottom)

1 To estimate your concrete needs, use the mathematical formulas shown here and in the text. If you flare the bottom of the hole, as shown on page 46, "guesstimate" the additional mix needed for the first hole. Then base your mixes for subsequent holes on your experience with the first.

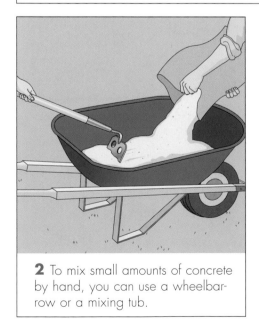

2 To mix small amounts of concrete by hand, you can use a wheelbarrow or a mixing tub.

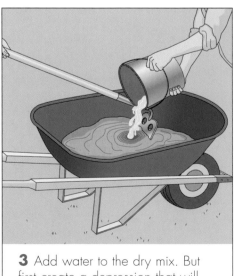

3 Add water to the dry mix. But first create a depression that will receive the water.

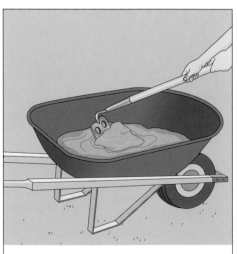

4 Mix thoroughly with a hoe. The concrete should hold its own form, as shown, without slumping down.

2 Mix by Hand. Dump the concrete mix into a wheelbarrow or a mixing tub. Since the ingredients may have separated a bit in the bag, first mix the dry ingredients thoroughly with a hoe or shovel. Then make a depression in the center to receive water.

3 Add Water. Fill a bucket with the amount of water specified in the instructions on the bag. Pour about half of the water into the depression you created in the dry mix.

4 Mix the Concrete. Thoroughly mix the water and dry ingredients. But add only small amounts of water as you mix, testing consistency as you go. As soon as you are able to form a stable mound with the concrete, stop adding water. If you've already added too much water, the mound will slump down; in that case, add more dry mix until you get the right consistency.

Using a Circular Saw

In building play structures, you'll probably pick up your circular saw almost as often as your hammer. This saw is capable of cutting straight and precisely, and it can serve for most types of joinery as well as decorative trim work. The most elaborate effects are simply variations on a few cuts.

Choosing the Blade. The most versatile blade for the do-it-yourselfer is a carbide-tipped combination blade, which some manufacturers refer to as a general-purpose blade. This blade will crosscut and rip both two-by stock and plywood. And with carbide tips, the teeth will stay sharp a long time.

If you plan to use the blade for only one purpose, such as crosscutting 2x4s, and don't mind taking a few minutes to change blades, you may be happier with several blades, each for a specific task. See "Choosing Circular-Saw Blades," page 23.

Kickback

Kickback is the term for that potentially dangerous saw reaction that occurs when the wood binds the teeth or when teeth on the rear part of the blade catch the edge of the saw cut, causing the saw to buck up or lurch backward toward you. To prevent kickback, as soon as you feel the saw start to bind or kick back, stop and correct the problem before continuing. Here are the major causes of kickback:

▲ **A Binding Board.** Sometimes the stresses in the wood cause the kerf to close. Binding also can occur if the cutoff is not falling free and is pinching the blade.

▲ **A Misguided Blade.** A circular saw is not designed to cut curves. If your cutting starts to stray from your straight cut line, do not try to veer back to the line. Instead, stop the saw, back up and start the cut again.

▲ **Backing Up the Blade.** Don't back up the saw while the blade is rotating. Always let the blade stop first.

▲ **Dull Blade.** A dull blade will heat up and bind, which can cause it to kick back. So it pays to have a spare blade handy.

Even the most experienced and cautious carpenters will encounter kickback from time to time. For this reason, it's important to adopt a method of cutting that eliminates the chance of injury. Whenever possible, hold the saw with both handgrips, first clamping the wood firmly in place. This gives you better control and keeps your forward hand in view and safely away from the blade. When using an angle square, as shown on page 51, you will need to hold the square in place with one hand while you saw. In this case, with the wood securely clamped and your eyes on the work, proceed with a firm grip. All the while, keep other parts of your body outside the plane of a potential kickback.

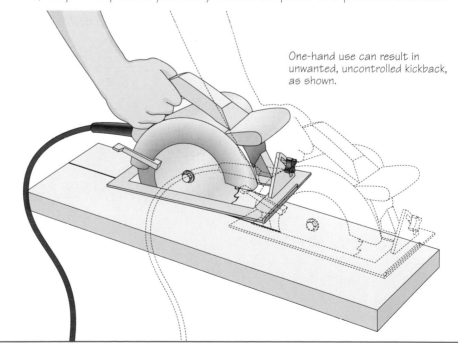

One-hand use can result in unwanted, uncontrolled kickback, as shown.

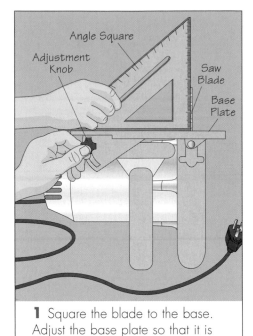

1 Square the blade to the base. Adjust the base plate so that it is perfectly square with the blade.

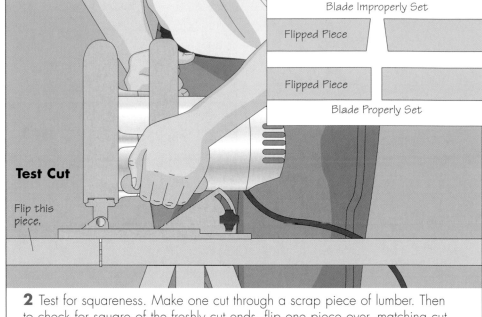

Test Cut

Flip this piece.

Blade Improperly Set

Flipped Piece

Flipped Piece

Blade Properly Set

2 Test for squareness. Make one cut through a scrap piece of lumber. Then to check for square of the freshly cut ends, flip one piece over, matching cut edge to cut edge. If they don't match squarely, reset the angle and try again.

Squaring the Blade

No matter what model of circular saw you have, don't expect the blade-angle markings stamped on the saw to be accurate. To ensure square cuts, use a square to set the blade at 90 degrees.

1 Square the Blade to the Base. Unplug the saw. Set the blade for maximum depth of cut. Then turn the saw over and loosen the angle-adjustment knob. Set a square against the blade and base, holding the square against the body of the blade without touching the teeth. Otherwise, the offset teeth can throw off your setting. Tighten the knob when the blade and base bear evenly on the square.

2 Test for Squareness. Crosscut a small block of scrap 2x4. Then flip over one of the cut pieces, matching cut edge to cut edge. If your blade is not square to the base, you'll see an angled gap that is twice the amount that your blade is out of square. If you see such a gap, repeat Step 1 and make another test cut. When the edges meet squarely, the blade is square to the base. If the stamped markings on your saw are inaccurate, scratch your own square mark onto the angle scale.

Making Square and Accurate Cuts

Each type of cut with a circular saw requires its own technique. Practicing these cuts on scrap wood will help you work more safely and efficiently.

1 Set Blade Depth. To produce the cleanest possible cuts and use a circular saw safely, avoid setting the blade so it projects far deeper than the wood. The farther the blade projects below the wood, the more heat it will generate and the greater the risk of its binding and kicking back. These concerns arise especially when cutting tricky materials, such as plywood.

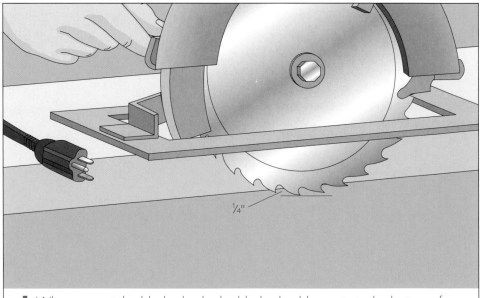

¼"

1 When you set the blade depth, the blade should penetrate the bottom of the board by about ¼ inch, or just enough to clear away the wood chips.

To set blade depth, unplug the saw. Swing the blade guard back so that you can clearly see the bottom of the blade. Adjust the blade so that about ¼ inch clears the bottom of the wood. Then tighten the depth-adjustment lock.

2 Position the Workpiece. Before the cut, your workpiece must be well-supported on a surface that won't move during cutting. To help avoid kickback, you must ensure that the piece you are cutting off can fall away without binding the blade. If you are trimming a small piece from a board, position the board across two sawhorses, clamp it firmly to the near sawhorse, and make the cut to the outside of the sawhorse, never between the horses.

When cutting relatively long pieces from a board, it is better to support the cut-off piece than simply let it fall to the ground. Working either on a stack of lumber or on the ground, place scraps of wood under each end of the board similar to that shown for cutting plywood on page 52.

3 Align Blade to Line. Use a square to strike a line where you want to cut the board. Make sure the workpiece is well supported on a stable surface and held firmly in place. Also ensure that the waste piece will fall away without binding the blade at the end of the cut.

Tip: For the most accurate cuts, first examine the teeth on your blade. The teeth on most circular saw blades are offset in an alternating pattern. If your blade is like this, position the blade along the waste side of the cut line. To do this, select a tooth that's offset toward the cut line and align the saw so that tooth just touches the line before you start the saw.

4 Make the Cut. After a bit of practice, you will soon be able to cut squarely by "eyeballing" a pencil line. To do this, keep your eye on the lead-

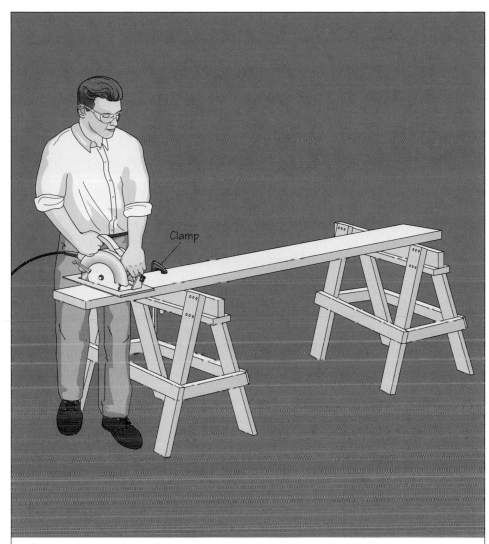

2 Support and clamp the workpiece before cutting. To support comparatively long pieces you will cut off, use the techniques in "Cutting Plywood," page 52.

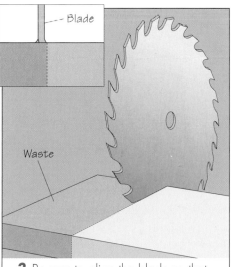

3 Be sure to align the blade so that you preserve the layout line itself. If you cut off the line, your piece may be too short.

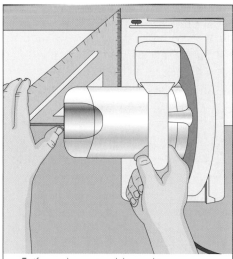

4 If you have trouble making square cuts, use a square to guide the saw. Press the square firmly against a clamped board.

ing edge of the blade, not the little notch on the front of the saw base.

If you are new to using a circular saw, you might use an angle square, as shown on the previous page, as a guide until you can follow cut lines accurately. Even when you gain confidence, an angle square can improve accuracy for joinery cuts that will show in the final project—for example, the end cut on a rail that will meet a post. The angle square can also ensure accuracy of 45-degree miter cuts.

First, use the square to mark the cut line. Slide the square along the piece you intend to use and hold the square firmly with your free hand against the edge of the stock. Set the base of your saw so that its edge bears against the square's edge. Adjust the saw and the square's position until the saw blade lines up with the cut line. Brace the square against the stock and make the cut, using the square's edge as a guide. Don't force the saw. Instead, use light, steady pressure, allowing the blade to determine the feed rate.

Cutting Plywood

Plywood presents unique cutting challenges. Because plywood sheets are large and because your cut lines are usually long, the sheet needs to be well supported. And because plywood flexes, it increases kickback hazard. A good way to cut plywood safely is to lay the sheet on top of some 2x4s placed on the ground or across a pair of sawhorses. Mark your cut line and adjust the blade.

Before making the cut, set up a straightedge to guide your saw. You can use a self-clamping straightedge or simply clamp a straight board to the plywood, as shown. Don't make the mistake of placing the straightedge directly on the cut line. Instead, measure the distance from the side of your saw's base plate to the

Ripping Lumber

When ripping lumber, use a rip guide. This is an adjustable plate that attaches to the saw's base, usually with a thumbscrew. The plate is designed to slide along the side of the board as you cut along the board's length. You'll need a little practice before cutting accurately with a rip guide, so work with scrap lumber until you get the knack.

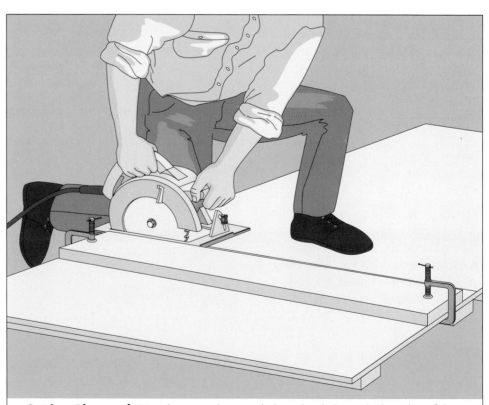

Cutting Plywood. Use clamps and a straight board to help guide the edge of the saw's base plate. It's often best to place plywood on scrap boards on the ground running parallel to the cut. Or you can place the work on a scrap sheet of plywood.

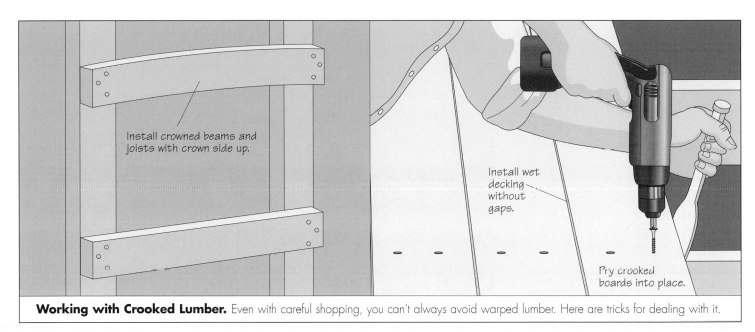

Install crowned beams and joists with crown side up.

Install wet decking without gaps.

Pry crooked boards into place.

Working with Crooked Lumber. Even with careful shopping, you can't always avoid warped lumber. Here are tricks for dealing with it.

blade. Then set the straightedge that same distance from the cut line.

If you are cutting near ground level, you will usually be able to move with the saw as you make the cut. If the blade binds, stop the saw and back it up so the blade will resume by the cut line. If you are cutting across sawhorses and advance the cut to a point that extends your reach too far for safe firm handed control, stop the saw and reposition the plywood to allow continuing.

Working with Crooked Lumber

One of the constant challenges of carpentry is trying to make something straight and square from a natural material that resists our best efforts. Almost every board you use will be at least slightly crooked, cupped, or twisted. So carpentry involves a continuing effort to force and fasten wood into positions it tries to resist. An experienced carpenter uses the forces within the wood to advantage.

The most common example is crowning in horizontal structural members such as beams and joists. To determine crowning, sight along the edges of a

board to decide which way it bows or crowns. Then install the board with the crown side up. This gives the board a head start in resisting sagging as a result of the weight bearing on it.

For decking, the best way to deal with crooked lumber is to avoid it. Even though decking on your play structures will be relatively short, try to choose straight boards anyway. If a long board is crooked, cut it to obtain its straightest section.

Yet even after judicious cutting of deck boards, you may still need to muscle the boards into position so they can be nailed or screwed down straight. The easiest way to do this is to pry the board into place with an inexpensive masonry chisel or a large screwdriver. Drive the nail or screw just short of penetrating the joist. Stick the chisel or screwdriver into the joist along the outside edge of the decking. Then pry the decking into place with one hand, as shown, while you drive the nail or screw with the other.

Installing Decking

Conventional wisdom has long been to install deck boards with the "bark side up," that is, with the arc of the growth

rings pointing up. The rationale is that the boards will cup in the same manner as the growth rings, shedding water rather than retaining it. For a variety of reasons, this behavior does not apply reliably to pressure-treated lumber, especially if it is treated with water repellent and fastened properly.

A better approach is to install the boards with their best side up. To better hold the decking to the joists, use deck screws rather than nails.

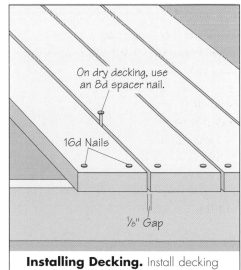

On dry decking, use an 8d spacer nail.

16d Nails

⅛" Gap

Installing Decking. Install decking boards with the best side up. Space the boards consistently. Dry decking should be installed with an ⅛-inch gap. Wet decking should be installed without gaps because gaps will open as the wood shrinks during drying.

Plan for shrinkage when laying deck boards. You want water and debris to pass through, but you don't want gaps between boards to be large enough for a child's toes or fingers to become caught. A gap of ⅛ inch is ideal. Because dry wood won't shrink, you can install it with an ⅛-inch gap between boards and expect the gap to remain fairly constant. However, wet boards and freshly pressure-treated boards will shrink after being installed. So you should install them with no gap. As that wood dries, you can expect a gap of ⅛ inch or more to open up. If you were to install wet boards and pressure-treated boards with an ⅛-inch gap, the eventual gap after drying would be an unwanted ¼ inch or more.

Driving Nails and Screws

There's more to nailing than just a well-aimed blow. The structural strength of your project depends on using nails of the right size and number in the right locations. For these projects, we'll use nails as the principal fasteners. They are cheap, strong, and easy to drive. However, screws are better when you want to ensure that wood members won't work loose, as sometimes occurs in a phenomenon known as nail withdrawal. This is most likely to be a concern with decking boards. Although ring-shank nails have nearly the same holding ability as screws, they can be very difficult to remove. When used in place of a nail, a screw should be the same length the nail would have been.

Overnailing (too many nails) can cause as many problems as undernailing. Overnailing can split lumber ends and thereby weaken joints; undernailing leaves too few fastening points. For this reason, building codes publish

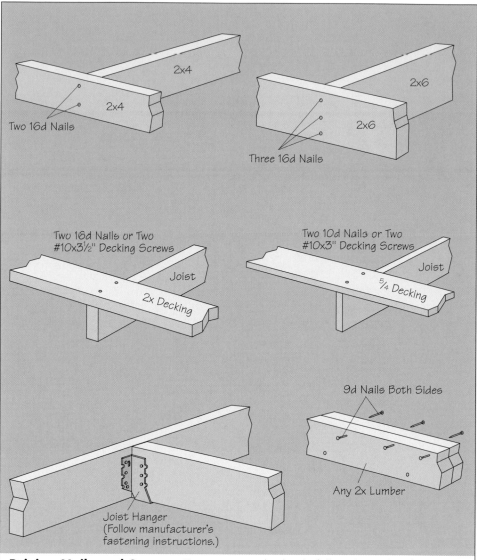

Driving Nails and Screws. For projects in this book, follow the nail and screw schedules shown in these illustrations.

what are known as schedules for nails and other fasteners. A schedule is simply a recommendation for the number and size of nails for fastening specified members together. The accompanying illustration shows nail and screw schedules for the most common connections in the play structure. You can follow the guidelines illustrated or, in the case of steel connectors, follow manufacturer recommendations. If you have further questions about options, consult local building authorities.

Select nail and screw lengths so the points don't emerge on the far side after driving. Points should remain buried in the wood. Otherwise,

exposed points could cause nasty cuts. Likewise, make sure the heads of all nails and screws are flush with or slightly below the face of the wood.

Avoiding Splitting. Splitting tends not to be a big problem with softwoods, although all boards have a tendency to split near their ends even if no nails or screws are driven there. Pressure-treated southern yellow pine is particularly prone to splitting when you drive nails at the ends. Even a minor split will affect the holding power of a nail, so try to avoid splitting during driving.

You can help avoid splitting the boards while nailing by using one of the following techniques:

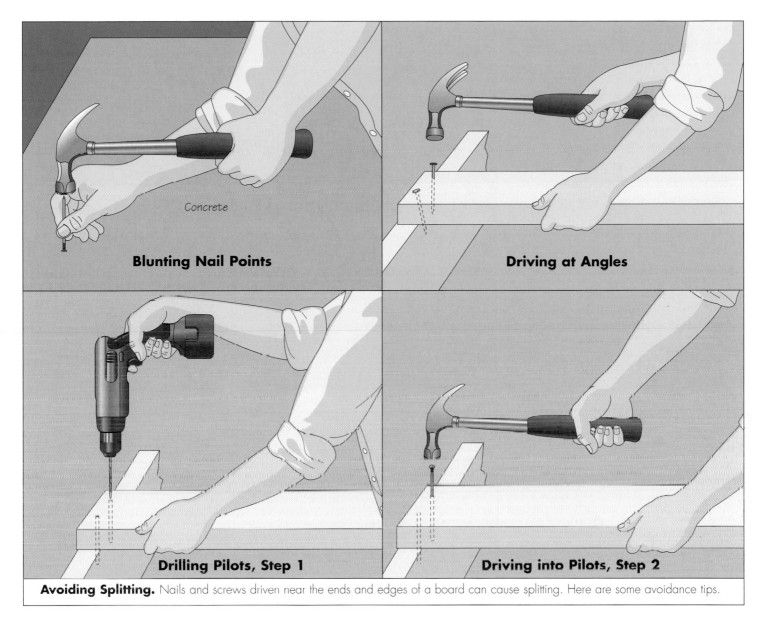

Blunting Nail Points

Driving at Angles

Drilling Pilots, Step 1

Driving into Pilots, Step 2

Avoiding Splitting. Nails and screws driven near the ends and edges of a board can cause splitting. Here are some avoidance tips.

▲ Blunt the tips of nails by striking them with a hammer. Illogical as this may sound at first, this works because the blunt nail head smashes wood fibers in its path, rather than wedging them and nearby fibers apart.

▲ Drill a pilot hole before driving the nail. Use a drill bit that is about 75 percent the diameter of the nail; a ⅛-inch-diameter pilot is good for a typical 16d common nail, and a ³⁄₃₂-inch bit works for a typical 8d nail.

▲ Drive nails into a board at opposing angles. In addition to reducing the chances of splitting, this technique will create a tighter connection that is less likely to pull apart.

Carriage Bolts and Lag Screws

Protruding hardware can cause serious injuries. Of course, it can cause cuts and bruises when bumped, but a bigger danger can arise when hardware, such as a bolt, snags clothing while a child is playing on a raised platform or near a slide.

Installing Bolts. Whenever installing through-bolts, try to use carriage bolts. They have a safe, smooth round head; but, for the sake of safety, their threaded end needs to be recessed (totally countersunk) in the wood. You

have several sequence options when drilling for recessed bolts. The method shown on page 56 is the simplest when appearance and positioning of the recess are more important than precise positioning of the bolt head. For another option, see p. 73.

Note: Purchase bolts that are slightly shorter than the combined depth of the joined wood members. Otherwise, cut them off so they will be flush with the wood after fastening.

To add life to the connection, coat the drilled holes with a water-repellent wood preservative before installing the bolts.

The nuts can work loose over time as a result of vibration, temperature swings, and wood shrinkage. Regularly check all nuts and bolts for tightness. To minimize the chance of nut loosening, use locknuts (or stop nuts), which contain a self-locking nylon bushing. The same effect can be achieved by coating the threads with a thread-locking compound before screwing on the nut.

Installing Lag Screws. A carriage bolt requires that you have access from both sides. But if only one side is accessible, you will need to use lag screws (also mistakenly called lag bolts). A lag screw requires two steps for the pilot hole, one step for the unthreaded part and another for the threaded part. The pilot for the unthreaded shank should be the same diameter as the shank, or slightly smaller, while the pilot for the threaded part should be the same as the solid core of the threaded part.

It is easier to drill the larger pilot hole first, but you must be careful not to drill too deep. Measure the distance from the bottom side of the screw head to the start of the threads. Mark this distance on your drill bit with a grease pencil or a small strip of masking tape so you can see precise penetration as you drill. The second pilot hole should be only as deep as the lag screw will penetrate; that is, measuring from the washer to the screw point. Remember to include a washer before you install the screw.

Here are some other rules of thumb for lag screws:

▲ When joining boards of different thicknesses, try to drive the lag screw through the thinner board into the thicker second board.

▲ At least half of the lag screw should penetrate the thicker (second) board.

Routing Wood Edges

Avoid sharp edges everywhere on the playground, including on the lumber. Although wood with sharp 90-degree edges may look impressive, it can impart a nasty cut and become damaged much quicker than wood with the corners "broken." Because most of the wood used on the projects in this book is standard dimension lumber, the edges have already been rounded over at least a little. You might be satisfied with the condition of the edges after touching them up with sandpaper.

Yet for a more uniform and distinctive appearance, and especially for those pieces, such as handrails, that kids will grasp regularly, you might want to round the edges with a router, using a roundover bit. For best results, choose a carbide-tipped router bit with a ball-bearing pilot. A bit with a cutting radius of ⅜- or ½-inch is ideal for use on 2-by lumber, although you could get by fine with a smaller cutting radius.

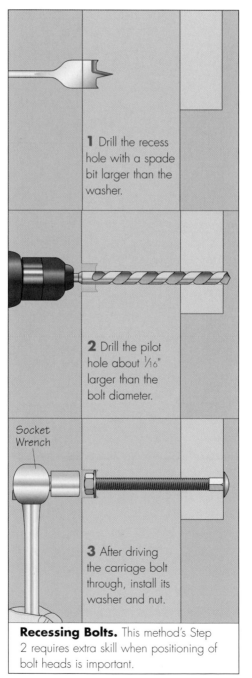

1 Drill the recess hole with a spade bit larger than the washer.

2 Drill the pilot hole about 1/16" larger than the bolt diameter.

Socket Wrench

3 After driving the carriage bolt through, install its washer and nut.

Recessing Bolts. This method's Step 2 requires extra skill when positioning of bolt heads is important.

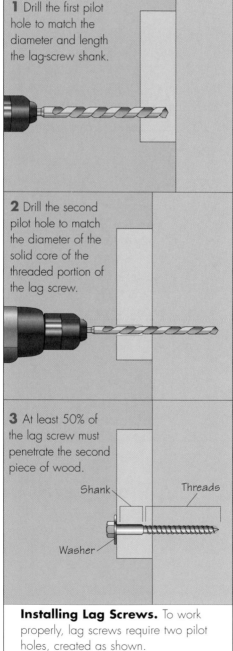

1 Drill the first pilot hole to match the diameter and length the lag-screw shank.

2 Drill the second pilot hole to match the diameter of the solid core of the threaded portion of the lag screw.

3 At least 50% of the lag screw must penetrate the second piece of wood.

Shank

Threads

Washer

Installing Lag Screws. To work properly, lag screws require two pilot holes, created as shown.

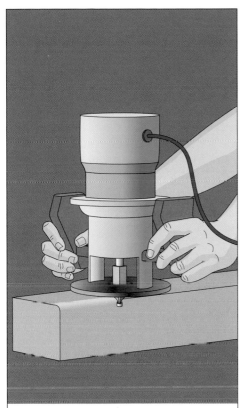

Routing Edges. The most effective tool for rounding edges is the router.

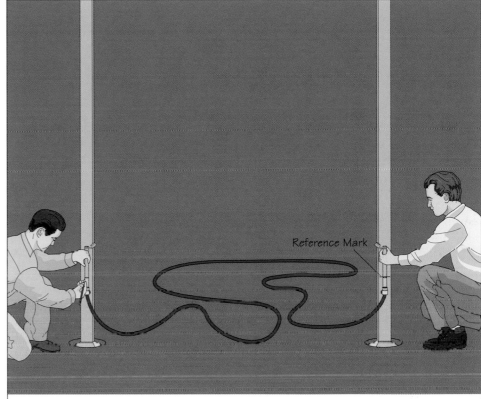

Reference Mark

Using a Water Level. When your carpenter's level won't reach, a simple water level works just as well in transferring your reference mark.

To install the router bit, unplug the router and turn it upside down. Drop the bit all the way into the collet, then back it out about ¹⁄₁₆ inch. Tighten the collet nut. Adjust the router for the desired depth of cut. Make a few passes on a piece of scrap wood to ensure that your adjustment is satisfactory. When routing edges, be sure to move the router from left to right (or counterclockwise around a perimeter). Hold the router with both hands, moving it at a comfortable but unforced pace. Always wear eye and ear protection.

Using a Water Level

A carpenter's level works well on closely spaced posts. But for widely spaced posts, a water level allows you to transfer level marks with deadly accuracy. The device depends on two laws of nature: gravity and atmospheric pressure. Within the hose, water will seek the same level at each end.

To make your own water level, use ³⁄₈-inch or ⁷⁄₁₆-inch clear vinyl tubing. If you build the Kids' Playland with all modules, you'll need 26 feet of tubing. Rinse the inside of the tubing with warm water and dishwashing detergent to remove any greasy film. Place one end of the tubing in a bucket of clean water. (If you like, you can add a couple drops of oil-free food coloring to make the water more visible.) Hold the other end lower than the bucket, then suck on it until the water starts siphoning in. As soon as water emerges from the lower end, plug that end with your thumb.

Hold both ends of the tubing side-by-side to ensure that the water is level. If it isn't, check the tubing for air bubbles or kinks. Run more water through the tubing to remove air bubbles.

Mark one post with a reference mark at the level you wish to transfer marks to all posts. Place one end of the tubing against the post, with the water

roughly aligned with the reference mark. To keep water from spilling while your helper moves to the post you wish to mark, both of you should place your thumbs over the tube ends. However, to function properly, the tube must be open on each end, and the water must be free of bubbles and able to move freely.

Have a helper position the other end of the tube against the unmarked post. After allowing the shifting water to come to a standstill, the helper should slowly move the tube up or down until the water level at your first reference mark aligns with your original mark. When it does, the helper's water level will be at the correct height. Have the helper mark the second post at that water level.

For best accuracy, continue using your first reference post to repeat the process on as many other posts as your tube will reach.

5

Finishing & Maintenance

The finish coating you choose will affect the appearance of your play structure. But more important, the finish can affect long-term durability and useability. That is, exterior wood must contend with temperature and moisture changes, the sun's ultraviolet rays, fungi, human use and abuse, and insects. This chapter discusses the variety of exterior finishing products and suggests their advantages and disadvantages.

For outdoor finishes, the principal options are sealers, stains, and paints. But it doesn't make sense to paint unless you are prepared to touch up and repaint regularly. Even a topnotch paint job won't survive the assaults of rambunctious kids. Yet, if you'd like to add extra color,

consider painting small parts of the structure that don't get abuse, such as the balusters on a railing.

Like paint, lacquer and varnish are poor play-structure finishes. They too function by forming a film on the wood, which can crack quickly under the stresses of wet-dry cycling. Although marine varnish is flexible enough to resist cracking, it is expensive. And because marine varnish is very glossy, it is not a good choice for play structures.

Durability

If you plan to dismantle the play structure within five years or so, the following strategy lets you avoid finish coatings almost entirely. First, use pressure-treated lumber for posts, beams, joists, and any other members that will be near or will be in contact with the ground. If you choose a premium line of pressure-treated wood, coated with water repellent at the factory, you won't need to apply additional moisture protection for a couple of years. For decking, guardrails, and other parts, you can use the same pressure-treated lumber or choose redwood or cedar heartwood. Left untreated, redwood and cedar will turn gray, but they won't rot or decay for many years.

Many people mistakenly believe that pressure-treated wood does not need to be finished. Although the chemicals used in normal pressure treating are intended to prevent rot and insect damage, they offer no protection against moisture and ultraviolet rays. Also, pressure-treated wood is prone to splitting, regardless of the finish. You can minimize deterioration by applying a stain or a water repellent with ultraviolet (UV) blockers.

If you use untreated wood for the decking and guardrails from a species that isn't rot resistant—such as pine, fir, or hemlock—apply a water-repellent finish that contains preservatives that prevent rot.

Sealers

Sold as "water repellents," sealers are usually clear or lightly pigmented coatings intended to protect the wood from excessive water absorption. Wood sealers contain a moisture inhibitor, usually paraffin wax, and are commonly sold as deck finishes.

You can choose a plain sealer or a sealer with additives that help protect the wood from fungi, mildew, insects, and ultraviolet rays. A sealer that contains UV blockers will maintain the natural wood color for a year or so, while a plain sealer will permit the wood to gray over time. A pigmented sealer will give the wood a moderate tint, without drastically altering its color.

Sealers from different manufacturers may contain different amounts of moisture inhibitor. A high concentration is around 3 percent and is the best choice if you plan to apply only one coat. A sealer with a lower concentration should be regarded as pretreatment, needing another coating.

Stains

Stains have more pigmentation than sealers. Color options include semitransparent and solid, both available in water-based and oil-based (or alkyd) formulations.

Semitransparent stains are moderately pigmented, adding color while allowing the wood grain to show clearly. Oil-based semitransparent stains are good choices for pressure-treated wood because they hide the greenish tint. For best results on pressure-treated wood, choose an oil-based stain that mimics red cedar or redwood.

Solid-color stains are essentially thinned paints. They color the whole board, penetrating crevices and defects, sometimes accentuating the grain. But because they form a thin film over the wood, solid-color stains pose the same maintenance problems as paint.

Paints

A dash of color can add a playful look to a play structure. But because a play structure takes a lot of abuse, paint that is abused can wear away quickly. Not only does deteriorated paint look ugly, it allows water to seep into the wood and damage it. If you decide to add some paint, consider limiting it to areas that won't receive much abuse. The most durable exterior finish is usually top-quality acrylic latex paint over an alkyd primer.

Sealers. When water beads on the wood surface, the water-repellent sealer is doing its job. When water soaks into the wood, it's time to apply more sealer.

Preparing the Surface

With any finish, the results look better and last longer if you first prepare the surface. If the wood is wet or dirty, the finish won't adhere well and you will need to refinish it sooner.

First, ensure that the wood is reasonably smooth. Wood that hasn't been pressure treated can be given a quick sanding by hand or with a power sander. Sanding allows better penetration of the finish. Because sawdust from pressure-treated wood contains toxic chemicals, sand only enough to remove serious nicks and sharp edges. Wear a dust mask and try to sweep up as much of the chemically treated sawdust as possible for disposal.

If the wood has started to age or if you're just overdue for a refinish job, a deck-cleaning solution can restore the natural color. Most home centers carry the cleaning solution.

Before applying the finish, spray-rinse the entire structure with water to remove sawdust and debris. Use a garden hose with a nozzle that produces a good stream. Then let the wood dry for a day or two.

When to Apply the Finish

Always follow the manufacturer's instructions on when and how to apply a finish. As a general rule, try to put some finish on the wood as soon as possible. That's because the sun's ultraviolet rays can start adversely affecting the wood almost immediately. If the wood was kiln-dried (KD) or, in the case of treated lumber, kiln-dried after treatment (KDAT) and has been kept dry, you can finish it right away. If the wood is wet, give it a few weeks to dry.

Before applying finish, "soften" any sharp edges and corners you missed prior to construction. The belt sander shown serves well for the purpose but won't reach into corners. For that, use a sanding block and sandpaper.

In most cases, water repellent should be applied annually. You can determine if the water repellent needs renewing by splashing water on vertical surfaces. If water beads on the surface instead of penetrating, the repellent is still doing its job. But if the water soaks in, it's time to apply more water repellent.

Applying the Finish

A brush ensures better penetration than either a roller or a multi-purpose sprayer, because it lets you work the finish into the wood. Besides, surfaces on the play structure are relatively small, making a brush about as quick as a roller and less wasteful than a sprayer, which tends to cause wasteful overspray. If you do use a sprayer or roller, follow with a brush where possible to work the finish in.

Be sure to read the manufacturer's instructions carefully. For example, some finishes should be recoated before the previous coat dries.

Applying the Finish. Although a pump sprayer is a quick means of applying the finish, you'll get better results if you go over the surface again, brushing the finish in.

General Maintenance

Clean the impact-reducing material of debris regularly, the frequency depending on season and use. Sand and gravel need to be raked regularly. Mulch and

wood chips should be renewed or replaced when they have begun to decompose or have lost resiliency.

To ensure long life and maximum safety of the Kids' Playland itself, inspect it at least monthly. Replace any metal parts that are especially rusty or otherwise damaged. Check all nuts, tightening as necessary. Inspect ropes and chains for evidence of aging and abuse. Also, remove splinters on all wood surfaces, and sand or remove sharp edges. Touch up nicks in the wood with spare finish.

Renovating

If the kids have begun showing less interest in the Kids' Playland, perhaps it is time to do a little renovating. You might consider replacing the swings with a tire swing, installing a tube slide instead of the straight slide, or adding some other component. Remember, the projects in this book are designed to allow your play structure to grow and mature right along with your children.

In your regular maintenance inspections, check all nuts and tighten them as necessary. Remember to check the out-of-sight locknuts atop the swing beam. Shown in the inset photo, the locknut's white bushing helps prevent the nut's working loose under stress.

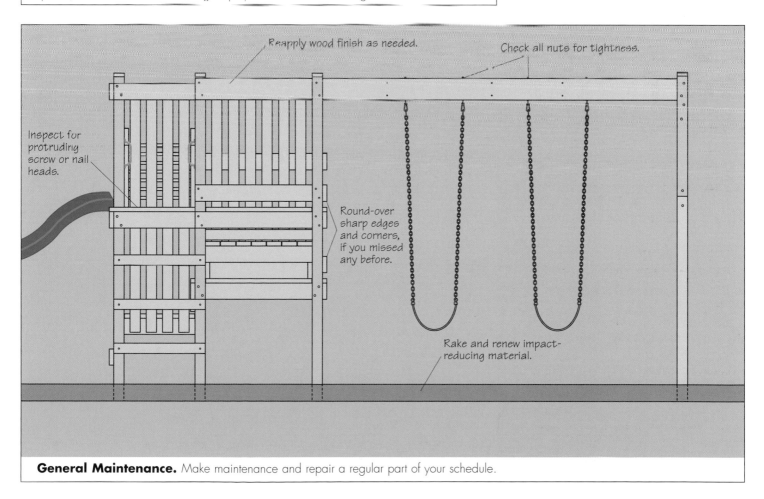

Reapply wood finish as needed.

Check all nuts for tightness.

Inspect for protruding screw or nail heads.

Round-over sharp edges and corners, if you missed any before.

Rake and renew impact-reducing material.

General Maintenance. Make maintenance and repair a regular part of your schedule.

Part 2

Kids' Playland

In some respects, the entire Kids' Playland—with Central Tower, Swing Beam, and Monkey Bar—is the most challenging project in the book. Yet, because it is modular, you can reduce the work by building one module, such as the Central Tower, and adding others later. For structural stability, the posts for all modules should be set in concrete fairly deep in the ground, and the posts need to be positioned precisely. Beyond that, construction is pretty straightforward, requiring mainly square cuts of lumber.

Even so, construction will go easier if you have a helper or two at those moments when you need to position the longer wood members.

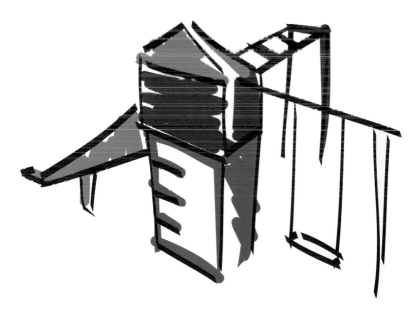

6 **The Kids' Playland and Its Central Tower 66**

7 **Swing Frame** **83**

8 **Monkey Bar** **92**

6

The Kids' Playland & Its Central Tower

The Kids' Playland is a multi-function, modular structure that can be adapted to please children of all ages. It provides the basic activities of any successful playground—swinging, sliding, climbing, relaxing, and socializing. All this in a layout that maximizes safety while using space efficiently.

The optional configuration shown on the next page can serve children of different ages and energy levels. The floor of the upper level of the Central Tower is 5 feet high—a good compromise height for younger and older children. Although a 5-foot-tall slide may be a bit high for toddlers, it will seem just right to kids over four years old. If you are more interested in satisfying preschoolers, the solution is simple—build at 4 feet and buy a slide designed for that height.

Deluxe Central Tower

The Deluxe Version of the Central Tower offers a series of height levels. The lower level serves as a launching pad for the Monkey Bar. The middle level and the additional step combine to offer a seat and space for relaxing play. The first two levels also provide transitions to the upper level. If you don't want the Monkey Bar, and instead prefer a simple ladder for access to the slide, you can opt for the Basic Version of the Central Tower shown on page 82. One virtue of a modular approach to the Playland is that you can later expand the Basic Tower to the Deluxe, shown here.

Our Monkey Bar slopes away from the Central Tower. This allows taller children to use mainly one end and shorter children, the other end. But if you prefer a Monkey Bar that is parallel with the ground, simply install longer posts at the outer end, or reduce the height of the bar where it joins the Tower.

The Swing Beam offers a full 10 feet of clearance between posts. This is plenty of room for two conventional swings, or for a single tire swing, or for a set of rings and a trapeze bar. However, if you are pressed for space or simply prefer a single conventional swing, you could shorten the beam span to 6½ feet.

Regardless of the configuration, allow sufficient area for the Safety Zone, which should be filled with impact-reducing material, such as wood chips, pea gravel, wood mulch, or sand. You need to decide on impact-reducing material and the configuration of the Safety Zone before you start construction. (See Chapter 1 "Layout Options" on page 12. There, overhead drawings will help you visualize the safety-zone requirements for optional Playland configurations. For comparisons of impact-reducing materials, including recommended minimum depths, see page 35. Excavate to at least that recommended minimum before beginning construction.)

Kids' Playland with Deluxe Version of the Central Tower

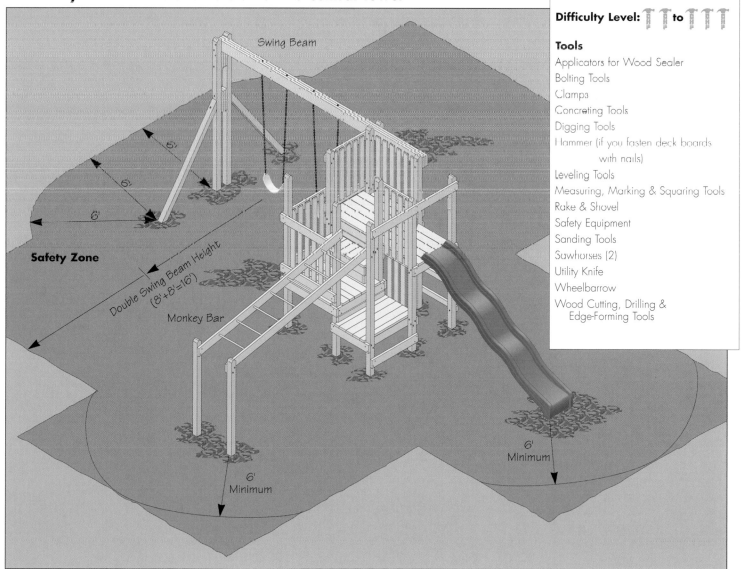

Swing Beam

Safety Zone

Double Swing Beam Height (8'+8'=16')

Monkey Bar

6' Minimum

6' Minimum

Difficulty Level: T T to T T T

Tools

Applicators for Wood Sealer
Bolting Tools
Clamps
Concreting Tools
Digging Tools
Hammer (if you fasten deck boards with nails)
Leveling Tools
Measuring, Marking & Squaring Tools
Rake & Shovel
Safety Equipment
Sanding Tools
Sawhorses (2)
Utility Knife
Wheelbarrow
Wood Cutting, Drilling & Edge-Forming Tools

Chapter 1 also contains thorough explanations on other safety features incorporated into the design of the various Playland components. As you proceed with construction, refer regularly to Chapter 4 for construction techniques mentioned, in passing, in this chapter and in those that follow.

The full Kids' Playland is constructed in three phases (Central Tower, Swing Frame, and Monkey Bar). The Central Tower is presented in this chapter, and the other components have chapters unto themselves. Although you can build the entire Kids' Playland at once, you can instead build one component at a time, as your time, budget, and energy allow. If you feel you'll eventually build all components, start with the Central Tower; then add the Swing Frame and the Monkey Bar.

The drawing on this page shows dimensions and string-line locations for laying out the full Playland.

Chapters 7 and 8 also explain how you can construct components as stand-alones. Because numerous options are offered in each chapter, review the entire book before finalizing your plans. Chapters 9 through 13 explain, in turn, how to build a Playhouse, three sandboxes, two balance beams, a Picnic Table, and a Teeter-Totter. Although these projects are not part of the Kids' Playland, they make great additions to a play yard.

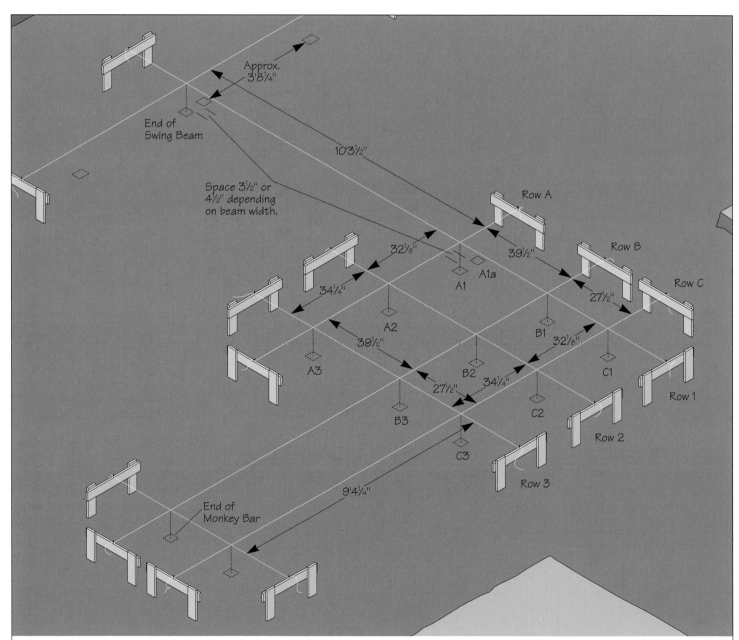

Kids' Playland Site Layout. Mark postholes with properly spaced string lines. The Deluxe Version of the Central Tower employs the nine post locations shown clustered in rows 1, 2, and 3, plus post A1(a) if you add the Swing Beam. The Basic Version of the Central Tower shown on page 82, employs just the six post locations shown in rows 1 and 2. (See page 85 for more on the Swing Frame Layout.)

THE CENTRAL TOWER

The Central Tower serves various play components, depending on the specific layout option you choose for the Kids' Playland. In the Deluxe Version of the Central Tower shown on previous pages, the upper level provides structural support for one end of the Swing Beam, as well as a platform for entering the slide. Again, if you'd prefer a simpler tower, you could build only the upper level by following instructions for the Basic Version shown on page 82.

Advantages of the Deluxe Version: It has twice the platform surface of the Basic Version. Also, the Deluxe has three levels. The lowest level platform serves the Monkey Bar. The middle level and the step can serve as platforms for sitting, eating, playing card games, or simply daydreaming. The changes in elevation also enhance the Tower's design balance and visual interest.

Preparing the Lumber

It is easier to do the bulk of sanding and smoothing of lumber before construction begins. With the right power tools, this step can be relatively simple and quick. Round-over the edges of the posts and the top edge of the top rails with a router equipped with a roundover bit. Then smooth all exposed surfaces with a power sander, removing any lumber-mill stamps as you go. In addition to providing a surface that is friendlier to small hands, the sanded wood will better absorb the finish you apply.

Lumber and Materials Order

Lumber	Qty	Size
4x4s	9	13' minimum
2x6s	12	8'
	1	10'
	7	12'
2x4s	2	10'
1x4s	1	6'
	7	12'

Hardware & More

	Qty	Size
Carriage bolts, nuts, washers	98	$\frac{3}{8}$"x5"
	2	$\frac{3}{8}$"x6$\frac{1}{2}$"
2x6 joist hangers, nails	8	2
Deck screws	250	3"
	150	2"
Plastic slide	1	10'

Handles
Concrete
Gravel
Finish
Impact-reducing material

Cutting List

	Qty	Size
4x4 posts	9	13' minimum
2x6 joists	1	21"
	1	25$\frac{5}{8}$"
	1	30$\frac{5}{8}$"
	3	31"
	1	35$\frac{5}{8}$"
	1	37$\frac{1}{8}$"
	5	37$\frac{3}{4}$"
	1	43"
	2	46"
	1	70$\frac{1}{2}$"
2x6 decking	3	35$\frac{3}{4}$"
	5	40$\frac{3}{4}$"
	6	46"
	5	73$\frac{1}{2}$"
2x6 rails	1	31"
	2	35$\frac{3}{8}$"
	2	38"
	2	44$\frac{1}{2}$"
	1	69$\frac{7}{8}$"
2x6 stair	2	9"
	9	12"
	2	33"
	2	36"
2x6 step	1	37$\frac{3}{4}$"
2x4 steps	3	31"
2x4 nailing cleats	6	4-5"
2x4 blocking	1	37$\frac{3}{4}$"
	1	43"
1x4 balusters	22	36"
	4	46"

Laying Out the Site

If you are planning to build the full Kids' Playland, see pages 44-46 and 67-68 for instructions on laying out the site for all components. This chapter addresses laying out the Deluxe Central Tower alone, but simplified layout for the Basic Tower is readily apparent along post rows 1 and 2. See "Setting Posts," on pages 46-47.

Note that the Site Layout drawing on page 68 labels the rows and posts. Be sure to refer to these labels regularly during construction.

Use batter boards and strings to establish the positions for all nine posts for the Central Tower (ten if you will add the Swing Beam now or later, page 86). Space the string lines exactly as shown in the Site Layout. Each intersection of string lines marks the center of a post. Drop a plumb line at each intersection and mark the ground with a small stake, such as a scrap piece of wood. When all posthole locations are marked, remove the strings, and dig nine 12-inch-diameter holes to at least 3 feet deep no matter where you live, and to an additional 6 inches below frost line if you live in northern states or Canada. Pour 6 inches of gravel into each hole.

Setting the Posts

The normal procedure for setting posts is to carefully brace each post before adding concrete to the hole. But with nine posts in close proximity and the need to space them accurately, you will be better off building a temporary frame that lets you align all posts at once.

1 **Mark the Temporary Frame.** Make the frame with the 8-foot 1x4s you bought to use as balusters. Since you'll reuse boards in the temporary frame for balusters later, mark them lightly in pencil now and use a minimal number of screws or nails. The drawing shows how to mark the 1x4s so that they won't need to be cut for use on the temporary frame. To position the nine posts, you'll need 14 total boards, six each with post positions marked 12 inches from the right end, plus two corner braces.

2 **Attach the Temporary Frame.** With a couple of helpers, you may be able to attach the 1x4s to the posts without needing any diagonal braces into the ground. But even if help is available, we recommend diagonal bracing for the first post, basing all other posts on the first.

Frame the four outside posts first (A1, A3, C1, and C3). Once they are up, the other posts will be easier to attach. Set post A1 into its hole. Then measure up the post about 12 inches and 72 inches above ground level, marking each location. While helpers or braces hold posts A1 and A3 upright, attach the 1x4 for Row A at 12 inches. Drive a 2-inch screw or a 6d duplex nail through the board into post A1; then use a level to position the board on post A3. Move up to the 72-inch mark on post A1 and repeat the process.

Brace or have a helper hold Row A upright while you set post C1 in its

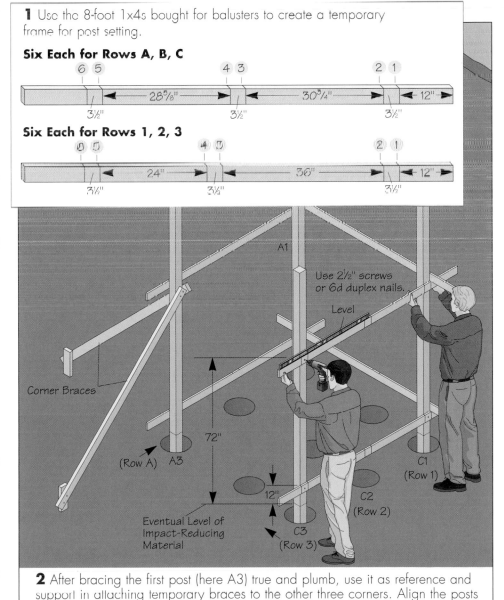

1 Use the 8-foot 1x4s bought for balusters to create a temporary frame for post setting.

Six Each for Rows A, B, C

6 5   4 3   2 1

← 28⅝" →   ← 30¾" →   ← 12"
3½"   3½"   3½"

Six Each for Rows 1, 2, 3

6 5   4 3   2 1

← 24" →   ← 36" →   ← 12"
3½"   3½"   3½"

A1

Use 2½" screws or 6d duplex nails.

Level

Corner Braces

72"

(Row A) A3

12"

Eventual Level of Impact-Reducing Material

C1 (Row 1)

C2 (Row 2)

C3 (Row 3)

2 After bracing the first post (here A3) true and plumb, use it as reference and support in attaching temporary braces to the other three corners. Align the posts with the reference marks on the 1x4s.

hole. Rest a 1x4 for Row 1 on top of one of the boards already attached to post A1; then use a level to position the board on post C1. Fasten the board to the two posts.

Repeat this process on Row C, placing post C3 in its hole. But place the boards directly beneath the overhanging boards on post C1. The two boards you will install on Row 3, then, should rest on top of the overhanging boards you've already installed.

With the four corners framed, ensure that all posts are plumb and that the structure is square. The structure will be square when the diagonal distances between corner posts are equal. Then continue adding posts and boards. When the frame is complete, check again for plumb and square.

Add concrete to each hole to 3 inches below ground level, sloping the concrete away from the posts, as shown on page 46. Let the concrete cure undisturbed overnight. Then remove the lower boards of the temporary frame so that they won't be damaged during subsequent construction. Leave the upper boards in place for now because they add stability to the posts. You can remove those boards one at a time when they would otherwise interfere with construction.

Marking the Reference Line. The best way to ensure that your decks are level is to establish a reference mark on one post and then transfer this mark to all posts supporting that deck. If you were to proceed instead from post to post, measuring from the

ground up, it is unlikely that the reference lines would be level.

With a tape measure (above the eventual level of impact-reducing material) make a mark on one post at 60 inches, which is the finished deck height of the upper level. Then use a 4-foot carpenter's level to transfer this mark to each of the posts. If you don't have a 4-foot level, you can rest a 2-footer on a longer, straight board, or use a water level, as shown on page 57.

Use a combination square to extend the reference point around all four sides of each post. Mark this line 60" so that it remains distinguishable from layout lines to come. In the following instructions, the dimensions for much of the construction will be given from this reference point.

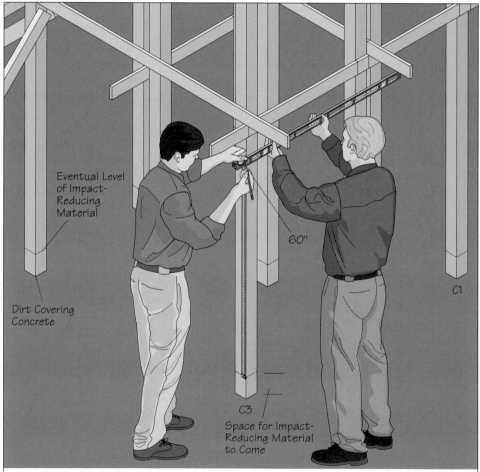

Marking the Reference Line. With the posts in concrete, establish level for each deck based on one reference mark, transferring that reference by means of a level, as shown, or by means of a water level. Note the allowance for the depth of impact-reducing material yet to come. See page 35 for recommended depths.

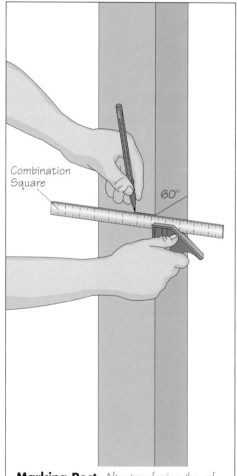

Marking Post. After transferring the reference line by means of a level, use a square to extend the reference lines around all of the posts.

Framing the Tower

The three levels on the Central Tower are framed independently. Each level has four rim joists that are bolted to posts. A total of four additional joists are needed, which are attached to the rim joists with joist hangers.

Because rim joists meet at right angles on most posts, with bolts running through posts at right angles, position bolts so they don't run into each other. The best approach is to stagger the bolts in a systematic manner, as described and illustrated below.

Note: Throughout this book, exact dimensions are given for each joist. These dimensions assume that each post is located exactly as shown in the layout and is perfectly plumb, and that the entire structure is perfectly square. Chances are, however, that your dimensions will vary somewhat, so be sure to measure each joist spacing before cutting.

The simplest and most prudent technique for attaching rim joists is to measure and cut each joist, one at a time. Then measure and mark the bolt-hole layout, and fasten the joist to the post temporarily with screws driven through the bolt-hole markings. To drill the bolt holes, remove one screw and drill a bolt hole in its place. Insert a bolt and hand tighten it, then remove the other screw and repeat the process. When you have installed all bolts for each level, go back and tighten the nuts with a socket wrench.

Staggering Bolt Holes. The rim joists must be bolted securely to the posts. If bolted correctly, your frame will be strong. But a careless approach to drilling bolt holes can weaken the posts and jeopardize the structural integrity of the entire tower.

There are several essentials: First, use the proper-size bolt. Throughout this project, ⅜-inch bolts are specified

Recessing Hardware

Avoid allowing any hardware to protrude in a way that a child might bump it or snag clothing on it. This requires that most of the washers and nuts be installed in recess holes drilled into the posts. Begin by temporarily fastening a 2x6 to its posts. Then follow the steps below.

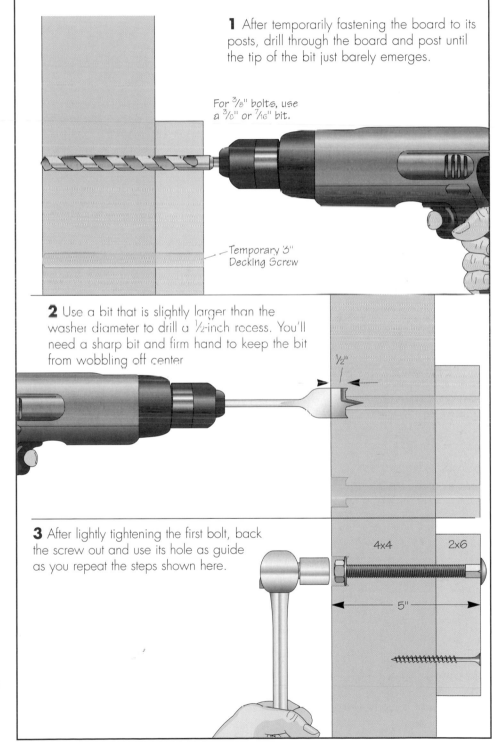

1 After temporarily fastening the board to its posts, drill through the board and post until the tip of the bit just barely emerges.

For ⅜" bolts, use a ⅜" or ⅞6" bit.

Temporary 3" Decking Screw

2 Use a bit that is slightly larger than the washer diameter to drill a ½-inch recess. You'll need a sharp bit and firm hand to keep the bit from wobbling off center

½"

3 After lightly tightening the first bolt, back the screw out and use its hole as guide as you repeat the steps shown here.

4x4   2x6

5"

for every application except the Swing Frame.

Second, as shown on the next page, bolts on the same side of a post should be staggered vertically, to minimize splitting of the post. Otherwise, bolts or other fasteners aligned vertically along the same grain lines in wood greatly increase the likelihood of splitting the wood.

Third, bolts passing through adjacent sides of a post must be staggered so they allow sufficient room for clearance. Bolt holes that cross too close to each other can interfere with bolt placement and weaken the post. The inset drawing on the next page shows a safe approach for staggering bolt holes in each post. Measure and mark the layout on each rim joist before drilling any holes.

1 Frame the Lower Level. The lower frame attaches to posts B2, B3, C2, and C3. On each post, measure down from the 60-inch reference point exactly 37½ inches. Mark this location; then align the tops of each joist with this line. Cut two 31-inch and two 37¾-inch rim joists and attach them to the posts as shown. Use ⅜x5-inch carriage bolts at each connection. Note that the bolts in accompanying drawings show on which sides the bolts should be inserted; the object is to try to drill recesses in the thick 4x4 posts, rather than into the joists.

After bolting the rim joists to the posts, cut and install the center joist using 2x6 joist hangers. Center this joist between the two longer rim joists.

2 Frame the Middle Level. The middle level attaches to posts A2, A3, B2, and B3. On each post, measure down from the 60-inch reference point exactly 25½ inches. Mark this location, and then align the tops of each joist with this line. Cut two

46-inch and two 37¾-inch rim joists and attach them to the posts as shown. Use ⅜x5-inch carriage bolts at each connection.

After bolting the rim joists to the posts, cut and install the center joist using 2x6 joist hangers. Center between the two longer rim joists.

3 Frame the Upper Level. The upper level attaches to posts A1, A2, B1, B2, C1, and C2. Measure down from the 60-inch reference

point exactly 1½ inches to determine the alignment for the tops of each joist. Again, based on your own post-to-post distances, cut rim joists of about 70½ inches, 43 inches, 37⅛ inches, 35⅝ inches, and 31 inches. Attach the joists to the posts as shown. Use ⅜x5-inch carriage bolts on all connections except at post B1, where you will need a longer 6½-inch bolt. Remember to drill the recess into the joist on the inside of the post. Cut inside joists of 30⅝ and 25⅝ inches; installing 2x6 joist hangers.

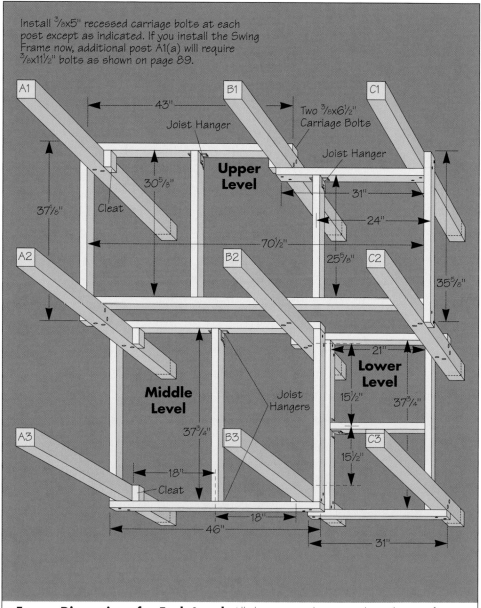

Install ⅜x5" recessed carriage bolts at each post except as indicated. If you install the Swing Frame now, additional post A1(a) will require ⅜x11½" bolts as shown on page 89.

Frame Dimensions for Each Level. All dimensions shown are based on perfect placements of all posts. Thus, you should consider the dimensions approximate, adjusting them as needed to match your exact post-to-post distances.

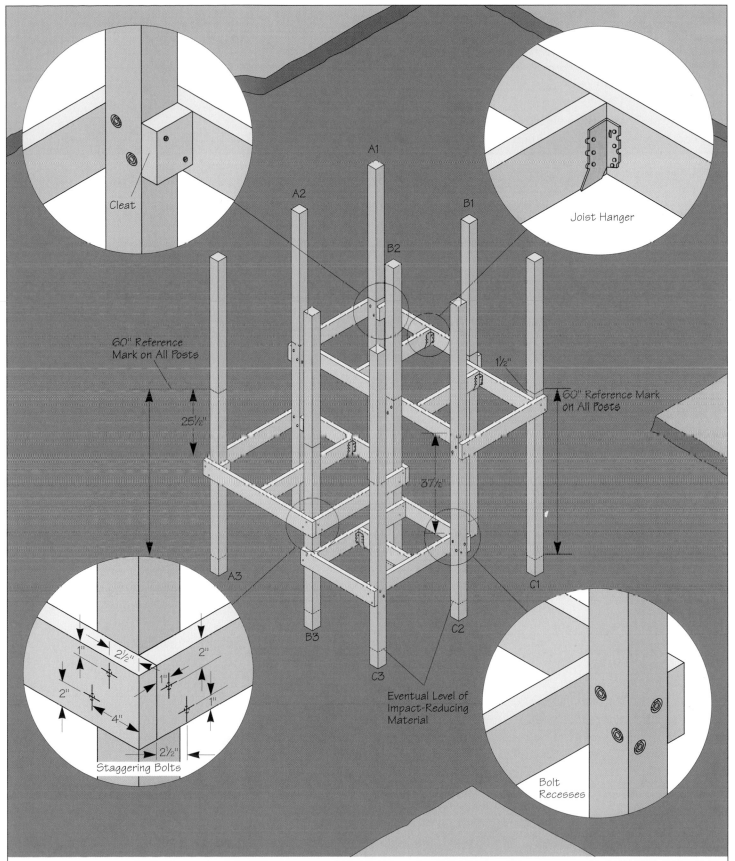

Cleat

Joist Hanger

60" Reference
Mark on All Posts

A1

A2

B2

B1

1½"

60" Reference Mark
on All Posts

25½"

37½"

A3

C1

B3

C2

C3

Eventual Level of
Impact-Reducing
Material

1" 2½" 2"

1"

2" 1"

4" 1"

2½"

Staggering Bolts

Bolt
Recesses

Framing the Central Tower. Frame each level independently. Note distances below the reference line. Begin by attaching rim joists to posts temporarily with screws. Then remove screws one at a time, replacing each with a bolt. Stagger bolts so they won't hit one another or weaken joints, and recess nuts on the post side. Cleats will support deck boards that will have no joists to rest on.

Installing the Decking

The framing allows for decking boards on the middle level to be installed perpendicular to those on the lower level. The decking boards on the middle and upper levels are installed parallel with each other, but the treads on the stair between the levels (to be built later) will run perpendicular to the decking. These contrasting decking patterns add design interest and also promote safety by drawing attention to the changes in levels. For tips on installation, see "Installing Decking," page 53.

Most of the decking boards will be full-width 2x6s. A few of the 2x6s will need to be ripped narrower to allow a good fit. You could instead insert an occasional 2x4 or 2x8; so, with careful planning, you may not need to rip any decking boards. The illustrations offer specific suggestions for board widths, assuming a ⅛-inch gap between all boards, and between boards and posts. Use these suggestions as a guide to determine the best widths of decking boards for each level on your tower.

Installing Cleats. Note that the middle level and the upper level require the installation of 2x4 cleats to create fastening surfaces for some decking boards. Cut these cleats from scrap 2x4s; each should be 4 to 5 inches long. Use 3-inch screws to fasten each cleat to its post, but only after you have tightened the nuts beneath them. Once or twice a year you should tighten all of the nuts on the structure. The screw-fastened cleats are easy to remove for this purpose and then reinstall.

Fasten the decking boards to the joists with 3-inch decking screws or 16d nails. Use two fasteners at each junction, spaced about 1 inch from the edge. When fastening a decking board near its ends, drill pilot holes first to prevent splitting.

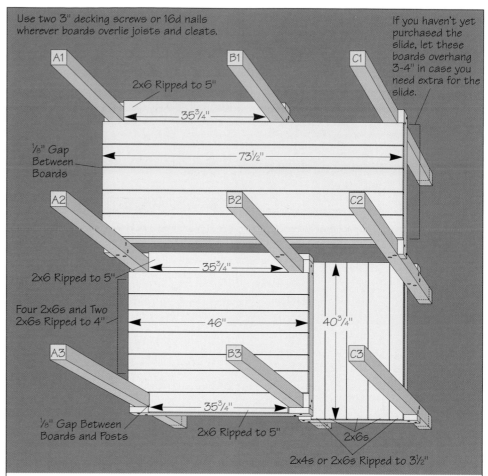

Installing Decking. Attach decking boards flush with the rim joists, equally spaced. Note that the middle and upper levels need nailing cleats for boards that won't rest on joists.

1 Install Lower-Level Decking. Each of the decking boards on the lower level is 40¾ inches long. Using 2x4s on each end along with three 2x6s allows for a good fit. Use two fasteners wherever boards overlie joists or cleats.

2 Install Middle-Level Decking. The two end boards must fit between the posts. Cut each to 35¾ inches to allow gaps. By ripping each board to exactly 5 inches, each will line up with the posts and simplify placement of the rest of the decking. Attach cleats to each post, as shown on page 74, before installing the end boards.

The other decking boards are 46 inches long. Two of the boards have been ripped to a width of 4 inches and are installed apart from one another among the full-width 2x6s.

3 Install Upper-Level Decking. The short board between posts A1 and B1 must be cut to a length of 35¾ inches. This board should also be ripped to a width of 5 inches. Attach supporting cleats to each post before installing this board.

The other five boards are full-width 2x6s. If you are planning to install a slide, you may need to let these boards overhang the slide's rim joist by several inches to allow the slide to be bolted to the deck. Check the instructions accompanying your commercially made slide before proceeding.

If you don't yet have the slide, install boards that are at least 77 inches long. Later, you can cut them if necessary to accommodate the slide.

Installing Middle- and Upper-Level Rails

The locations for the 2x6 rails are all based on the decking surface. The rails are fastened to the posts in the same manner as the rim joists. Since children will touch top edges of the top rails regularly, the edges should be rounded and smoothed.

Cut the rails to length and then fasten them temporarily to the posts with screws. Next, remove the screws one at a time as you replace them by drilling bolt holes and installing bolts. As with the joists, the washers and nuts should be recessed on the post side of the connection, and the bolts should be offset and staggered, as shown on page 75.

The middle level has two top and two bottom rails, which meet at post A3. The bottom of the bottom rails should be positioned 2 inches above the decking surface, and the top of the top rails should be 42 inches above the surface of the decking.

The rails on the upper level are a bit more complicated to prepare and install. The two bottom rails, which meet at post A1, are also located 2 inches above the decking surface. However, the tops of the three top rails are at 41½ inches; this allows the top rail between posts A1 and A2 to align with the bottom edge of the Swing Beam, when it has been installed.

Note: If you do not intend to install the Swing Beam right away, you will need to install a 44½-inch top rail between posts A1 and B1.

The rail between posts C1 and C2 actually continues to post C3. It serves as a handle to help guide children onto the slide while also providing lateral bracing. Note that if you do not intend to install a slide immediately, you will need to install a 35⅝-inch bottom rail between posts C1 and C2.

For safety reasons, the balusters in this bay are installed differently.

Only a top rail is installed between posts C2 and B2. That is because the balusters in this bay will be installed on the back side of the rail, and they will extend and be fastened to the joist beneath the decking. (See "Special Baluster Treatment" and the drawing on page 78.)

Installing Balusters

The 1x4 balusters are installed vertically, attached to the inside top and bottom rails. The actual width of a 1x4 (3½ inches) is the maximum gap recommended by the U.S. Consumer Product Safety Commission. Local code may require less. Other choices for balusters include 1x6s and 2x2s.

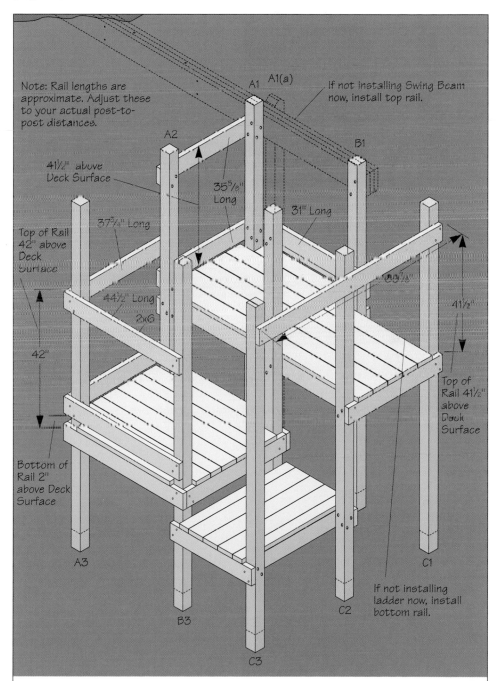

Note: Rail lengths are approximate. Adjust these to your actual post-to-post distances.

41½" above Deck Surface

Top of Rail 42" above Deck Surface

37¾" Long

44½" Long 2x6

42"

Bottom of Rail 2" above Deck Surface

A2

A1 A1(a)

If not installing Swing Beam now, install top rail.

B1

35⅝" Long

31" Long

41½"

Top of Rail 41½" above Deck Surface

If not installing ladder now, install bottom rail.

A3

B3

C3

C2

C1

Installing Rails. Bolt the rails to the posts in the same manner as the rim joists. The top rail on the upper level is positioned to align with the Swing Beam. See the text for rail installation guidance if you do not intend to install the Swing Beam now.

All balusters are 1x4s (3½" wide).

A1

1⅞" Gap

A2 28⅝"

A3 30¾"

B1

2¼" Gap

B2

C1

C2

Top Rail

1"

2" Decking Screws or 6d Nails

36"

Bottom Rail

Break edges at top and bottom.

B3

C3

A3

B3

C2

C1

42" Balusters

C3

Make this bay's balusters extra long (46"), with gap less than 2".

Tape Measure

2¼" 3½"

Spacing Option:
Measuring

2¼"
Spacer Jig

Spacing Option:
Using a Spacer Jig

Installing Balusters. To space balusters evenly, calculate the baluster gap, as explained in text. Break the sharp edges before fastening balusters to the rails. Install balusters above the lower level so that little hands and fingers can't reach the upper deck.

Special Baluster Treatment

As a safety measure, the balusters between posts B2 and C2 should be installed a bit differently. To understand the following explanation, consult the drawing above.

If the balusters at the upper level were installed conventionally, there would be a gap between the decking and the bottom rail. This gap would be large enough for a child to slip its fingers through, where they might be stepped on by someone on the upper deck.

To remove this hazard, run the balusters all the way from the top rail to the joist beneath the upper level decking. Also, keep the gap between these balusters less than 2 inches. Using these precautions, you will have made it more difficult for little hands from the lower level to find their way onto the upper deck.

For appearance's sake, try to maintain a consistent spacing. The following explains how to calculate the gaps.

Calculating the Baluster Gap. Calculate baluster spacing for each bay (that is, each section of railing between two posts). First, decide on the approximate gap you want (3½ inches is the maximum allowed by the U.S. Consumer Products Safety Commission). Add this figure to the width of one baluster (3½ inches when using 1x4s):

$$3\tfrac{1}{2} + 3\tfrac{1}{2} = 7$$

Measure the distance between the posts (30¾ inches in the bay between posts A2 and A3), and divide that dimension by the baluster width plus gap amount:

$$30\tfrac{3}{4} \div 7 = 4.4$$

Round this figure up to the nearest whole number (5) to determine the total number of balusters needed. (By rounding the figure up, you ensure that the gap will be less than the maximum allowable 3½ inches.)

Multiply the number of balusters by the width of each baluster:

$$5 \times 3\tfrac{1}{2} = 17\tfrac{1}{2}$$

Subtract this figure from the spacing between posts:

$$30\tfrac{3}{4} - 17\tfrac{1}{2} = 13\tfrac{1}{4}$$

Divide this figure by the total number of gaps you will need (which will always be one more than the total number of balusters):

$$13.25 \div 6 = 2.21, \textit{which can be}$$
$$\textit{rounded fractionally to } 2\tfrac{1}{4} \textit{ inches}$$

Use the above math logic and new gap dimensions for each of the bays.

Spacing the Balusters. There are two ways to space the balusters. The first option is to use a tape measure to lay out the baluster locations on the top and bottom rails. (See previous page.) The second option is to make a spacer jig by ripping a board to the size of the gap between balusters, and attaching a T-brace at a right angle, designed to rest on the top rail.

The advantage of using a spacer jig is that you don't need to worry about a miscalculation when measuring a layout. Rest the spacer against the first baluster while you attach the next one, and so on. The modest disadvantage is that you need to make a new spacer for each bay.

Break the sharp edges on the tops and bottoms of the balusters by rounding

them over with a router or cutting a 45-degree bevel, as shown.

Be sure to use right-length fasteners. When attaching 1x4 balusters to 2x6 rails, use 2-inch decking screws or 6d (2-inch) nails.

As shown, the open area between the lower level and upper level should be blocked with balusters. Attach 1x4s vertically to the joists on both levels between posts B2 and C2. Space the 1x4s just as you did the balusters directly above.

Building and Installing the Stair

A simple stair facilitates movement from the middle level to the upper level. This stair is large enough to serve as a seat. Build the stair in two stacked sections, using a series of overlapping 2x6s, fastened with 3-inch decking screws. Fasten the bottom section to posts A2 and B2 with 3-inch decking screws. Then

set the top section directly on top of the bottom one and fasten it to the posts.

For the treads, rip an 8-foot 2x6 to 5-inch width. Next, cut the seven 12-inch long treads. Set the treads on the stair frame so that they are equally spaced. Then drive 3-inch deck screws through the treads into the frame.

Installing the Lower-Level Rung

The rung from the ground up to the lower level is simply a 2x6 bolted to posts C3 and C2. Use a good piece of lumber for the rung, one that is relatively free of knots and splits. Cut it to 37¾ in

Measure from the top of the decking surface down each post 12 inches and make a mark. Align the top of the rung with these marks before bolting it to the posts with ⅜x5-inch carriage bolts, with the washers and nuts set in recesses in back of the posts.

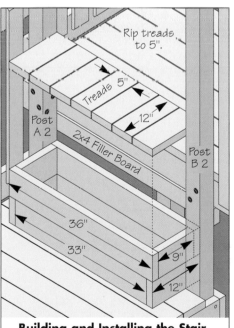

Building and Installing the Stair. Construct the stair to the upper level with two stacked boxes. Fasten the boxes to the posts. Fill the gap between the stair and the upper level with a 2x4.

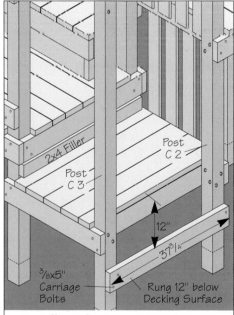

Installing the Lower-Level Rung and Blocking. A single 2x6 ladder rung provides the step up to the lower level. Fill the gap between the lower level and the middle level with a 2x4.

The gaps between the lower and middle levels and between the middle and upper levels should be blocked enough to keep a child's head and feet from slipping through. In both places, attach a 2x4 to the posts, as shown in "Installing the Lower-Level Rung and Blocking" at the bottom of page 79.

Installing the Ladder to the Upper Level

The ladder rungs to the upper level are each 31-inch 2x4s. Cut the rungs from clean, knot-free lumber. On posts C1 and B1, measure down from the top of the decking surface 16 inches, 31 inches, and 46 inches, and mark each location. Align the top of each rung with its marks before bolting it to the posts with ⅜x5-inch carriage bolts, setting the washers and nuts in recesses in back of the posts.

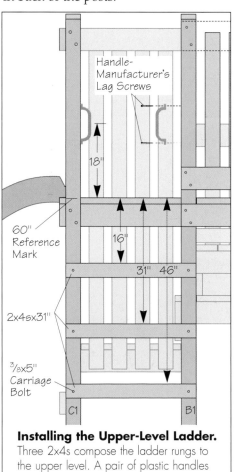

Handle-Manufacturer's Lag Screws

18"

60" Reference Mark

16"

31" 46"

2x4sx31"

⅜x5" Carriage Bolt

C1   B1

Installing the Upper-Level Ladder. Three 2x4s compose the ladder rungs to the upper level. A pair of plastic handles facilitate the child's final step.

Installing Upper-Level Handles. Handles can be considered an option on the Central Tower. The most useful location for a pair of handles is above the ladder to the upper platform, where they can help children hoist themselves from the top rung to the decking surface. Center the handles about 18 inches above the decking, as shown.

The best handles in this location are those specifically designed for use on playground equipment, usually available at playground retailers. Because these handles will be under a good deal of stress when they are being used, they should be fastened to the posts with lag screws, following the manufacturer's instructions. Smaller door handles, fastened with normal wood screws, are not strong enough for this use.

Attach other handles as you feel the need, for example, at the entrances to the slide and the lower level and above the stair to the upper level.

Installing the Slide

Most of the plastic slides install in a similar manner. Avoid a slide that can be attached only to a tower made by the slide's manufacturer.

Also ensure that the slide is suitable for your deck height. Typically, slides 8 feet long should be attached to decks 48 inches high or less, while slides of 10 feet are intended for 60-inch-high decks (such as the one on the Central Tower). Most slides are bolted to the deck through holes the manufacturer drilled through flanges. Most slides are staked into the ground.

Read manufacturer instructions carefully, and use only hardware recommended. Trim the overhanging decking boards as directed.

If you'd rather not install a slide at this time, as shown on page 67, consider using the space to install a sliding pole, shown on the next page.

Cutting and Treating Post Tops

The post tops do not need to be cut at all, especially if they are reasonably level. If you do plan to cut them, make sure that you leave sufficient room to attach the Swing Frame or Monkey Bar. From a safety standpoint, the posts need only be as high as the top rails on the Central Tower.

When you cut off the top end of a pressure-treated post, you remove much of the chemical treatment. To increase water runoff, cut the top ends in a modified peak. Then soften sharp edges with a sander. To prolong the life of the cut end, saturate it with wood preservative and then a sealer.

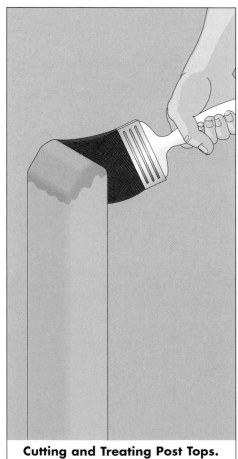

Cutting and Treating Post Tops. Treat cut post ends by applying wood preservative and then sealer.

Finishing Touches

You can now proceed to install the Swing Frame and the Monkey Bar, if that is your intention (see upcoming chapters). Before allowing the Central Tower to be used, apply the finish of your choice, and install the impact-reducing material as described in Chapter 4.

The open area beneath the upper level is just about the right size to appeal to young children as a shady spot to sit and relax—and it is. The problem with children playing in this area is that the frame for the upper deck is within easy reach, and protruding nails or screws, the sharp edges of joist hangers, and splintering lumber could all cause injury.

To make this open area safer, there are two options. The first is simply to close it off with diagonal bracing, not shown here. Although your Central Tower shouldn't require any additional bracing (your local building inspector may say otherwise), you can install several 2x4s diagonally between posts. Diagonal, rather than horizontal, installation reduces the likelihood that adventurous souls will use the 2x4s as steps to climb from the outside. To further discourage climbing, attach the diagonal 2x4s to the insides of the posts and joists with nails or decking screws. The most useful locations for this barrier are between posts A1 and A2, A1 and B1, and C1 and C2.

The second option is to allow access to the space beneath the upper level but block access to protruding hardware in the framing above. You don't want to completely cover the framing because that will inhibit water from draining. Instead, staple chicken wire or small-mesh plastic fencing to the undersides of joists.

The Sliding Pole

A sliding "firefighter's" pole is always a hit with kids. On the Central Tower, a sliding pole is a good choice if you aren't installing a slide. The pole must be installed far enough away from the structure to make the descent safe yet close enough to allow safe access. Make the pole using galvanized steel plumbing pipe and fittings; you should use at least 1-inch (nominal) pipe, which has an outside diameter of about 1½ inches.

Attach the flange to the post with 3-inch lag screws, not simple wood screws, to ensure a secure connection. The pole should be braced at the bottom by burying it at least 24 inches deep. To bury the pole, dig a hole 6 to 8 inches in diameter. With the 10-foot pipe resting on a large, flat rock in the hole, assemble the pipe and fittings as shown. Backfill the hole with dirt, tamping it firmly every 6 inches with a 2x4. To add a dash of color, paint the pole brightly before installation. Be sure to surround the bottom of the pole with extra impact-reducing material.

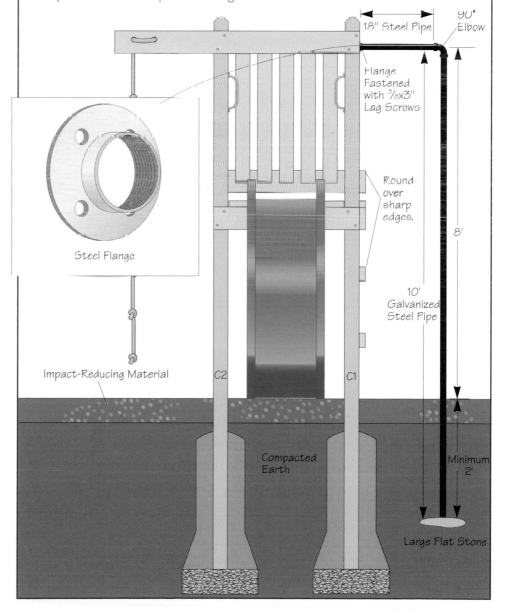

Steel Flange

18" Steel Pipe

90° Elbow

Flange Fastened with ⅜x3" Lag Screws

Round-over sharp edges.

8'

10' Galvanized Steel Pipe

Impact-Reducing Material

C2

C1

Compacted Earth

Minimum 2'

Large Flat Stone

The Basic Version of the Central Tower

The accompanying Basic Version of the Central Tower has about half the footprint of the Deluxe Version. Yet with a little planning, the Basic Version can offer a worthy variety of activities.

Referring back to the Playland Site Layout on page 68, you'll note that placement for the six posts needed for the Basic Version is shown along rows 1 and 2. Thus the layout for the Basic Tower allows you to expand it to the Deluxe Tower at a later date, following the layout and instructions in this chapter. In either case, you need to set the posts in concrete and fasten the joists, decking, rails, and balusters in the same way.

The drawing of this Basic Version shows optional accessories. In addition to a climbing rope, climbing nets are available at reasonable cost from manufacturers of playground equipment. Follow manufacturer instructions for installation

Like the Deluxe Version, the Basic Version of the Central Tower can be built with a deck height of 48 inches, which is better than 60 inches for younger children. A 48-inch deck height is ideal for an 8-foot-long slide.

The Basic Version can include a swing frame large enough for a single swing. If you are building the deck at the lower 48 inches, you might prefer a lower swing-beam height as well. (See Chapter 7 for more on the Swing Frame.)

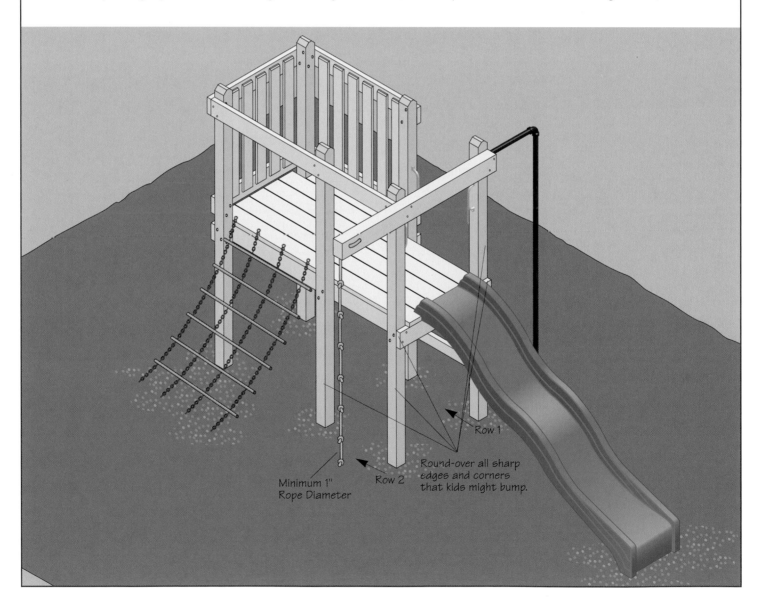

Minimum 1"
Rope Diameter

Row 2

Row 1

Round-over all sharp
edges and corners
that kids might bump.

7

Swing Frame

Swings are almost as vital to a children's playground as tires are to a car. Surely no other project in this book would be used as much by so many children— and adults.

And yet many backyard swing sets sit idle while their intended users head for the swings at school or at the park. There's a good reason for this preference: Many backyard swings are small, flimsy structures made of tubular metal and allow only a short swing arc. They are best for very young children who can't propel them themselves. Once kids leave the kiddie seat and learn to kick and pump on their own, they crave speed and altitude.

The plans in this chapter show how you can make a swing frame that kids won't ignore.

Swing-Frame Basics

The swing beam—the horizontal member that supports the swings—is 8 feet above the impact-reducing material, allowing a substantial and satisfying swing arc. On one end, the beam is fastened to three posts on the Central Tower; on the other end, it is fastened to a double post with an A-frame. With this arrangement, even an aggressive swinger won't affect the stability of the structure.

For safety's sake, the beam is over-sized to support kids and parents alike. And the distance between posts allows swings to be spaced far enough apart to ensure that two simultaneous swingers won't collide.

Although called a Swing Frame, this project can be used for a number of optional swinging and gymnastic accessories. The full-length Swing Frame is long enough to allow for the safe use of a tire swing. But because a tire swing moves in all directions, it should be the only accessory suspended from the beam; all others should be removed. Also, the bottom of the tire should be at least 24 inches above ground, thereby minimizing the chance for the user to bump a post.

As alternatives, rings, trapeze bars, and climbing ropes can be attached to the Swing Frame. But again, any accessory that allows swinging from side to side should be the only accessory attached at any one time. Changing accessories can be a breeze if you first attach a series of eyebolts on the beam and use quick-release fasteners.

You'll find additional instructions if you need or prefer a swing frame suitable for only a single swing, or if you decide to build the Swing Frame as a stand-alone unit. Regardless of the design you choose, bear in mind that swings are perhaps the most dangerous component on any playground. The person using the swing can be injured

Lumber and Materials Order

Lumber	Quantity	Size
4x4	3	13' minimum
	2	10'
2x8	3	16'
	1	10'
Hardware and More		
Fasteners		
Carriage bolts, nuts,		
washers	6	⅜"x5"
	2	⅜"x8"
	4	½"x8"
	11	½"x12"
Carriage bolt or threaded rod	1	½"x16"
Eyebolts, locking nuts,		
washers	4	⅜"x8"
S-hooks	8	⅜"x2½"
Spring-loaded clips	4	⅜"x3½"
Chain		
Swing seats		
Concrete		
Gravel		
Impact-reducing material		
Finish		

from an accidental fall as well as from intended "jumps" from the swing while it is moving. But the most serious swing accidents occur to children who run into the path of a moving swing, colliding either with the person using the swing or with the seat.

Take these safety precautions:

▲ Extend the impact-reducing material at least double the swing height in front and in back, and 6 feet outside each post.

▲ Locate the swing away from any pathways that children are likely to use to reach the other parts of the Kids' Playland. This can be accomplished by placing the swing adjacent to bushes or a fence, or by adding a simple rope fence around the perimeter.

▲ Use safe, flexible seats on the swings that have no protruding hardware and no hard edges. (For a more complete discussion of safety, see Chapter 1.)

Site Layout

If you are building the Swing Frame when you build the Central Tower, you can dig all postholes then, especially advised if you rent a power auger. The illustrations show the string-line layouts, based on whether the Central Tower is in place. Note that dimensions differ on the two illustrations, indicating different alignments with Post A–either splitting the middle or locating the edge of the post.

Swing-Frame Basics

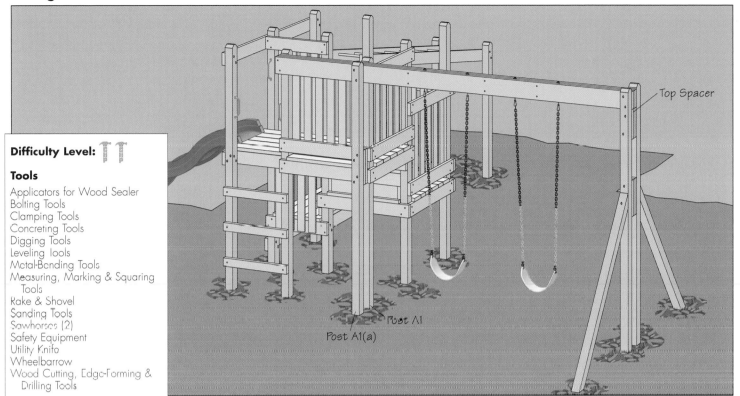

Difficulty Level: ⚒ ⚒

Tools

Applicators for Wood Sealer
Bolting Tools
Clamping Tools
Concreting Tools
Digging Tools
Leveling Tools
Metal-Bending Tools
Measuring, Marking & Squaring
   Tools
Rake & Shovel
Sanding Tools
Sawhorses (2)
Safety Equipment
Utility Knife
Wheelbarrow
Wood Cutting, Edge-Forming &
   Drilling Tools

Top Spacer

Post A1

Post A1(a)

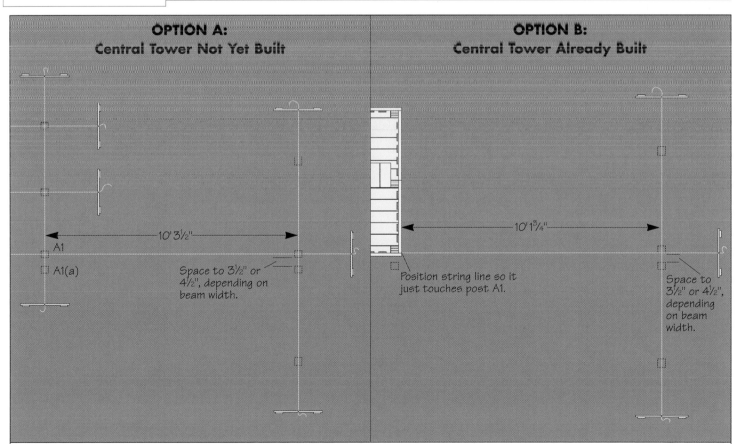

OPTION A:
Central Tower Not Yet Built

10' 3½"

A1

A1(a)

Space to 3½" or
4½", depending on
beam width.

OPTION B:
Central Tower Already Built

10' 1⅝"

Position string line so it
just touches post A1.

Space to
3½" or 4½",
depending
on beam
width.

Site Layout. If you will dig postholes for the Swing Frame at the time you dig holes for the Central Tower, use the layout shown in Option A. However, if you dig postholes after constructing the Central Tower, use Option B. If you build the Central Tower only and anticipate adding the Swing Frame later, allow sufficient room for an eventual post A1(a) and its concrete footing.

Preparing the Swing Posts

Because the outer posthole and the posthole for posts A1 and A1(a) will receive two spaced 4x4 posts, they must be larger than holes for single posts. The depth should be the same, at least 3 feet, plus at least 6 inches below frost line in northern regions. The oval surface dimensions should be 12x20 inches. After digging the holes to proper depth for your locality, shovel gravel into the bottom to a 6-inch depth. See "Setting Posts," page 46, on postholes.

The outer set of swing posts has two spacers, one near the middle and the other near the top, that will support the beam. The spacers are composed of 14½-inch lengths of scrap lumber, either three 2x4s for the triple 2x8 beam or a 4x4 for a 4x8 beam. Only the middle spacer is installed at this point; the top spacer is installed after the posts are set in concrete. To position the middle spacer for the outer posts, insert one of the posts into the posthole, resting it on the 6 inches of gravel. Measure upward from the eventual level of the impact-reducing material

66 inches and make a mark for the center of the middle spacer block, as shown. Lay the swing posts on a flat surface, and center the spacer on the mark, and then temporarily clamp the assembly together.

Raise the doubled swing posts in their hole and brace them temporarily, as shown. Use string lines from the Central Tower to align the posts with the Central Tower, as well as plumb, adjusting braces as necessary. Do not add concrete yet.

Preparing the Beam

The ideal beam for the Swing Frame is a 14-foot 4x8. But 4x8s can be hard to find in many locales. And they can be quite heavy, especially if pressure treated and still wet.

The plans call for a built-up beam composed of three 2x8s bolted together. Structurally, two 2x8s are nearly as strong as a single 4x8 even though they are ½ inch thinner. Yet, by adding a third 2x8, you'll have solid wood for the drilling of eyebolt holes and other supporting hardware. Also, working with individual 2x8s is much easier on your back than working with a 4x8. The following instructions assume that you'll have a strong helper or two for lifting the beam into place. But if you work alone, you could instead position the 2x8s one at a time and then clamp them together before drilling bolt holes.

The dimensions in the plans call for a 14-foot beam, and if you are careful in your measurements and construction, you can buy a 14 footer. We recommend, however, that you buy 16-foot boards and cut them to finished length only after the Swing Frame is completed. That way, you won't need to worry that slightly out-of-place posts will leave you with a beam that is too short. Also, many lumberyards carry 2x8s in 12- and 16-, not 14-, foot lengths.

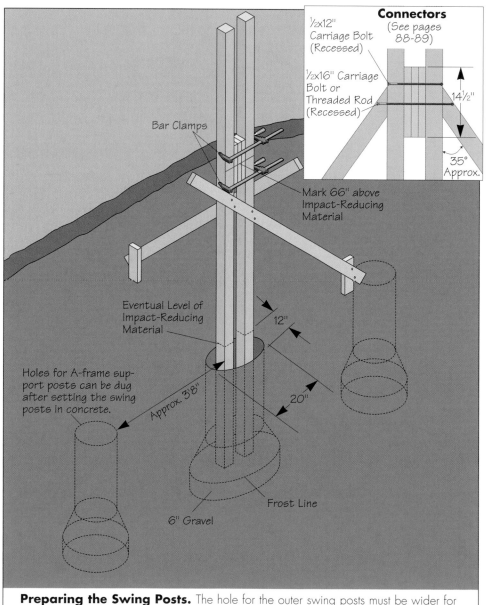

Connectors
(See pages 88-89)

½x12" Carriage Bolt (Recessed)

½x16" Carriage Bolt or Threaded Rod (Recessed)

14½"

35° Approx.

Bar Clamps

Mark 66" above Impact-Reducing Material

Eventual Level of Impact-Reducing Material

12"

Holes for A-frame support posts can be dug after setting the swing posts in concrete.

Approx. 38"

20"

Frost Line

6" Gravel

Preparing the Swing Posts. The hole for the outer swing posts must be wider for the double posts than for the A-frame support posts.

1 Make a Built-up Beam. On a level surface, clamp the three 2x8s together, with all sides and ends flush. Drill six ⅜-inch bolt holes, as shown. The two ½-inch holes on the left end will be used to attach the beam to post B1 on the Central Tower. Offset these holes slightly to minimize the chance of splitting the post. The ⅜-inch holes do not need to be offset, because they are not attached to posts. Insert and tighten the ⅜x5-inch bolts. Later, you will drill six more bolt holes for swing-post attachment.

2 Drill Holes for Eyebolts. Next, lay out and drill holes for the eyebolts that will suspend the swings. The illustration allows recommended spacings between swings and posts, measured 48 inches above ground level, when swing chain tapers inward toward the seat. Tapered swing chains are safer because they help keep the swing moving in intended back-and-forth arcs, perpendicular to the beam, rather than veering much. The dimensions given are suitable for most commercially available swing seats, but consult the seat manufacturer's instructions before you drill any holes.

3 Install the Hardware. The plans call for using ⅜x8-inch eyebolts. Be aware that different manufacturers measure eyebolt lengths differently. For some, the 8-inch dimension is an overall length, while for others the 8-inch length refers to the shaft below the eye. Look for eyebolts with at least an 8-inch shaft. One possible alternative for a light-duty toddler swing is ⅜-inch lag-screw eyebolts, shown on the next page.

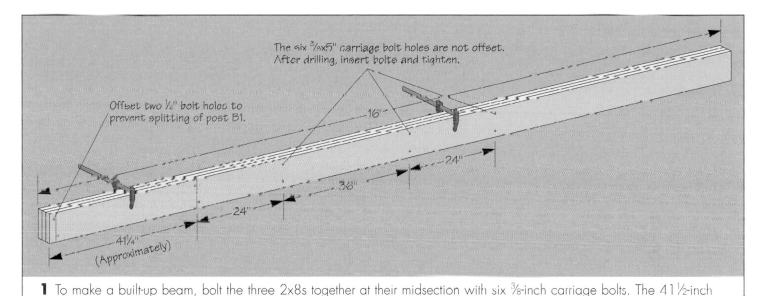

The six ⅜x5" carriage bolt holes are not offset. After drilling, insert bolts and tighten.

Offset two ½" bolt holes to prevent splitting of post B1.

16'

24"

36"

24"

41¼" (Approximately)

1 To make a built-up beam, bolt the three 2x8s together at their midsection with six ⅜-inch carriage bolts. The 41½-inch spacing for the four eventual ½-inch bolts at the Central Tower is approximated here; drill only the two holes shown.

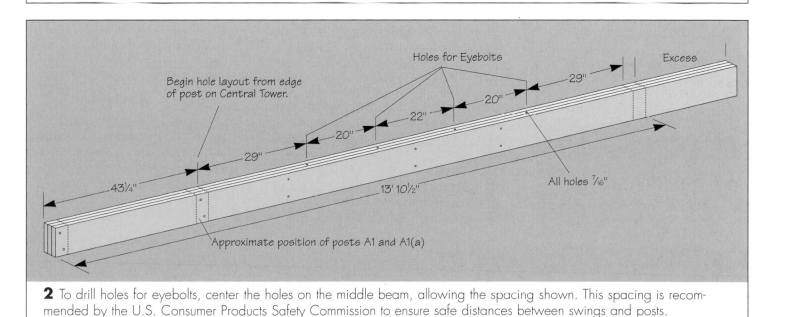

Begin hole layout from edge of post on Central Tower.

Holes for Eyebolts

Excess

29"

20"

22"

20"

29"

43¼"

13' 10½"

All holes ⁷⁄₁₆"

Approximate position of posts A1 and A1(a)

2 To drill holes for eyebolts, center the holes on the middle beam, allowing the spacing shown. This spacing is recommended by the U.S. Consumer Products Safety Commission to ensure safe distances between swings and posts.

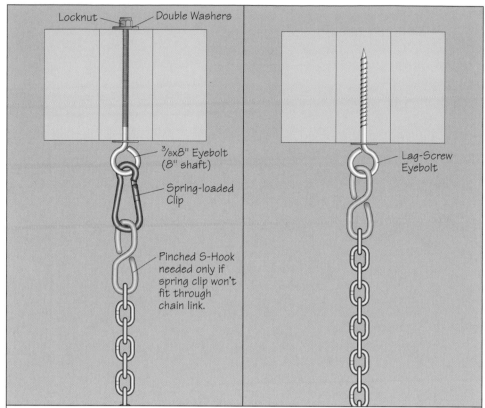

Locknut — Double Washers

⅜x8" Eyebolt
(8" shaft)

Spring-loaded
Clip

Pinched S-Hook
needed only if
spring clip won't
fit through
chain link.

Lag-Screw
Eyebolt

3 Install the hardware. Secure the eyebolts with double washers and a locknut on top of the beam. Because eyebolts will bear more weight than lag screws, lag screws should be used only for light loads, such as toddler swings. Use spring-loaded clips and S-hooks to attach the seats and chain to the beam.

For the ⅜-inch eyebolts, drill ⅞-inch holes as straight as possible through the middle board in the beam. Attach the eyebolts with double washers on top and a single washer on the bottom, as shown, fastening them with ⅜-inch locknuts.

Installing the Beam

At the Central Tower, on the three posts that will support the swing, measure and mark 36 inches up from the upper deck surface. The bottom of the swing beam will align with these marks. With a helper or two, raise the beam into position using the temporary cleats shown as supports. When the beam is aligned with the layout mark on post A1, adjust the ends for level; then clamp the beam at each end. (At the outer posts, clamp the beam to only one post, not

both. Otherwise, the temporary cleat would prevent a tight "sandwiching" of the beam between posts.)

At the outer posts, drill two offset ½-inch holes through posts and beam, drilling recesses on the second post. (See "Recessing Hardware," page 73.) Install ½x12-inch carriage bolts and tighten the nuts.

At post B1 on the Central Tower, use the beam's two ½-inch holes as guides to continue the holes through the post, drilling recesses on the backside of the post before installing bolts and nuts.

At post A1(a), remove the temporary cleat and drill two offset ½-inch holes through the posts and beam. Drill recesses on the backside of A1 before installing bolts and nuts.

Back at the outer posts, remove the temporary cleat. Then clamp, drill, recess, and bolt the top spacer, shown

on page 85, so that it is flush with the bottom of the beam.

Recheck that the outer swing posts are plumb. Then fill the posthole with concrete to 3 inches below grade, sloping the concrete's surface away from the posts to promote rain runoff. Let the concrete cure overnight, and do not allow anyone to use the Central Tower during that time.

Then dig postholes for the A-frame; attach the supports as shown on page 86, and fill the holes with concrete to 3 inches below grade, again sloping the surface away from the posts.

Installing the Swings

In addition to the seat and chain, each swing requires two ⅜ x 3½-inch spring-loaded clips. (For more information on clips, see "Clips and Hooks," on page 38.) If you have clips, you would need S-hooks here only if the clips won't fit through small chain links. With a large pliers, close the ends of the S-hooks tightly so that they cannot slip off the clips or chain. If you can't close the S-hooks with a large pliers, remove the clips from the eyebolts and use a hammer or a vise to close them. Attach the seats to the chain with S-hooks (also closing them) or as directed by the manufacturer.

Ensure that the eyes of the eyebolts are perpendicular to the length of the beam, as shown. Proper position of all hardware will provide the best swinging motion.

Install swing seats just low enough so your children's feet can touch the ground (14 to 18 inches is usually ideal). You can add extra sets of S-hooks in the chain and then close them to allow easy raising or lowering of the seat by means of the spring-loaded clips. Be sure to close the S-hooks completely.

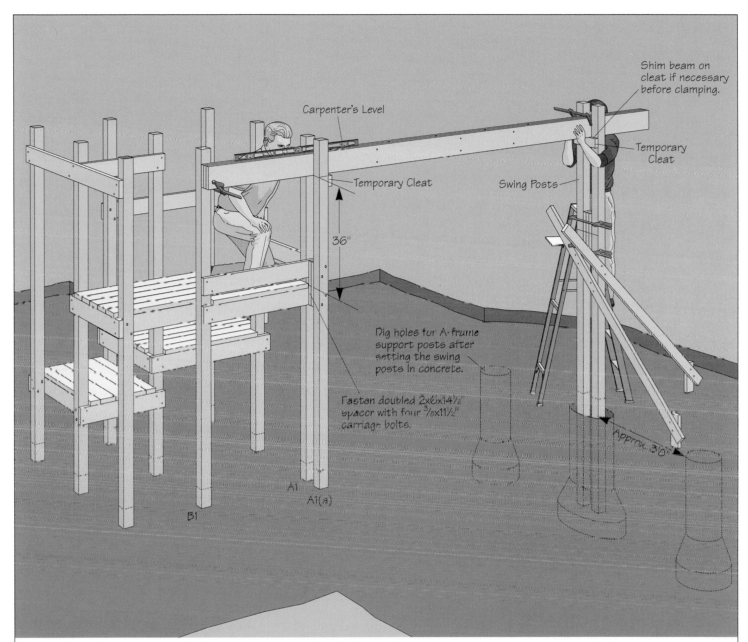

Shim beam on cleat if necessary before clamping.

Carpenter's Level

Temporary Cleat

Temporary Cleat

Swing Posts

36"

Dig holes for A-frame support posts after setting the swing posts in concrete.

Fasten doubled 2x6x14½" spacer with four ⅜x11½" carriage bolts.

Approx. 3'6"

A1
A1(a)

B1

Installing the Beam. Rest the beam on temporary cleats before leveling and clamping the beam at its intended position. Ensure that you have enough strong help, and begin by hoisting the Tower end of the beam to the person atop the Tower.

Swing Substitutes

You can also use the installed eyebolts to suspend rings or a 20-inch trapeze bar, a commonly available size. For the quick switches of accessories, attach the proper length of chain for each with closed S-hooks. Then simply remove each by means of spring-loaded clips.

For a tire swing, use only a swivel manufactured specifically for that purpose. Attach the swivel to the beam, centering it between the posts. Install the tire so its bottom is at least 2 feet above the ground.

Swings take a beating. And their hardware gets stressed. On a regular basis, inspect all hardware and replace parts that are worn or rusting. Especially check the nuts that secure eyebolts, and tighten or replace as needed.

Caution: *The U.S. Consumer Product Safety Commission considers trapeze bars and exercise rings to be athletic equipment and does not recommend them for playgrounds. If you install such equipment, be cautioned that it allows children to turn themselves upside down, increasing the chances for headfirst falls.*

As to a tire swing, because it can rotate in all directions, avoid installing it where it could impact support posts or another swing apparatus. At very least, ensure that there's extra-thick reduced-impact material wherever swing arcs could project a child. As this area becomes compressed with use and weather, refresh it regularly.

Stand-Alone Swing Frame

To construct a stand-alone swing frame, you need to set double 4x4 posts in concrete on both sides. Then follow instructions here. (You can build a double swing frame by using the heftier beam and bolt sizes indicated with earlier instructions.)

Dig two 12x20-inch postholes to at least three feet, plus at least 6 inches below frost line in northern regions. Insert the 4x4 middle spacers, and then place both sets of posts in the holes. When the posts are spaced properly and plumb, brace them securely.

Measure up one post 8 feet above the eventual surface of impact-reducing material and make a mark. Using a line level or else a carpenter's level on a long straight board, transfer this mark to the other set of posts. Install the top spacers, with their tops aligned with the marks.

Lay out the beam for the eyebolt positions, as shown on page 91. Drill $7/16$-inch holes for the eyebolts and install the eyebolts with double washers on top, a single washer on the bottom, and locknuts. See "Install the Hardware" on pages 87-88.

Lift the beam into position, resting it on the top spacers. Check once again that the beam is level. (If it isn't, place shims between the beam and one spacer.) Drill holes through posts and beams for the ½-inch carriage bolts. Install and tighten the bolts, washers, and nuts.

Fill the holes with concrete to 3 inches below ground level, sloping the surface away from the posts. Leave the bracing in place overnight while the concrete cures.

Attach the swings as described on page 88. Dig the four holes for the A-frame. Pour concrete into the holes to about 5 inches below ground level. Then proceed as shown at right.

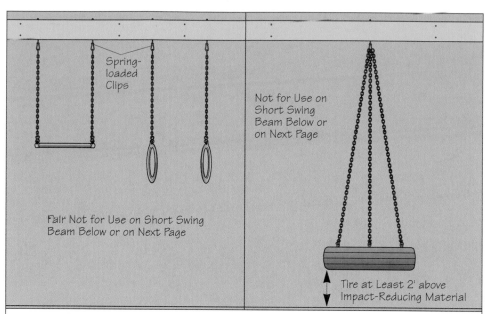

Spring-loaded Clips

Fair Not for Use on Short Swing Beam Below or on Next Page

Not for Use on Short Swing Beam Below or on Next Page

Tire at Least 2' above Impact-Reducing Material

Trapeze bars and exercise rings are considered athletic, rather than playground, equipment. They pose additional risk of headfirst falls. Because a tire swings in all directions, it should be the only swing suspended from the beam at one time.

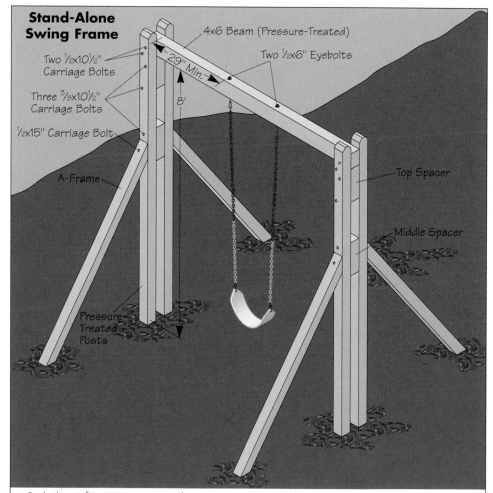

Stand-Alone Swing Frame

4x6 Beam (Pressure-Treated)

Two ½x10½" Carriage Bolts

Three ³⁄₈x10½" Carriage Bolts

½x15" Carriage Bolt

Two ½x6" Eyebolts

29" Min.

8'

A-Frame

Pressure-Treated Posts

Top Spacer

Middle Spacer

Sink the A-frame posts into the wet concrete so the angled tops abut the swing posts exactly opposite each other. Drill through the assembly, securing it with a ½x15-inch carriage bolt or threaded rod, first recessing for washers and nuts.

Swing Frame for a Single Swing

If all you need—or have room for—is a single swing, the accompanying illustration gives the necessary dimensions and materials. Use a 12-foot 4x6 for the swing beam. You can cut it to finished length after installation. Make the three 12-inch spacers from scrap 4x4s. Note that since the 4x6 beam for a single swing is an inch thinner than the built-up beam for the double swing, bolt lengths must be shortened accordingly.

This swing frame will also accommodate a single trapeze bar or a set of rings. But it is not wide enough for a tire swing, which swings in all directions

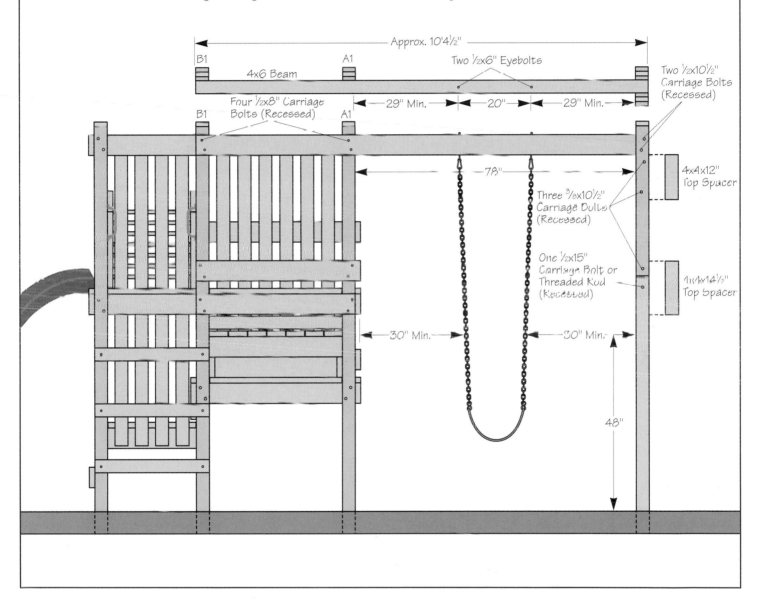

8

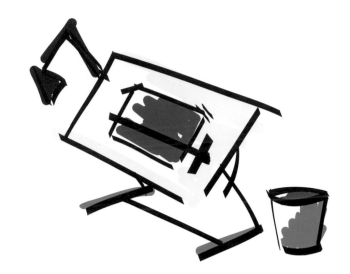

Monkey Bar

Although kids love whooshing down a slide and "flying" on a swing, those activities don't offer much physical challenge. A monkey bar is fun too, but it also requires strenuous effort that develops strength and coordination. Thus, it is an excellent component for the Kids' Playland.

Better yet, the Monkey Bar is easy to add and to afford. Two posts on the Central Tower support one end of the Monkey Bar, so the only strenuous work is the digging of two holes to support posts on the outer end. The lower deck on the Central Tower serves as the launching pad.

The plans show a sloping monkey bar, descending from 84 inches at the Central Tower to 60 inches at the outer end. This is a good height for most kids 6 years and older. The slope makes the bars more of a challenge ascending than descending. For younger kids install the bar lower, so that they can reach the bar nearest the Tower, simply by stretching, rather than by jumping. At the lower end, a jump height for younger kids still provides a reaching height for older kids.

Bar Vantages

The bar slope shown is optional. Feel free to instead install horizontal bars at a lower height for children younger than 6 years or so.

The first bar nearest the Central Tower is set some distance from the posts. This is an important safety feature—don't place the first bar directly over the platform at the Tower. Children should need to reach out to grasp the first bar. That way, should they fall, they will fall to the impact-reducing material and not against the platform. The ground beneath should be covered with extra-thick impact-reducing material, which you should maintain regularly.

For individual bars themselves, we recommend hardwood dowels, although you could use galvanized pipe. The biggest advantage of wood dowels is that they won't become too cold or too hot in extreme weather. Wood is also more comfortable to grasp in any weather.

If you use plumbing pipe, or a thicker dowel, be sure to drill mounting holes to match their diameter. The best diameters for dowels are 1 to 1½ inches. Larger diameters are hard for children to grasp.

Laying Out Postholes

If you didn't mark the Monkey Bar postholes when laying out the Playland initially, set the two 2x6 rails on the ground, on edge and with their ends flush with the back edges of the Central Tower posts, as shown on page 94. If necessary, temporarily fasten the rails to the posts to hold the rails upright. On the outer end, adjust the rails so their outside faces are exactly 24 inches apart, also squaring them with the near wall of the Central Tower.

Measure back on each rail 6 inches then out 1¾ inches, as shown. These

Sloping Monkey Bar

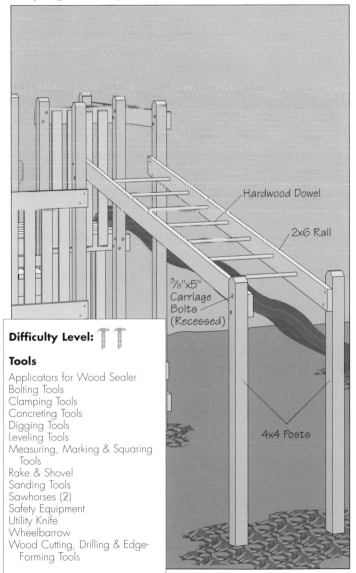

Hardwood Dowel

2x6 Rail

⅜"x5" Carriage Bolts (Recessed)

4x4 Posts

Difficulty Level:

Tools

Applicators for Wood Sealer
Bolting Tools
Clamping Tools
Concreting Tools
Digging Tools
Leveling Tools
Measuring, Marking & Squaring
  Tools
Rake & Shovel
Sanding Tools
Sawhorses (2)
Safety Equipment
Utility Knife
Wheelbarrow
Wood Cutting, Drilling & Edge-
  Forming Tools

Lumber and Materials Order

	Qty	Size
4x4	2	10' minimum
2x6	2	10'
Hardwood dowels	4	1"x4'

Hardware & More

Decking screws	14	3"
Carriage bolts, washers, nuts	8	⅜"x5"

Concrete

Gravel

Construction adhesive or polyurethene glue

Impact-reducing material

Finish

Cutting List

Dowels	7	22½"

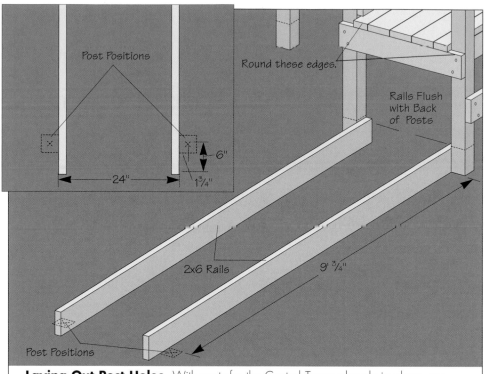

Laying Out Post Holes. With posts for the Central Tower already in place, use the 2x6 rails to mark the post locations for the Monkey Bar.

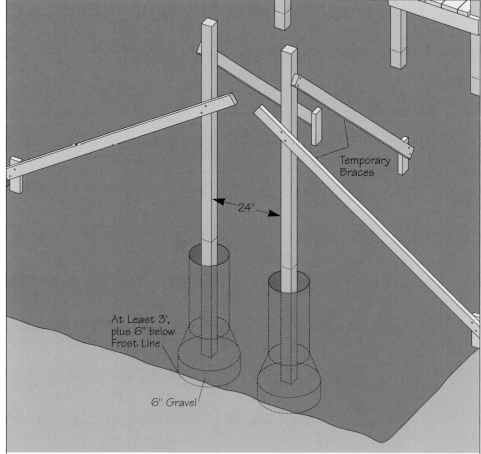

Preparing the Posts. Position the posts in the holes, but don't add concrete until after you have attached the rails.

locations will be the centers of the two new postholes. Mark them with a small piece of wood. Remove the rails and set them aside.

Preparing the Posts

Dig the two postholes to at least 3 feet and an additional 6 inches below frost line in northern regions. See "Setting Posts" on page 46 for more on posthole digging. Set the posts in the holes, 24 inches apart and 9 feet ¾ inch from the posts on the Central Tower, as shown. Plumb the posts and brace them securely, but do not fill the holes with concrete yet.

Building the Bar

The bar is assembled by inserting dowels into matching holes drilled halfway into the face of each rail. The dowels are held in place with glue and screws. The dimensions given here assume that spacing between posts on each end of the Monkey Bar is exactly 24 inches. If this spacing is off by even a fraction of an inch—and don't be surprised if it is—now is the time to determine it and make necessary adjustments.

1 **Check the Post Spacing.** At the Central Tower, measure from the decking surface up each post 60 inches, or a lesser height, and make a mark at that spot. Now carefully measure the distance between the posts at the mark. If it is exactly 24 inches, you can proceed with the instructions exactly as given.

If the spacing between posts is a bit over or under 24 inches, cut the dowels to a length that makes up the difference. For example, if the spacing is 23½ inches, subtract ½ inch from the dowel length. In this case, your dowels would be 22 inches

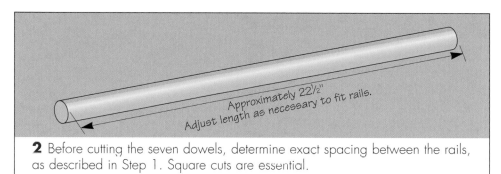

2 Before cutting the seven dowels, determine exact spacing between the rails, as described in Step 1. Square cuts are essential.

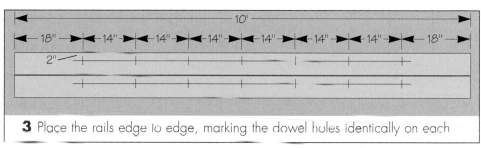

3 Place the rails edge to edge, marking the dowel holes identically on each.

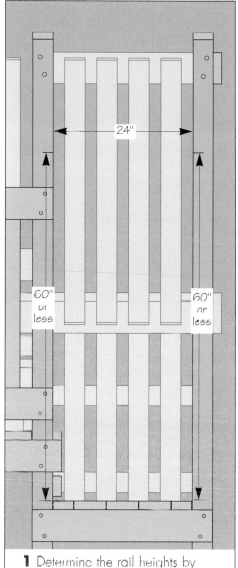

1 Determine the rail heights by measuring from the deck surface of the lower level.

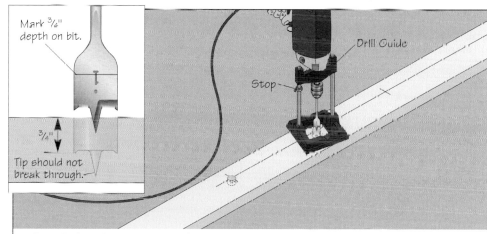

4 Drill dowel holes only half way through the rail. A drill guide with stop at ¾ inch ensures uniform depths.

long. Likewise, for example, if the spacing between posts is 24¾ inches, you would cut dowels 23¼ inches long. This is the only adjustment necessary to ensure that the bars fit snugly between the posts.

2 Cut the Dowels. Cut a total of seven dowels to a length of 22½ inches or the length calculated in the previous step. For best results, make the cuts as square as possible. A table saw or power miter saw will produce the most accurate results. If you must use a hand saw, take a little extra time to produce the squarest ends you can.

3 Prepare the Rails. Lay both 2x6 rails on a flat surface. On the inside face of each, mark a layout line along the length of the board 2 inches from the top edge. Now mark the dowel hole layout along this line, 18 inches from the end of each board and then every 14 inches on center.

4 Drill the Dowel Holes. On each board, drill 1-inch-diameter holes exactly ¾ inch deep. Ensure that the tip of your wood-boring bit won't break through the outside face of the board. The best way to control the depth of each hole is to use a drill press or a drill

guide with the stop set for a ¾-inch depth. If you don't have access to either of these, mark the bit with a marker and drill carefully.

5 Attach the Rails and Dowels. Spread a small amount of exterior glue around each dowel hole on one rail. Insert dowels into each hole, giving them a light tap with a hammer if necessary. Then apply glue to the dowel holes on the other rail, and fit the rail over the dowels.

After you have joined all dowels and rails, drill deck-screw pilot holes 3 inches deep through the top of the

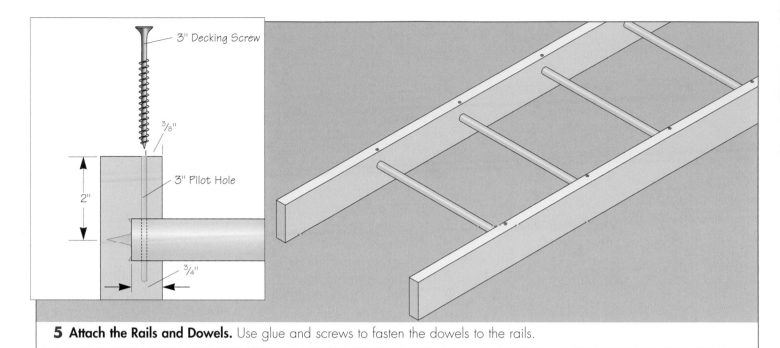

5 Attach the Rails and Dowels. Use glue and screws to fasten the dowels to the rails.

rails at each dowel location, ⅜ inch from the inside edge. Then finish the assembly by driving 3-inch deck screws into each pilot hole.

Assembling the Monkey Bar

Attach the bar temporarily to the posts. If you like, adjust the height of the bar at either end to suit the needs of your children. Mark cutoff lines on the rails and posts. Then take the bar down and make the cuts.

1 Mark the End Posts. Measure up one end post 60 inches, or to a lower height for kids 6 years and younger, and make a mark. With a level, transfer this mark to the other post.

2 Temporarily Attach the Bar. With a helper, raise the rails between the posts. Center the rails on the height marks you made on the end posts and the marks you made earlier on the posts at the Central Tower (60 inches or less above the deck). Temporarily attach the rails to the posts with clamps or screws.

Check the end posts for plumb and make adjustments as necessary. Pour concrete into the holes to 3 inches below ground level, tapering the surface of the concrete away from the posts. Let the concrete cure undisturbed overnight. Then top off the holes with dirt.

Mark and cut off the rails at the end posts, using the posts as a guide. At this time you can either cut off the end posts at the tops of rails or leave them long enough to allow your raising the rails as your kids grow taller.

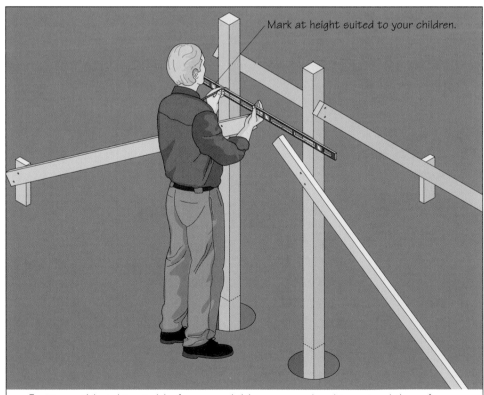

1 At a rail height suitable for your children, use a level to extend the reference line to the second post.

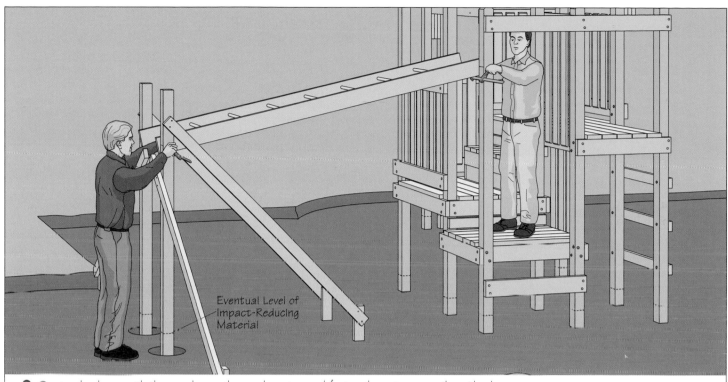

2 Center the bars with the marks on the end posts, and fasten them temporarily with clamps or screws.

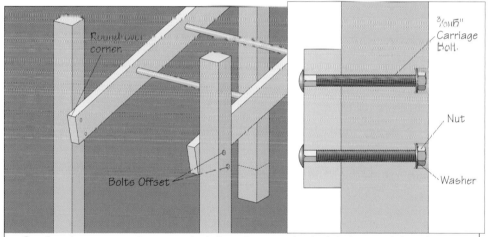

3 After the concrete has cured, drill and recess the bolt holes, and then fasten the bars to the posts.

4 For a step to help smaller kids reach the first bar, we recommend a 24-inch diameter truck tire (not shown) filled with impact-reducing material.

Remove the bar and make all of the necessary cuts. Round-over and smooth all sharp or rough edges.

3 Permanently Attach the Bar. Clamp or temporarily screw the bar to the posts. Drill two ⅜-inch holes through each rail and post junction, offsetting them so they don't split the posts. Drill ½-inch deep recesses on the outsides of the posts, as shown. Fasten with 5-inch carriage bolts, washers, and nuts.

4 Create a Launch Pad. Rather than adding a wood step on the end posts to allow smaller kids to reach the first dowel, lay a 24-inch-diameter truck tire (not shown) flat between the posts and fill it with impact-reducing material, after roping the tire to the posts on each side. This lets smaller kids reach the first bar, and it provides a cushioned landing pad when kids descend from the Tower end. Remove the tire after your kids outgrow the need.

Part 3

Stand-Alone Projects

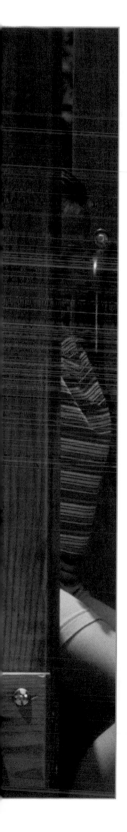

This part of the book explains how to build five popular play components. You might decide to build them all because kids like to move from one activity to another.

The Playhouse will be popular with kids of all ages, with the bonus that it could become a storage shed after your kids outgrow it. You'll also find several sandbox designs. The balance beam allows simulated aerial feats without the height hazards. Our kids'-size Picnic Table encourages rest and socializing, though it's big enough to accommodate parents. And our final project, the Teeter-Totter, is just right for kids about 4 to 6 years old.

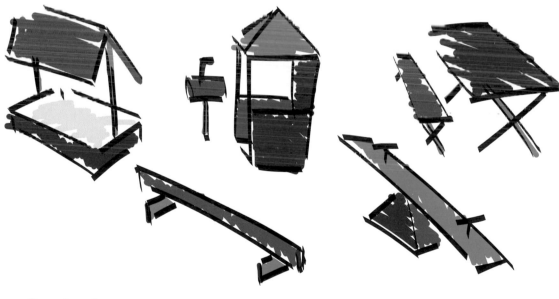

9   **Playhouse**   **101**

10   **Sandboxes**   **114**

11   **Balance Beam**   **123**

12   **Picnic Table**   **127**

13   **Teeter-Totter**   **132**

Playhouse

The Playhouse has something for everyone. For kids, it offers an elevated, covered, and reasonably private outdoor room that can serve a range of functions from clubhouse to quiet haven. For parents, the Playhouse offers most of the attractions of a tree house, but without the combined dangers of height and structural uncertainty. Besides, the Playhouse need not be so private that younger kids are completely hidden from view, and it is reasonably easy to construct.

The plans call for a deck surface only 20 inches above ground. Because the deck is low, the ground beneath the Playhouse doesn't require special impact-reducing material. The low profile also means that the Playhouse can be built without need to bury posts in concrete. With bolts and screws for most of the joinery, this structure can be dismantled easily when it has outlived its purpose.

Choose the lumber with an eye toward how long you want the structure to last. To postpone rot at ground level, you will probably want to use pressure-treated lumber for the posts. But the rest of the structure can be built with untreated lumber, which you can then finish with a good water-repellent or semi-transparent stain on a regular basis. Even unfinished lumber can provide many years of service.

Preparing the Site

The Playhouse can be placed directly on grass. But a better approach might be to remove the sod beneath the structure, lay down some landscape fabric, and then fill the excavation with gravel. Since the grass will probably die from lack of sunlight anyway, gravel will be more attractive than bare ground. Additionally, the gravel bed will help as you level the structure, and it will prevent water from pooling beneath it.

Since you don't need to dig postholes for this project, layout steps are simpler than those for the Kids' Playland. Nor is it necessary to rely on batter boards and strings to keep the sides properly aligned.

The basic plans for the Playhouse show a relatively low deck height. This offers several advantages: It eliminates concerns about kids falling from great heights to the ground, posts don't need to be braced or buried in concrete, and kids usually won't mind that their Playhouse isn't

higher. If you prefer to build the deck a little higher, you can do so following essentially the same design. But with a deck height of more than 20 inches, up to about 36 inches, you should add 2x6 base supports and 2x4 cross bracing all around, as shown on page 113, as well as at least 6 inches of impact-reducing material under the doorway and around the entire structure.

If you want a deck higher than 36 inches, embed the posts in concrete. For that, see "Setting Posts," page 46.

Playhouse with Roof of Beveled Siding

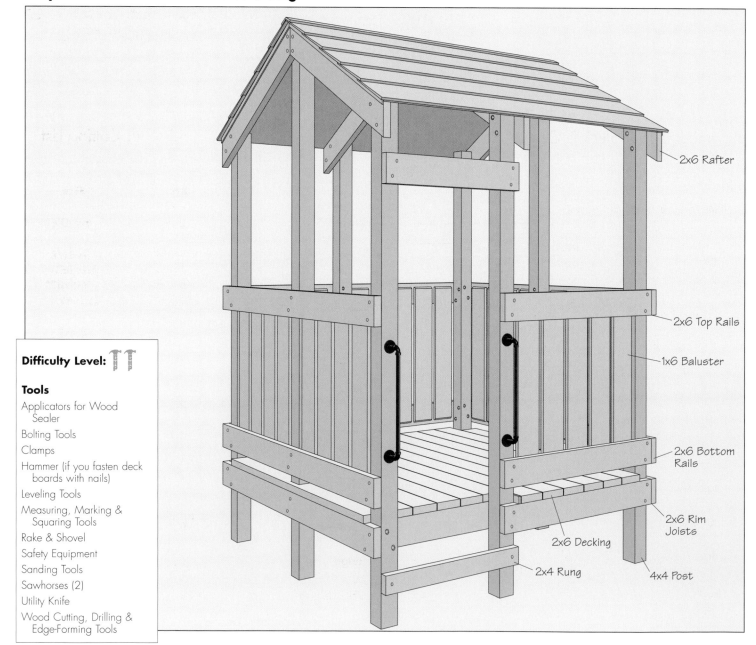

2x6 Rafter

2x6 Top Rails

1x6 Baluster

2x6 Bottom Rails

2x6 Rim Joists

2x6 Decking

2x4 Rung

4x4 Post

Difficulty Level:

Tools

Applicators for Wood Sealer

Bolting Tools

Clamps

Hammer (if you fasten deck boards with nails)

Leveling Tools

Measuring, Marking & Squaring Tools

Rake & Shovel

Safety Equipment

Sanding Tools

Sawhorses (2)

Utility Knife

Wood Cutting, Drilling & Edge-Forming Tools

Preparing the Lumber

It is easier to do the bulk of smoothing and sanding of lumber before construction begins. With the right power tools, this step can be relatively quick and simple. First, round-over the edges of the posts and the top edge of the top rails with a router equipped with a roundover bit. Then smooth all exposed surfaces with a power sander, removing any mill stamps on the lumber as you go. In addition to providing a surface that is friendlier to small hands, the sanded wood will better absorb the finish you apply later.

Use a router with roundover bit, as shown, or a belt sander to soften edges and corners that kids might accidentally bump into.

Lumber and Materials Order

	Qty	Size
4x4s (pressure-treated posts)	6	8'
	2	10'
2x6s (joists, rails, rafters, ridge)	15	12'
	4	8'
2x4s (step)	1	8'
1x6s (balusters)	10	10'
Roof covering (Choose among options.)		@50 sq. ft.
Carriage bolts, nuts, washers	14	⅜"x7"
	12	⅜"x5½"
	62	⅜x5"
Lag screws	8	⁵⁄₁₆x4"
2x6 joist hangers, nails	2	
Deck screws	200	3"
	150	2½"
Finish		

Cutting List

	Qty	Size
Posts	2	4x4x9'6"
Joists	1	2x6x70"
	1	2x6x68½"
	5	2x6x69"
	1	2x6x41½"
Rung	1	2x4x31"
Door Header	1	2x6x31"
Decking	5	2x6x65"
	8	2x6x70"
Top/Bottom Rails	2	2x6x70"
	2	2x6x41½"
	2	2x6x69"
	2	2x6x68½"
Rafters	6	2x6x48"
Ridge	1	2x6x62"
Balusters	29	1x6x36"

Building the Side Walls

The side walls (Sides B and D in the accompanying drawing) are virtually identical, except that the rim joist and both rails on Side D are 1½ inches longer. Study the illustrations to familiarize yourself with the details. As shown, each wall is assembled on the ground before being raised.

The four 4x4 corner posts should each be 8 feet long. From 10-foot 4x4s, cut the two center posts to 9 feet, 6 inches. Lay the posts on the ground, then measure from the bottom and mark layout lines for tops of the rim joist and two rails at 18½ inches, 27½ inches, and 60 inches, as shown. Space the posts 28¼ inches apart, making sure that the bottoms are in line.

Next cut the rails and rim joists. Using 2x6s, cut three boards 70 inches long for Side D and three others 68½ inches long for Side B. Place the cut 2x6s across the posts with their top edges aligned with the layout marks. Check that the boards for Side D overlap the outside posts by 1½ inches on each side; those for Side B should not overlap the corner "door post."

Mark the bolt-hole locations on each board. The bolts must be offset vertically on each post side and staggered to allow for bolting through adjacent sides of the post so that the bolts don't hit one another. See the section "Staggering Bolt Holes" on page 73 for detailed instructions. Temporarily fasten the boards to the posts with 3-inch screws, which you will replace with bolts once the walls are raised. The holes left by the screws will serve as pilots for drilling the bolt holes, so take care to drive the screws as straight as possible.

Now cut the four outside rafters, using 48-inch 2x6s. To do this, lay one board across the tops of a center post and a corner post, with the top of the rafter flush with the edges of the posts, as shown. Use a sliding bevel gauge to

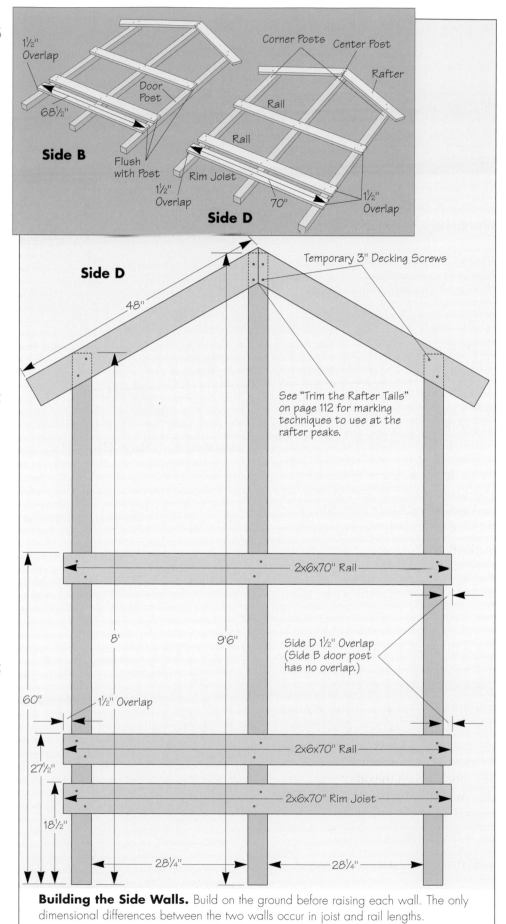

Building the Side Walls. Build on the ground before raising each wall. The only dimensional differences between the two walls occur in joist and rail lengths.

determine the angle to plumb-cut the rafter peaks, about 60 degrees. (For marking savvy, see "Trim the Rafter Tail" on page 112.) Mark and cut the angle. Check fit and alignment of each rafter. If the plumb cuts aren't perfectly in line, adjust your bevel gauge a few degrees. Mark and cut the remaining rafters and fasten with screws.

Raising the Side Walls

Cut seven 2x6s to 69-inch lengths. Five will serve as floor joists and two will serve as rails for the back wall. Mark the bolt-hole locations on each board, again making certain that they are offset and staggered.

Carefully raise each wall into position and brace each plumb and parallel with its opposite wall; alternatively, a couple of helpers could hold the walls in place. Temporarily attach the back-side top rail with 3 inch screws. Then attach the outside joist on the back wall and the long joist on the inside of the posts on the front wall. With a helper or two, shift the walls until diagonal posts are equidistant, making the structure square. Level the structure by digging under posts or shimming them up, checking joists with a carpenter's level.

Framing the Front Wall

Cut three 2x6s to 41½ inches to serve as the rails and outside joist on the front wall. Mark layout lines on a 4x4 post at the same distances from the bottom as on the other posts, as shown. With a helper or two, hold the inner door post upright while you drive temporary screws through the rails, ensuring that each board is flush with the outside edge of each post.

Now cut and attach the 2x6 doorway header and the 2x4 step. Each is 31 inches long.

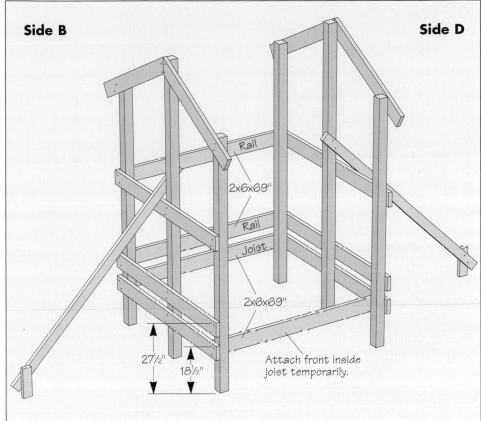

Raising the Side Walls. After raising the side walls, temporarily attach rim joists and, for the back wall, rails as well.

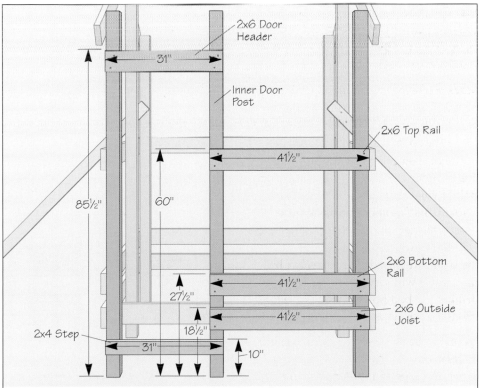

Framing the Front Wall. After marking layout lines as indicated on the posts, temporarily fasten the 41½-inch rails and joist to the inner door post. Then temporarily attach the 2x6 door header and 2x4 step.

Attaching the Back Wall Post

Mark layout lines on a 4x4 post, as you did on the front wall. Measure and mark vertical layout lines on each board, as shown here. Raise the post, aligning it with all marks, and fasten it temporarily with 3-inch screws.

Completing the Roof Frame

Cut a 62-inch 2x6 ridge board and attach it with 2x6 joist hangers to the center posts. Keep the top of the ridge aligned with the tops of the posts. To attach the joist hangers, use fasteners recommended by the manufacturer.

Using 48-inch 2x6s, plumb-cut the two middle rafters at the ridge boards. To lay out the cut, set a sliding bevel

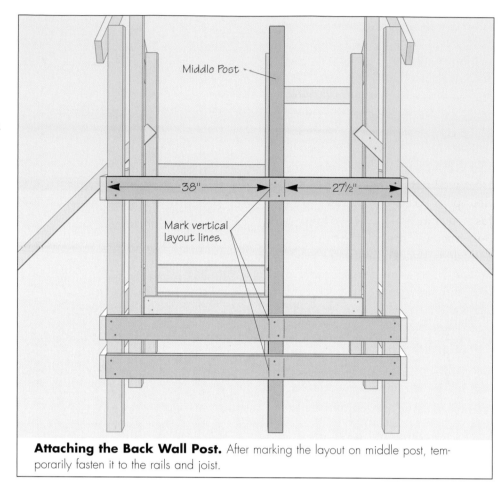

Attaching the Back Wall Post. After marking the layout on middle post, temporarily fasten it to the rails and joist.

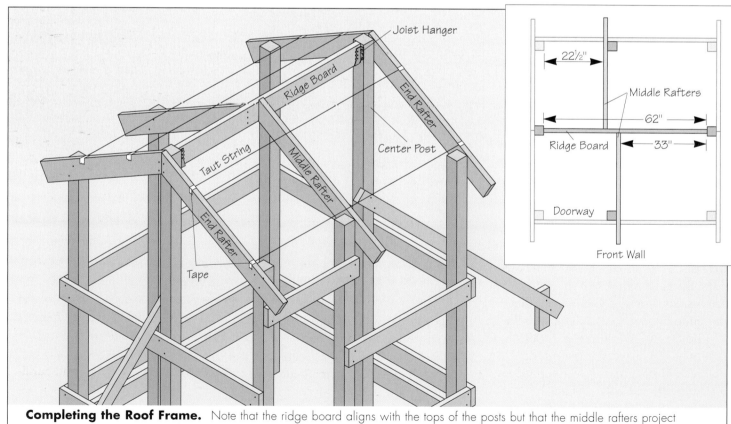

Completing the Roof Frame. Note that the ridge board aligns with the tops of the posts but that the middle rafters project above the ridge board to the same height as the end rafters. Align tops of the middle rafters with the taut strings.

gauge to the angle used on the outside rafters. To help align the middle rafter heights with the outside rafters, tape two equally spaced, taut strings across the end rafters on each side to serve as guides. To make fastening easier at the ridge board, attach the middle rafters to the middle posts, spacing them as shown. Be sure to place the front-wall rafter on the outside of the door post. Position the rafters so they just touch the strings. Drive three 3-inch screws through the faces of the ridge into each rafter and two 3-inch screws through each rafter into the post.

The tips of the rafters will sit slightly above the ridge. Ensure that no parts of any post rise above a rafter, where they would interfere with the roofing.

Checking Plumb and Square

With a carpenter's level, check adjacent sides of every post to ensure that each is plumb. Then measure the distances between diagonal posts. If the diagonals are equidistant, the frame is square. If they vary by ¼ inch or more, carefully shift the frame until it is square.

Bolting the Frame

You will use ⅜-inch carriage bolts to fasten all joists, rails, and rafter tails to posts. The end rafters must be bolted at the ridge with ⁵⁄₁₆x4-inch lag screws. For safety, any bolt ends that protrude into an accessible part of the Playhouse should be recessed. Bolts that will be covered by decking do not need to be recessed. The top view on the next page indicates bolt lengths needed. For detailed guidance on bolt installation, see "Recessing Hardware," on page 73.

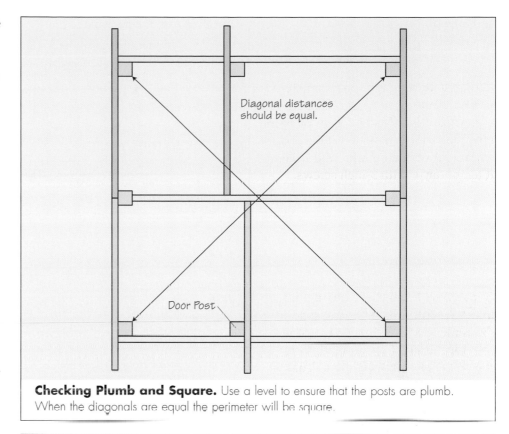

Checking Plumb and Square. Use a level to ensure that the posts are plumb. When the diagonals are equal the perimeter will be square.

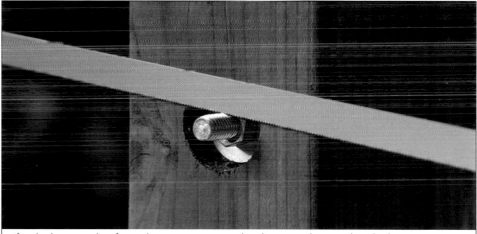

If a bolt protrudes from the recess, use a hacksaw or heavy-duty bolt cutter to cut the bolt flush with the wood. Use a mill file to soften sharp edges.

Whenever possible, drill recess holes into the posts because they are thicker than the boards. Use two bolts at each board-and-post intersection.

Because you will need to temporarily remove the bottom rails in order to attach decking, do not yet bolt the bottom rails to the posts. To create the bolt holes for the rails, remove one of the screws. Then drill a ⅜-inch bolt hole, using the screw hole as a pilot. Drill all the way through for bolts that

do not need to be recessed. However, if you need to drill a recess hole, drill only until the tip of the wood bit pokes through on the back side of the post. Use that hole to pilot a 1⅛-inch spade bit, drilling the recess ½ inch deep. Slide a bolt through the hole, slip a washer over the end, and hand-tighten the bolt. Then move to another screw. This procedure is illustrated on page 73. It will proceed much faster if you have access to a hand brace and auger bit to drill recesses and two power drills, one with a bit to remove screws and one for the bolt holes. Of course, this will proceed even faster with three power drills.

After inserting all of the bolts, check the posts and frame one more time for plumb and square. Begin tightening the bolts with a socket wrench. Recess 5-inch bolts for all rails and the doorway header. Attach the 2x4 rung with one 5½-inch bolt on each side.

Installing Decking

Install the 2x6 decking boards perpendicular to the joists. If you are using relatively dry boards, install them with an ⅛-inch gap between them. If you are using boards that still contain quite a bit of moisture (particularly if they are wet pressure-treated boards), install them with no gap; as these boards dry, the gaps will open up. The same spacing principle applies for decking around posts. See "Installing Decking" on page 53 for more details.

The decking should be installed flush with the outside faces of the joists on all sides. This deck is small enough so you can cut all decking boards and position them before you begin fastening.

You may need to rip a few boards somewhat narrower to allow for the best spacing. One strategy, as shown in the illustration, is to rip the two end boards to 5 inches. Then notch them to fit around the center post.

If you need to rip any more boards, width differences will be less noticeable if you take small amounts off them rather than a large amount off a single board. Alternatively, you could use a 2x4 or a 2x8 to complete the decking. From an aesthetic standpoint, maintaining a consistent gap between boards is more important than maintaining a consistent width of all boards.

Plan View of Deck Joists

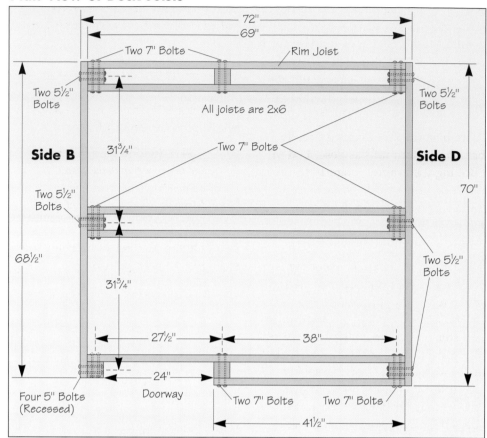

Installing Decking. Lay out all decking boards before fastening them. Rip small amounts off of several boards, as needed, to maintain consistent spacing.

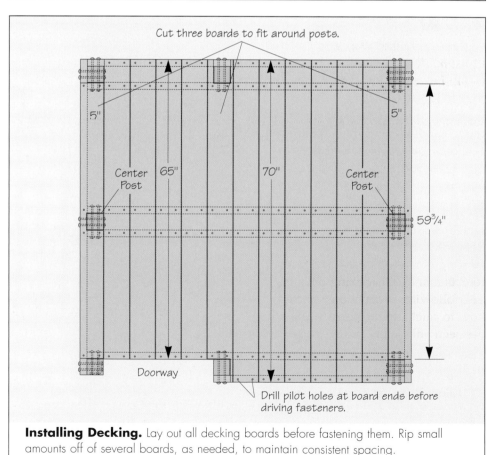

Attach the decking with 3-inch deck screws or 16d nails. Screws and ring-shank nails provide the best holding power, although screws would be much easier to remove when you decide to disassemble the Playhouse. To prevent splitting at board ends, drill pilot holes before installing the fasteners.

After installing all decking boards, bolt the bottom rails as described in "Bolting the Frame," page 107.

Installing Balusters

The 1x6 balusters are installed vertically and are attached to the insides of the top and bottom rails. The plans call for a very small gap between the balusters to maximize the sense of privacy inside the Playhouse. These are all arbitrary choices, of course. For example, you could choose to use 1x4s or 2x2s for baluster stock and space them with somewhat wider gaps to allow you to see your children better from the outside.

Caution. Although the U.S. Consumer Product Safety Commission specifies that gaps in playground equipment be no greater than $3\frac{1}{2}$ inches, to prevent entrapment, local code may require even smaller gaps, perhaps no greater than $2\frac{1}{2}$ inches. So check with local building authorities.

The balusters could instead be attached to the outsides of rails. Regardless of the style, consistent spacing between the balusters results in a better-looking project. The following instructions explain how to calculate the correct gap between balusters.

1 Calculate the Gap. You'll need to calculate baluster spacing separately for each bay—that is, each section of railing between two posts. First, decide on the approximate gap you want ($1\frac{1}{2}$ inches in our example). Add this figure to the width of one baluster ($5\frac{1}{2}$ inches when using 1x6s):

$$5\frac{1}{2} + 1\frac{1}{2} = 7$$

Measure the distance between the posts, in this case $34\frac{1}{2}$ inches, and divide that dimension by the baluster width plus gap amount:

$$34\frac{1}{2} \text{ divided by } 7 = 4.9$$
Round this figure up to the nearest whole number, in this case 5, in order to determine the total number of balusters needed.

Multiply the number of balusters by the width of each baluster:

$$5 \text{ times } 5\frac{1}{2} = 27\frac{1}{2}$$

Subtract this figure from the spacing between posts:

$$34\frac{1}{2} - 27\frac{1}{2} = 7$$

Divide this figure by the total number of gaps you will need (which will always be one more than the total number of balusters):

$$7 \div 6 = 1.166, \text{ which can be rounded fractionally to } 1\frac{5}{32} \text{ inches.}$$

2 Mark and Attach Balusters. There are two ways to position the balusters. One way is to measure out the baluster locations on the top and bottom rails. The second way is to make a spacer jig by ripping a board to the

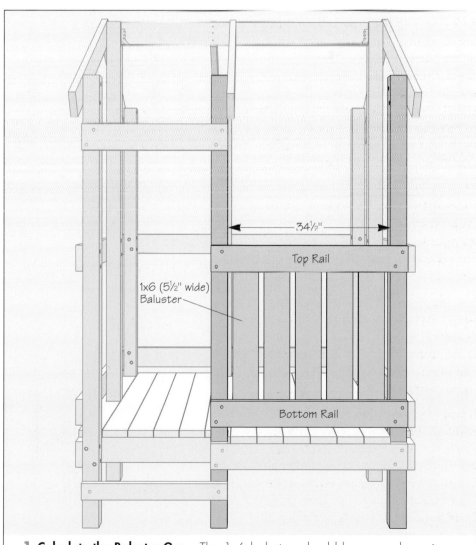

1 Calculate the Baluster Gap. The 1x6 balusters should be spaced consistently between each pair of posts.

exact width of the gap between balusters and attaching it at a perfect right angle to board that rides on the top rail.

The advantage of a spacer is that you don't have to worry about a miscalculation when measuring the layout. Simply suspend the spacer from the rail, resting its vertical member against the previous baluster as you attach the next one.

Before attaching the balusters, break the sharp edges on their tops and bottoms with a router or by cutting a 45-degree bevel, as shown.

Be sure to use fasteners of the correct length. When attaching 1x6 balusters to 2x6 rails, use 2-inch deck screws or 6d (2-inch) nails.

Roofing

There is a variety of roof styles to choose from. This section explains considerations in choosing a roof and then shows how to install each type. The slope, or pitch, of the roof is determined by the length of the center posts. On our design, the center posts rise 18 inches above the end posts, which provides a moderate slope of about 30 degrees.

You could make the roof line more dramatic by increasing its slope. But a steeper roof offers more visibility of the roofing materials, inside and out. To increase the slope, you can simply increase the length of the center posts. Of course, this changes the roof angle and consequently changes the plumb cuts at rafter ends. A steeper roof also increases the square footage of the roof surface.

Do you want the roof to be fully or only partially covered? A fully covered roof will keep out both sun and rain. A partially covered roof will offer partial shade and an airier appearance, and it is the easiest and least expensive roof to install.

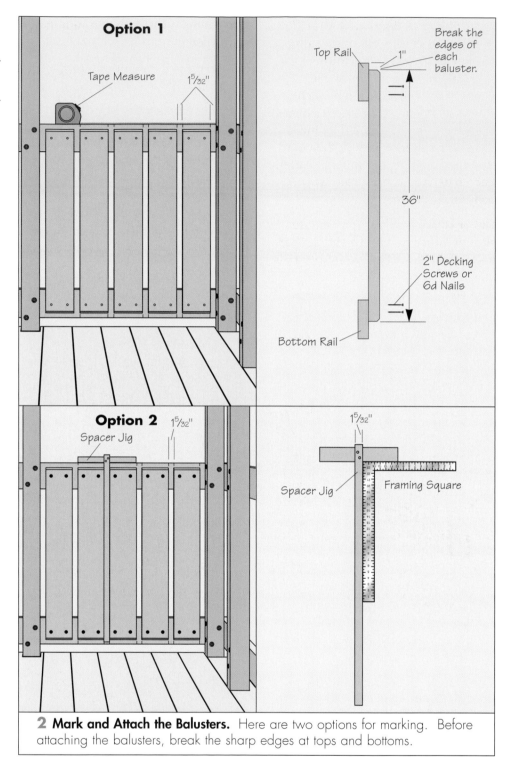

2 Mark and Attach the Balusters. Here are two options for marking. Before attaching the balusters, break the sharp edges at tops and bottoms.

Most parents prefer a covered roof. By blocking all sun and rain from above, you will increase the amount of time your children will want to spend in the Playhouse. Although the sides will be open to the weather, a fully roofed structure offers good protection from the sun and a gentle summer rain.

Caution: *The Playhouse roof is designed to be solid enough to withstand snow loads and the elements. But it is not designed to be walked on. Thus, unless you install 3/4-inch exterior plywood underlayment, you must do all of your roofing work from a ladder.*

Bevel Siding as Roofing. Bevel siding, the kind used as horizontal siding on houses, can make an attractive roof, and it is simple to install. Adjust the exposure so that each course is equal, but be sure to overlap the boards by at least 1¼ inches. Use 8d box nails to fasten the boards through the plywood into the rafters. Each nail should penetrate two boards, as shown.

Slat or Lattice Roofing. You can use slats or lattice to create a simple, partially open roof. Slats are simply 1x4s nailed to the rafters. The spacing between slats is entirely up to you. Less spacing provides more shade.

Drive two 8d box nails through the slats at each rafter.

Standard panels of lattice (not shown) are made with ½-inch-thick slats, and are sold in 4x8 sheets. You can choose between pressure-treated and untreated lattice. Cut one sheet of lattice to fit each side of the roof. Drive 4d box nails through the lattice into each rafter, spacing the nails every 6 inches. Trim the ridge with 1x4s, ripping ¾-inch off one of them to account for the overlap.

Plywood Roofing. You can cover the roof with only plywood, if you prefer. In this case, look for an exterior-grade with two good sides. Since the nails will be driven only into the rafters, you can use ⅜-inch sheets or, in snow country, ½ inch. Another option with plywood is to cut a series of strips, and install them in an overlapping manner, as shown for bevel siding. In either case, paint the roof with a good-quality exterior enamel. Install the plywood with 8d nails every 6 inches along each rafter.

Textured plywood is popular for siding on houses and garages. For the Playhouse, you could use this for roofing. Choose a pattern you like and install the sheets with the

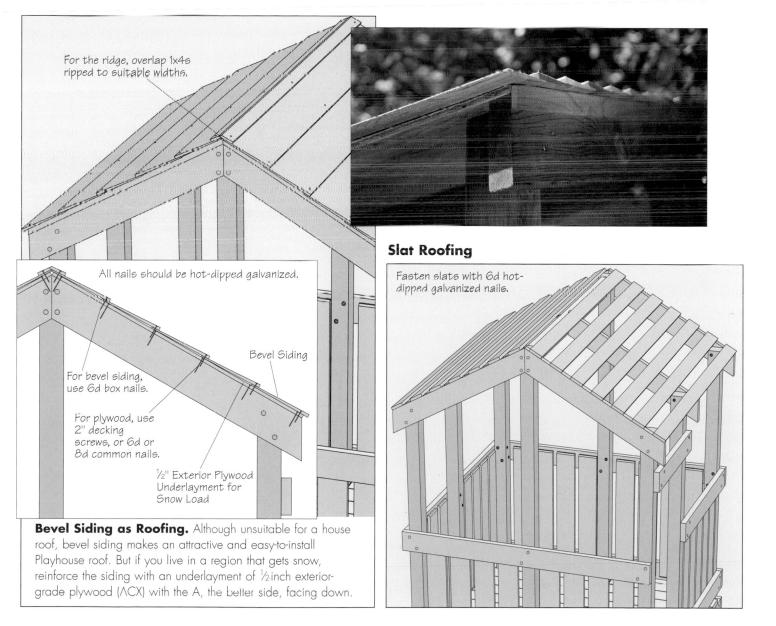

For the ridge, overlap 1x4s ripped to suitable widths.

Slat Roofing

Fasten slats with 6d hot-dipped galvanized nails.

All nails should be hot-dipped galvanized.

For bevel siding, use 6d box nails.

Bevel Siding

For plywood, use 2" decking screws, or 6d or 8d common nails.

½" Exterior Plywood Underlayment for Snow Load

Bevel Siding as Roofing. Although unsuitable for a house roof, bevel siding makes an attractive and easy-to-install Playhouse roof. But if you live in a region that gets snow, reinforce the siding with an underlayment of ½-inch exterior-grade plywood (ACX) with the A, the better side, facing down.

grooves running up and down the roof, not horizontally. This will promote water runoff.

Final Touches

Finishing. Apply the finish of your choice. For advice on types of finishes, see Chapter 5.

Handbars. A couple of handbars in the doorway will make climbing into the Playhouse a little easier for most kids. For this you can use common galvanized plumbing materials to fashion large handbars. For each handbar you will need two ½-inch floor flanges, two 1-inch nipples, two 90-degree elbows, and about an 18-inch length

Plywood Roofing

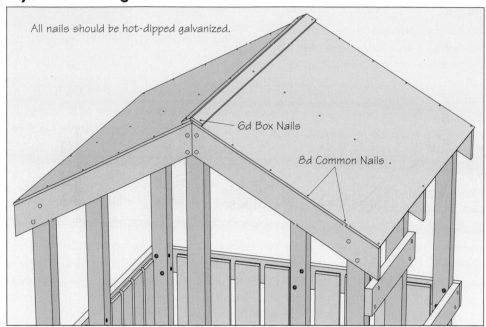

All nails should be hot-dipped galvanized.

6d Box Nails

8d Common Nails

Trim the Rafter Tails

The rafter tails will look better if you cut them plumb, although this step is optional. First decide how much you want the roof to overhang. Measure the amount of overhang horizontally from the post to the rafter and mark each rafter. The illustration shows a 3-inch overhang.

To make a plumb cut at the end of each rafter, place the bevel gauge on top of the rafter, aligning the metal blade against the near post. Set the gauge's locking wing nut and copy that

angle to the overhang mark where you wish to cut each rafter, thereby providing plumb cutting lines.

For a more finished look, you can conceal rafter ends by attaching a fascia board. Do this by cutting a 1x6 to span the rafters. Then align it, by means of a framing square, as shown, so that the top of the fascia board doesn't project into roofing material yet to come. Drive three 6d nails or 2-inch decking screws through the fascia into each rafter.

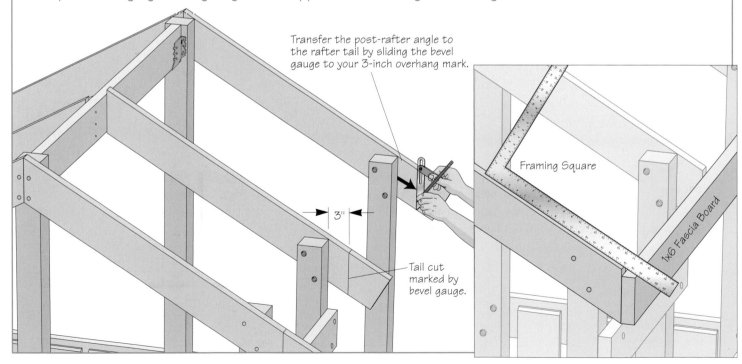

Transfer the post-rafter angle to the rafter tail by sliding the bevel gauge to your 3-inch overhang mark.

3"

Tail cut marked by bevel gauge.

Framing Square

1x6 Fascia Board

of threaded pipe. Thread the parts together, and then drive screws through the flanges into the posts on both sides of the doorway. For a touch of color, before installing the handbars paint them with a metal or auto-body paint, after first removing the oily residue on the pipe with hot water and either household soap or automotive cleaner.

As options, playground stores and some home centers carry plastic handles for use on structures. You could also buy a pair of large garage-door or barn-door handles. All handles should be fastened with screws.

Customizing the Playhouse. For features such as clubhouse signs, flags, and flagpoles, try to involve your children. They will be more proud of a sign or flag that they created than something conceived and created completely by adults.

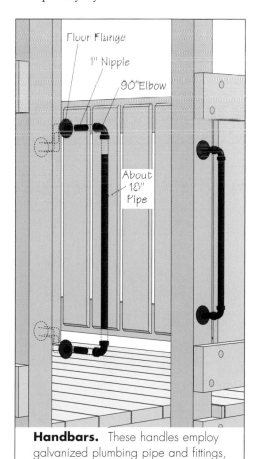

Floor Flange
1" Nipple
90° Elbow
About 18" Pipe

Handbars. These handles employ galvanized plumbing pipe and fittings, but commercial handles for play structures would serve well too.

A Taller Playhouse

If you prefer a somewhat higher deck, you can follow the same Playhouse design on preceding pages. However, with a deck height of more than 20 inches, up to about 36 inches, you need to add 2x6 base supports and 2x4 cross bracing all around, as shown here. You should also add at least 6 inches of reduced-impact material around the entire structure, especially where kids are more likely to fall below the doorway.

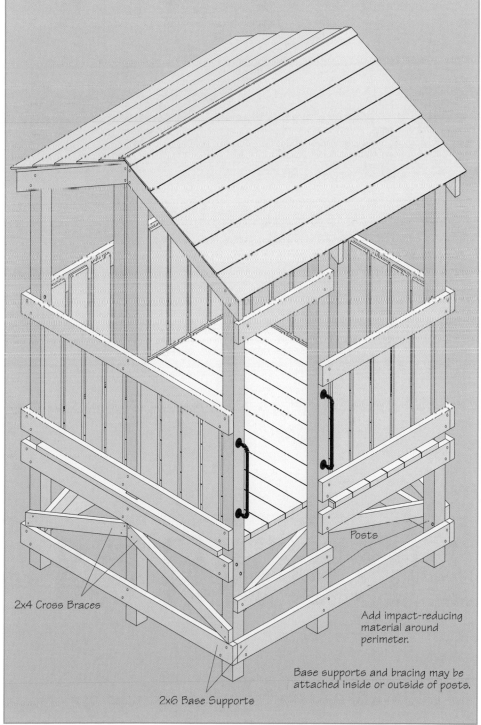

2x4 Cross Braces

Posts

Add impact-reducing material around perimeter.

Base supports and bracing may be attached inside or outside of posts.

2x6 Base Supports

10

Sandboxes

Available almost everywhere, sand seems to attract people of all ages. Adults spend billions annually to visit sandy beaches, while children barely old enough to sit up can enjoy hour after hour in the sand—shoveling, piling, and sifting.

Backyard sandboxes can stimulate creativity in children, whether for the building of sand castles or the construction of whole villages, complete with roads, traffic, and toy citizens. Sandboxes also promote cooperative play, helping teach children how to "build" toward a common goal.

A sandbox can be the simplest of all building projects. If you dig a shallow depression in the ground and fill it with sand, kids will find a way to have fun with it. The three sandbox projects in this chapter give structure to the enterprise, offering styles and sizes that should satisfy nearly any need.

Design Options

Of the three designs, the Covered Sandbox is the most elaborate, yet it is no more difficult to construct than the others. The roof is partly functional and partly decorative. It will block some sunlight but isn't intended to keep out rain. Perhaps more importantly, the roof lends a sense of enclosure that makes kids feel they have a space of their own. This sandbox is best suited to preschoolers. Once the kids grow tall enough to bump their heads on the roof, you can simply remove it. Then cut the roof supports flush with the top of the seats. Round-over and sand sharp edges.

The Timber Sandbox requires the least labor of the three projects, yet it offers the largest play surface—nearly 64 square feet. Its size allows several children to play without interfering with one another.

The Basic Sandbox is quick to make and the least expensive. The design is ideal if you want to keep the sandbox below ground level. Unlike the Timber Sandbox, which allows sitting around the perimeter, the Basic Sandbox's only comfortable seats are at the corners. These corner seats also help brace the box.

Siting and Other Basics

Try to position the sandbox away from play components where there's more action. This makes sense first because sand play tends to be relatively stationary and quiet, but more importantly, for the sake of safety. To avoid mishaps, seated children should be isolated from those going full tilt. For example, never place a sandbox near a swingset or near the bottom of a slide with the intention of having it also serve as impact material there. Doing so would greatly increase the chances for collisions.

Sandbox Design Options

Basic Sandbox Sunk Below Grade

Covered Sandbox

Timber Sandbox

Difficulty Level:

Tools

Applicator for Wood Sealer

Digging Tools

Leveling Tools

Measuring, Marking & Squaring Tools

Safety Equipment

Sanding Tools

Sawhorses (2)

Utility Knife

Wood Cutting, Drilling & Edge-Forming Tools

Others that may apply

Bolting Tools

Clamps

Hammer

Also, a sandbox that is regularly exposed to direct sunlight will stay drier and will catch less falling debris than a sandbox under a tree.

Covering the Sandbox. If your sandbox becomes a litter box for cats, you will need to cover it when not in use. A small plastic tarp held in place by a few bricks or large stones may be effective but unsightly. The better way to keep unwanted critters out, while also allowing the sand to dry, is to use the plastic mesh shown below.

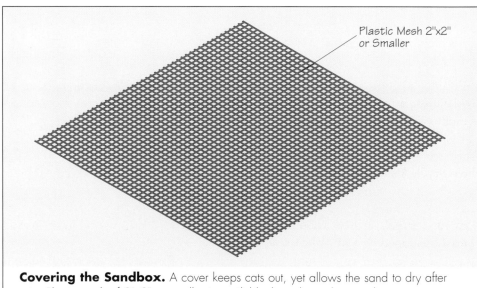

Plastic Mesh 2"x2" or Smaller

Covering the Sandbox. A cover keeps cats out, yet allows the sand to dry after rain. Plastic mesh of 2"x2" or smaller is available through garden suppliers.

Choosing the Sand. Sand is graded according to cleanliness and particle size. Home centers carry bags of sterilized "play sand," which is packaged in 40-pound bags for children's sandboxes. You can also use washed masonry sand, available at masonry supply outlets. It is often cheaper to buy sand by the truckload. Both play sand and masonry sand are fine grained, which is often preferred for sandbox play because it holds together better when wet.

However, sand with slightly larger particles has some advantages. It is less likely to penetrate clothing and so get carried into the house. It won't blow away as easily, and it won't as readily clog up moving parts of toy tractors and trucks. Regardless of grain size, the important thing is that the sand be washed free of all organic materials, such as silt and clay.

For best results, the sand should be at least 8 to 10 inches deep, which is the minimum for "serious" digging. Deeper is better, up to about 20 inches. This depth also allows you or the kids to bring wetter sand up to the surface for modeling.

Construction Details. Any wood that will be in contact with ground or sand should be pressure treated or be from a rot-resistant species. If you use untreated wood for the seats, round the edges and sand the wood relatively smooth before sealing it. Also ensure that no fasteners protrude.

Maintaining the Sandbox. Whether the sandbox is covered or not, rake it regularly and remove any debris. If the sand stays wet much of the time, raking will help dry it. Also, make a rule that there's to be no glass and no sharp metal, such as nails, used near the sandbox. If glass gets broken and worked into the sand, replace all of the sand.

If the sand hasn't been used for a long time and seems dirty, consider replacing it.

Covered Sandbox

1 **Build the Roof Frame.** Use 2x4s for all parts of the roof frame. Vertical roof supports tie the sandbox to the roof. Rafters provide a fastening surface for the roofing slats, and braces strengthen the entire frame.

The two roof supports are 54 inches long. Make 15-degree angle cuts on both sides to form the peak. Or cut the posts after installing the rafters.

The four rafters are 25⅝-inches long. Make parallel 15-degree plumb cuts on both ends.

To make the four braces, start with 17¼-inch 2x4s. Make a 45-degree angle cut on the upper end, which will join the rafter, and a 30-degree cut on the lower end, which will connect with the roof support. Place each pair of cut braces together as intended to meet. Draw a horizontal line about 1 inch up from the bottom point, as shown. Cut the braces along this line.

On a flat surface, lay the rafters and braces on each support. Check for a good fit between all pieces. Then fasten rafters and braces to the support

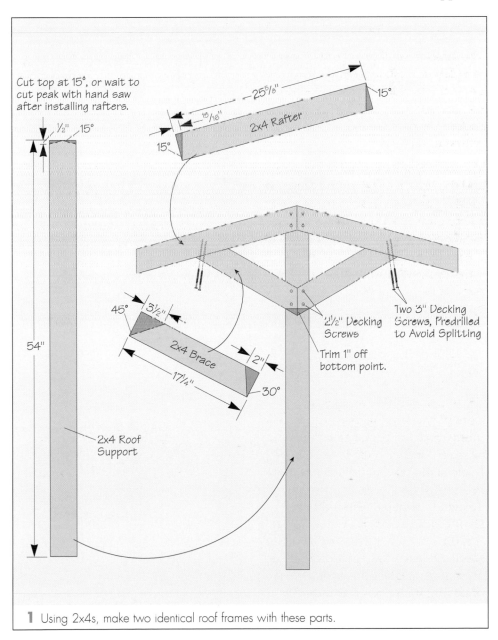

1 Using 2x4s, make two identical roof frames with these parts.

by driving 2½-inch deck screws through the face of each. Attach the braces to the bottom of the rafters by driving 3-inch deck screws up through the bottom of the brace.

2 Build the Box. Use 2x10s to build the box for the sand. Cut two pieces to 48 inches each, two to 45 inches, and four to 20¾ inches.

Assemble the box as shown using 3-inch and 2½-inch deck screws. Make certain that none of the screws breaks through the wood on either side of the box.

3 Join the Roof Frame and Box. With the box resting on a flat surface, set one of the roof supports in the gap between the 2x10s inside the box. The support should fit snugly, but use a framing square to check the alignment. Clamp the support in place. Then drill three bolt holes through the box and support, offsetting the holes as shown to avoid splitting the wood. Then drill recess holes on the inside of the support and fasten with ⅜x3-inch carriage bolts and recessed washers and nuts. Repeat with the other support.

After construction, round-over all sharp corners and edges.

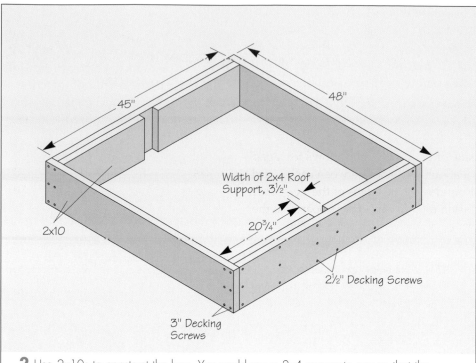

2 Use 2x10s to construct the box. You could use a 2x4 spacer to ensure that the inside gap is wide enough for the roof supports.

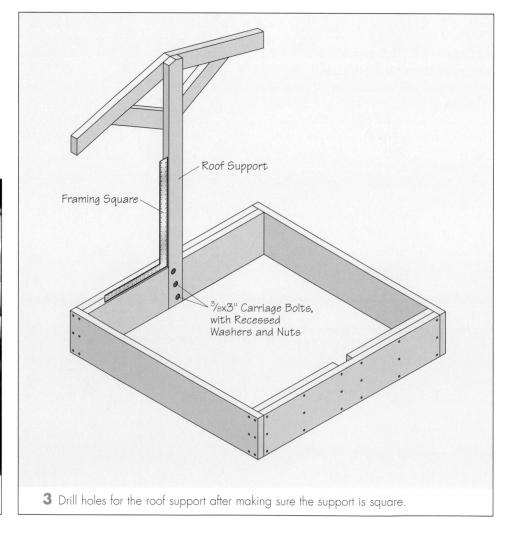

3 Drill holes for the roof support after making sure the support is square.

4 **Finish the Roof.** Measure the span from the outside faces of the rafters. If it varies from 48 inches, be sure to cut slats and fascia boards to that length.

The number of slats and the size of the gap between them are up to you. Our drawings show five 1x4 slats on each side of the roof, which allows for a gap of about 1½ inches between each board. Round-over the edges of the 1x4s. Then fasten the slats and fascia boards to the rafters with 1½ inch deck screws.

5 **Attach the Seat and Finish Up.** Adding a separate seat of untreated lumber is probably a good safety precaution if you used pressure-treated lumber for the box itself. And the 1x4s add some width to the sitting area. Round-over the edges of the 1x4s. Cut notches to fit around the roof supports, and fasten the seats with 1½-inch deck screws spaced about 6 inches apart.

Apply the finish of your choice to the sandbox. Then fill it with sand.

Lumber and Materials Order

Lumber	Qty	Size
2x10	3	8'
2x4	1	8'
	2	10'
1x4	8	8'
Fasteners		
Deck screws	32	3"
	52	2½"
	64	1½"
Carriage bolts, washers, nuts	6	⅞"x3"
Other		
Sand	@10-12 cu. ft.	

Cutting List

	Qty	Size
Roof supports	2	2x4x54"
Rafters	4	2x4x25⅝"
Rafter Braces	4	2x4x17¼"
Roof slats	10	1x4x48"
Fascia boards	2	1x4x48"
Box	2	2x10x48"
	2	2x10x45"
	4	2x10x20¾"
Seat	2	1x4x40"
	2	1x4x41"
Plastic mesh (to cover sand)	1	42"x42"

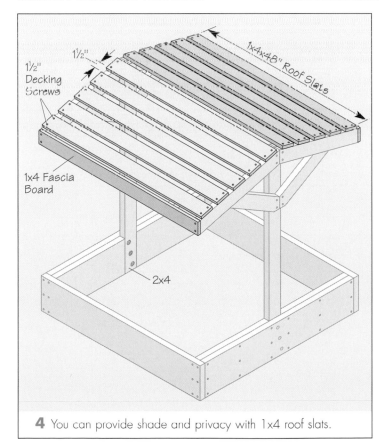

1½" Decking Screws

1½"

1½"

1x4x48" Roof Slats

1x4 Fascia Board

2x4

4 You can provide shade and privacy with 1x4 roof slats.

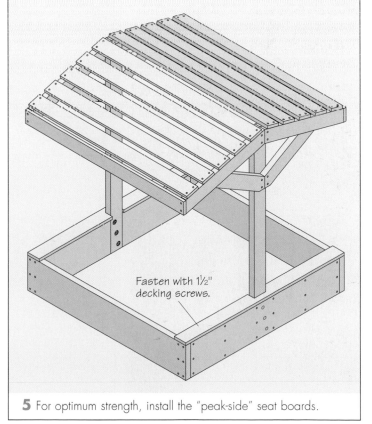

Fasten with 1½" decking screws.

5 For optimum strength, install the "peak-side" seat boards.

Timber Sandbox

Choose landscape timbers carefully. Look for straight 8-foot timbers of uniform length and thickness. (Rough-sawn timbers can vary slightly.) Our plans specify galvanized or stainless-steel 40d nails, 5 inches long. But be sure to use nails long enough to penetrate the top timber and at least half of the timber below it.

1 **Set the First Row.** Lay the first row of timbers in place with the ends overlapping as shown. To ensure that the timbers form a perfect square, position them using a framing square and then measure the diagonals. When the diagonals are identical, the timbers are square.

2 **Set the Second Row.** Set the second row in place, again with the ends staggered as shown. To avoid splitting the wood, drill ⁵⁄₃₂-inch pilot holes 3¾ inches deep before driving each nail. Drive 5-inch nails through the top into the bottom timbers. Use one nail at each corner and three more, evenly spaced, along each side, as shown.

3 **Complete the Sandbox.** Add the third row of timbers, with the ends aligned like those of the first row. Be sure the third row is square before nailing as in Step 1. Fill the box with 6 to 8 inches of sand. This will require 32 to 42 cubic feet.

For a deeper sandbox, add a fourth row of timbers and fill with 48 to 52 cubic feet of sand. If you prefer, you can also use pressure-treated 4x4s to build this deeper sandbox. Use rustproof nails. Apply a sealer to the top surface.

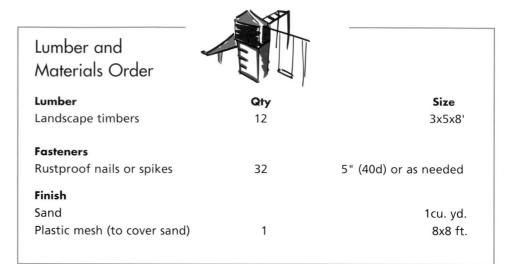

Lumber and Materials Order

Lumber	Qty	Size
Landscape timbers	12	3x5x8'
Fasteners		
Rustproof nails or spikes	32	5" (40d) or as needed
Finish		
Sand		1cu. yd.
Plastic mesh (to cover sand)	1	8x8 ft.

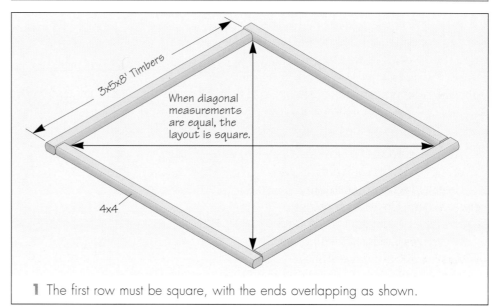

1 The first row must be square, with the ends overlapping as shown.

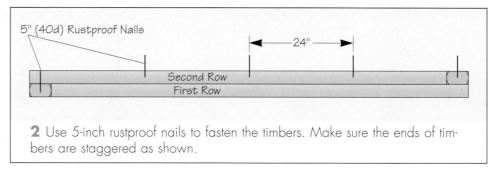

2 Use 5-inch rustproof nails to fasten the timbers. Make sure the ends of timbers are staggered as shown.

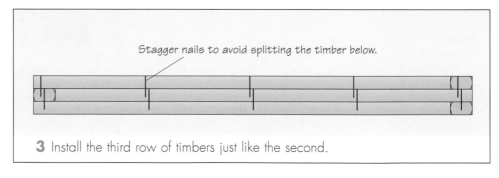

3 Install the third row of timbers just like the second.

Basic Sandbox

This 6x6-foot sandbox is about midway in size between the previous sandboxes. Feel free to adjust the size to suit your needs. The sides are built with double 2x6s, although you could substitute with individual 2x10s or 2x12s. You could construct this sandbox on ground level or, with a bit of extra digging, below grade.

1 **Build the Box.** Cut the 2x6s to 6-foot lengths. Then round-over one corner of the 4x4 before cutting it into four 11-inch lengths. With each 4x4's rounded corner positioned toward the center of the sandbox, attach the 2x6s to the 4x4s with 3-inch decking screws. Stagger the 2x6s at each corner, as shown.

2 **Attach the Seats.** The seat for each of the corners is composed of two 2x4s installed with a ½-inch gap between them. Create each pair of boards, using the layout shown. Round-over the edges and install with a ½-inch overhang, using 3-inch deck screws.

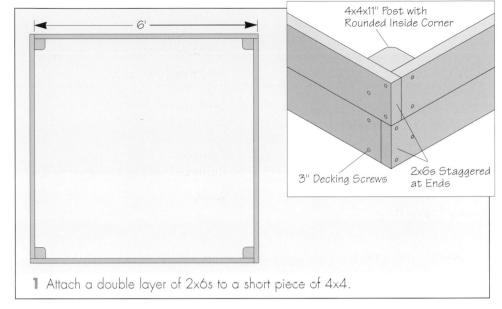

1 Attach a double layer of 2x6s to a short piece of 4x4.

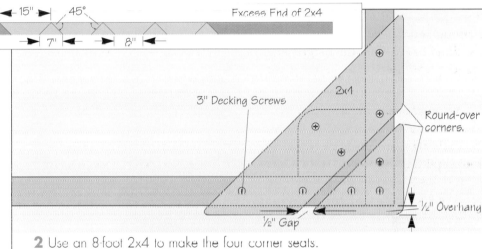

2 Use an 8-foot 2x4 to make the four corner seats.

Lumber and Materials Order
(Basic Sandbox)

Lumber	Qty	Size
2x6	4	12'
4x4	1	8'
2x4	1	8'
Fasteners		
Decking screws	68	3"
Finish		
Sand		@30 cu. ft.
Plastic mesh	1	60"x60"
Cutting List		
Sides	8	2x6x72"
Support posts	4	4x4x11"
Seats	1	As shown

An angle square helps guide the circular saw for common cuts of 45° and 90°. It's also useful for marking other angles.

A Sunken Sandbox

A below-grade sandbox is less obtrusive than other types because it blends with the surface of the yard. First, build the Basic Sandbox described earlier. However, in place of standard deck screws, use stainless steel screws, and use only lumber that has been treated for ground contact.

1 Dig the Hole. Dig a hole deep enough to allow for a 6-inch bed of gravel beneath the box and its sand. For our sandbox built with double 2x6s plus the seats, this requires a hole 16½-inches deep. Also, dig the hole about 6 inches wider than the box on all four sides. When filled with gravel or sand, this added border will allow you to mow easily.

2 Prepare the Hole. Fill the bottom of the hole with 6 inches of gravel. Then cover the gravel completely with landscape fabric, which will prevent the sand from filtering into the gravel.

3 Complete the Sandbox. Set the sandbox into the hole so that the spacing outside the boards is consistent on all sides. The top boards should be about ½ inch above surrounding grade. Fill the border with either sand or gravel. This promotes drainage away from the wood and allows you to cut the grass around the sandbox with little danger of having the mower hit any boards. Lastly, fill the sandbox with the desired amount of sand.

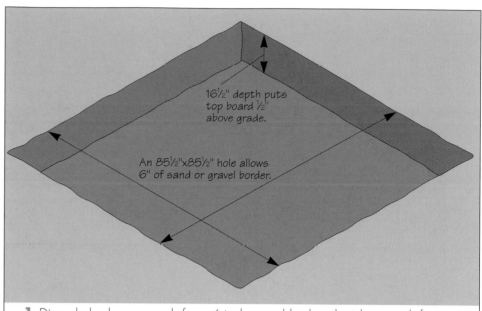

16½" depth puts top board ½" above grade.

An 85½"x85½" hole allows 6" of sand or gravel border.

1 Dig a hole deep enough for a 6-inch gravel bed and wide enough for a border that will allow neat mowing.

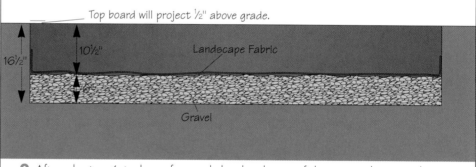

Top board will project ½" above grade.

16½"   10½"   Landscape Fabric

Gravel

2 After placing 6 inches of gravel, lay landscape fabric over the gravel to keep the sand from mixing with it.

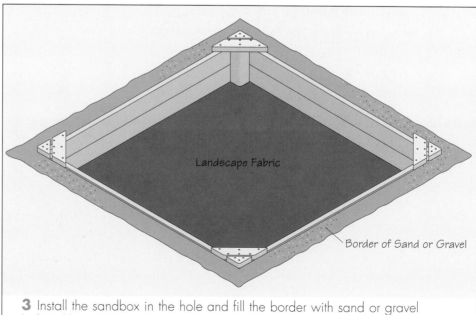

Landscape Fabric

Border of Sand or Gravel

3 Install the sandbox in the hole and fill the border with sand or gravel before filling the box with sand.

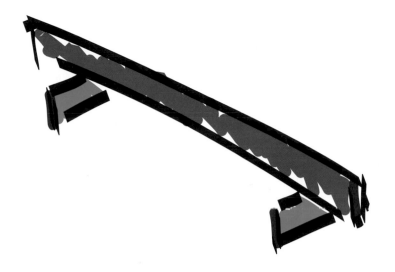

11

Balance Beam

Ask children what they would like in their playground, and chances are that few will mention a balance beam. But if you include a balance beam, few, if any, of those kids will ignore the beam when they walk by.

Although kids don't usually use a balance beam for long periods of time, they will use it regularly. Children love to perform balancing acts, and if you don't supply them with a playground component for the purpose, they are likely to find a more dangerous structure to serve as their "tightrope." In this chapter, two basic beam designs allow beams of optional widths, the narrower widths of course increasing the challenge to kids.

So the beams don't become tripping hazards, try to place them in border locations, where there is little if any other traffic.

The Portable Beam

This beam is low, so it doesn't require underlying impact-reducing material. Even though it is lightweight and portable, it is sturdy enough to support children of all ages. To avoid tipping, position the Portable Beam only on a level surface. Also, keep the beam at least 6 feet from any other surface or structure that could cause injury from a fall.

1 Prepare the Beam. The beam is composed of a full-length 4x4 post. Round-over the two top edges and sand the top and sides.

2 Make the Supports. From the other 4x4, cut three 24-inch-long supports. Lay out each support for the 3½x1½-inch notch in the center. With a saw, make a series of kerfs 1½ inches deep, within the layout lines. Clean out the notch with a chisel.

Break the edges of the supports either by rounding them over on a band saw or by beveling the corners, as shown, and sanding edges round.

3 Assemble the Balance Beam. Set the supports on the post at the dimensions shown. Drill pilot holes for two lag screws into each support. Stagger the pilot holes to prevent splitting. With a washer under each head, insert and tighten the lag screws.

The Portable Beam

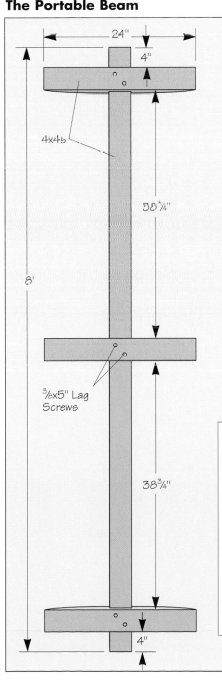

24"
4"
4x4s
38¾"
8'
⅜x5" Lag Screws
38¾"
4"

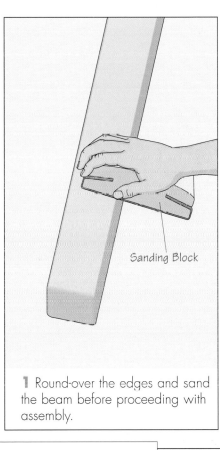

Sanding Block

1 Round-over the edges and sand the beam before proceeding with assembly.

Cut corner

Rounded over

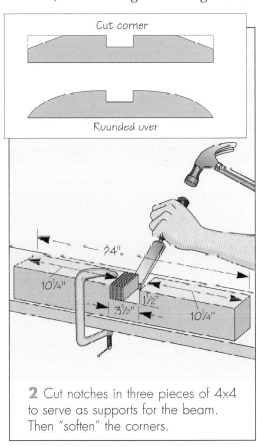

24"
10¼"
3½"
1½"
10¼"

2 Cut notches in three pieces of 4x4 to serve as supports for the beam. Then "soften" the corners.

Difficulty Level:

Tools
Applicator for Wood Sealer
Bolting Tools
Clamps
Measuring, Marking & Squaring Tools
Sanding Tools
Sawhorses (2)
Safety Equipment
Wood Cutting, Drilling & Edge-Forming Tools

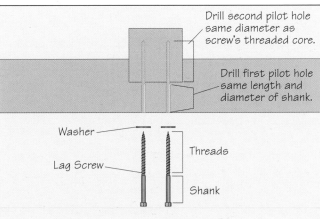

Drill second pilot hole same diameter as screw's threaded core.

Drill first pilot hole same length and diameter of shank.

Washer
Lag Screw
Threads
Shank

3 Fasten supports to the beam with lag screws through the bottom.

Place the Portable Beam on a level spot, outside normal traffic.

Making Narrower Beam Widths.
Reminder: Nominal sizes and actual sizes of lumber differ. Here's a listing of nominal and actual sizes that will yield beams of various widths:

Nominal	Actual
$\frac{5}{4}$ x 4"	1 x 3½"
2 x 4"	1½ x 3½"
4 x 4"	3½ x 3½"

Mindful that labeled, nominal lumber dimensions are greater than finished lumber dimensions, you can make a 3-inch-wide beam by joining two 2x4s face to face. Fasten the boards with 2½-inch deck screws, placing two screws every 6 inches on alternating sides. Adjust the width of support notches accordingly.

You could instead also use two $\frac{5}{4}$x4 boards to make a 2-inch-wide beam. Join them with 1½-inch deck screws.

Finally, you could vary the width of the beam simply by beveling the corners on a 4x4 to the width you like.

Permanent Balance Beam

If you prefer to mount a beam higher off the ground, you should support it on posts embedded at least 36 inches and surround it with an impact-reducing material to cushion falls. If you wish to embed the posts in concrete, see "Setting Posts" on page 46.

A 4x4 beam can be attached to 4x4 posts using appropriately sized one- or two-piece post caps, available from building suppliers. Attach the post caps with fasteners recommended by the manufacturer. Break all sharp edges on the post caps with a smooth file or with emery cloth. Round-over beam top corners and aboveground post corners. Sand the top and sides.

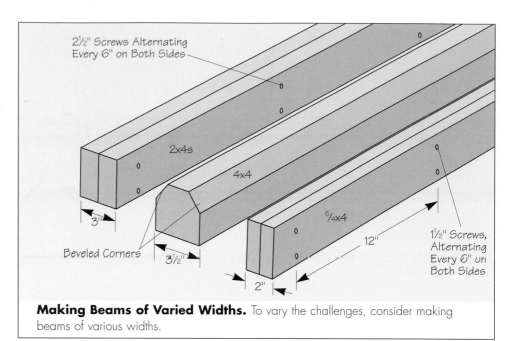

Making Beams of Varied Widths. To vary the challenges, consider making beams of various widths.

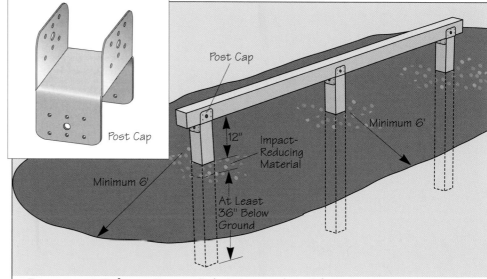

Permanent Balance Beam. Sink 4x4 posts about 3 feet in concrete to create a permanent beam, which can be set at the height you prefer. Be sure to extend impact-reducing material at least 6 feet from all parts of the beam.

Lumber and Materials Order
(Permanent Balance Beam)

	Quantity	Size
4x4	3	8'
Post Caps & Fasteners	3	4x4
Finish		
Cutting List		
Supports	3	4x4x48"

12

Picnic Table

This traditional A-framed picnic table is scaled down for children, yet it is sturdy and durable. Although most children will find the table height ideal, the table isn't so low that adults couldn't sit comfortably. Made from standard 2x4 and 2x6 lumber, this project requires a minimum of cutting. Carriage bolts and screws accomplish all joinery.

You can build the picnic table from woods that are durable outdoors, whether pressure-treated lumber, cedar, or redwood. The table shown in the photo employs redwood lumber throughout. Yet because the legs are in contact with the ground, pressure-treated lumber for the legs, at least, would be more durable. Regardless of the wood used, you should treat it with a semitransparent, water-repellent stain. Should the seat and tabletop begin to weather, they can be sanded and refinished. Or if they eventually show some rot, they can easily be replaced.

Assembling the Frame

The two identical A-shaped end braces are composed of 2x6 seat supports, 2x4 tabletop supports, and 2x6 legs. The four legs are from 32-inch-long 2x6s cut to 60 degrees at each end, as shown.

Working on a flat surface, lay the legs so their outside corners are 52¼ inches apart at the bottom and 23½ inches apart at the top. Center the table-top support flush with the top edges of the legs and the seat support 9½ inches above the bottoms of the legs. When all of the pieces are in place and centered, drill ⅛-inch pilot holes through the supports and legs. Use the pilot holes as guides to drill the recesses for the bolts and washers on the insides of the legs. A 1⅛-inch-diameter recess, drilled ½-inch deep, should suffice, but measure your washers first to be sure they match the intended recess diameter.

Place the supports back on the legs, using the ⅛-inch drill bit to position them properly. Drill ⅜-inch holes through the supports and legs. After drilling each hole, insert a ⅜-inch carriage bolt, washer, and nut. This will keep the pieces in alignment while you drill the next hole. When all the bolts are in place, tighten the nuts securely.

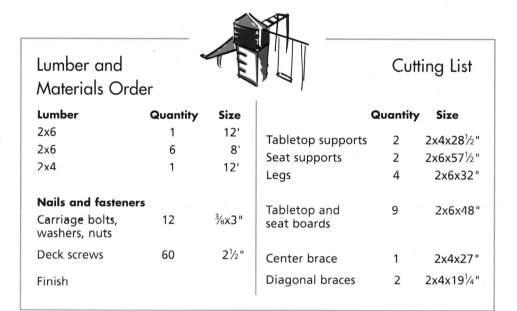

Lumber and Materials Order				Cutting List		
Lumber	**Quantity**	**Size**			**Quantity**	**Size**
2x6	1	12'		Tabletop supports	2	2x4x28½"
2x6	6	8'		Seat supports	2	2x6x57½"
2x4	1	12'		Legs	4	2x6x32"
				Tabletop and seat boards	9	2x6x48"
Nails and fasteners						
Carriage bolts, washers, nuts	12	⅜x3"		Center brace	1	2x4x27"
Deck screws	60	2½"		Diagonal braces	2	2x4x19¼"
Finish						

Difficulty Level:

Tools

Applicator for Wood Sealer
Bolting Tools
Clamps
Measuring, Marking & Squaring Tools
Safety Equipment
Sanding Tools
Sawhorses (2)
Utility Knife
Wood Cutting, Drilling & Edge-Forming Tools

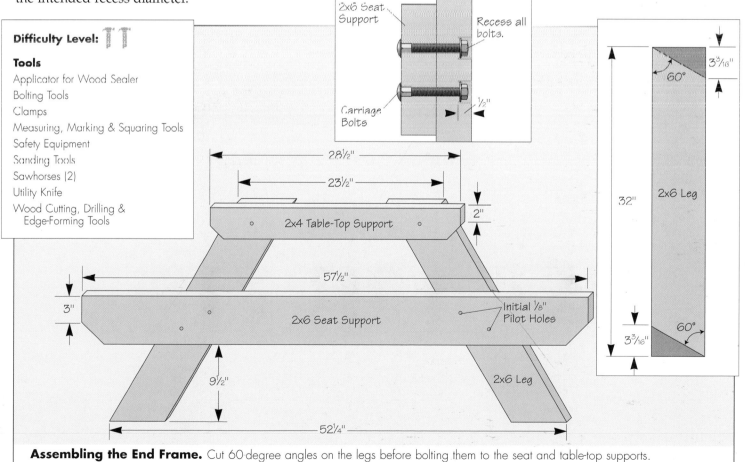

Assembling the End Frame. Cut 60-degree angles on the legs before bolting them to the seat and table-top supports.

Assembling the Seats and Tops

The four seat boards and five table-top boards are each 48-inch 2x6s. Draw a squared line across each board 8¾-inches from each end. Then start two screws along each line about 1 inch inside the edge, without driving them through the seat board.

If working alone, hold up one of the end braces and finish driving one screw through an outside seat board into the center of the support, flush with the end of the support. Next, attach the outside board to the other seat on the same end brace. Then attach both boards to the other end brace. This job is easier if you have a helper or two to hold up the end braces.

Using a framing square to assure that the supports are perpendicular to the

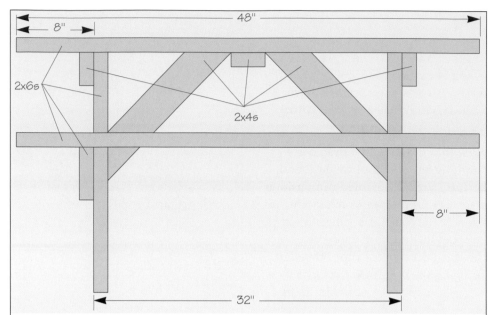

The drawings in this chapter show exact dimensions except those for the two diagonal braces, which are approximated. To determine exact brace dimensions, create cardboard templates after assembling all other components. For this, see the next page.

seat boards, drive each of the remaining screws. Next, attach the inside seat boards on both sides, being sure to leave a ¼-inch gap between them and their outside board.

Position table top boards, keeping outside boards flush with ends of support boards. Keep gaps between boards ¼ inch. Screw the boards to the end braces.

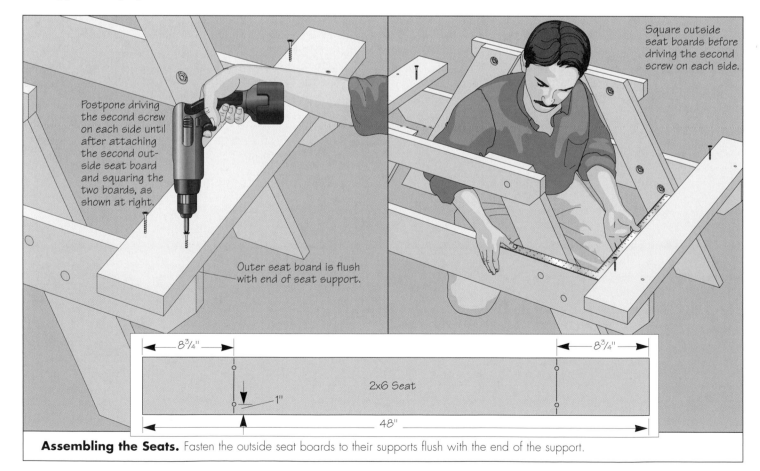

Postpone driving the second screw on each side until after attaching the second outside seat board and squaring the two boards, as shown at right.

Outer seat board is flush with end of seat support.

Square outside seat boards before driving the second screw on each side.

Assembling the Seats. Fasten the outside seat boards to their supports flush with the end of the support.

Attaching the Braces

The 2x4 bracing on the table is composed of two diagonal braces and one center brace. The center brace is 27-inches long, its sharp end corners broken by a 45-degree bevel.

Note that the diagonal braces are cut at different angles on each end. Because your assembled dimensions may vary from ours at this point, the 20¾-inch length suggested for the diagonal braces should be regarded only as an approximation. To avoid wasting wood, first transfer your measurements and angles to a piece of cardboard; then cut the cardboard with a utility knife. Set the template in place on the table and check the fit. Trim the template until the edges are flush with their mating surfaces. When you have found just the right length and angles for the cardboard template, trace its pattern onto the 2x4s.

Turn the table over and screw the braces into place, driving screws through the diagonal braces at an angle into the seat support and table top. Be careful not to drive screws through the topside of the table itself or through the seat supports.

Smoothing and Finishing

Round-over cut edges and smooth any rough edges. Then apply a water-repellent finish or exterior stain.

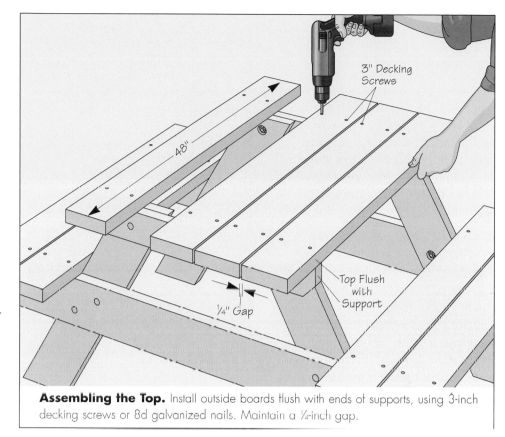

Assembling the Top. Install outside boards flush with ends of supports, using 3-inch decking screws or 8d galvanized nails. Maintain a ¼-inch gap.

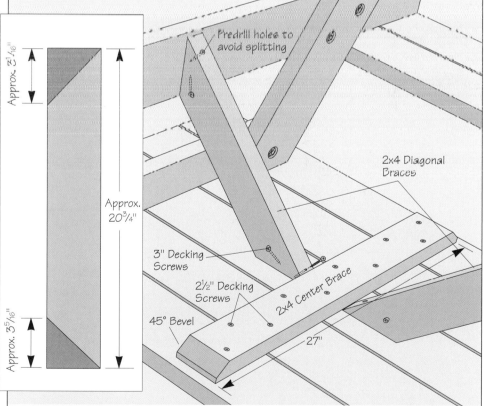

Attaching the Braces. If your assembly has only slightly different dimensions than prescribed, angles and lengths of your braces may need to be different from those shown. For best results, create test-fitted cardboard templates for each brace and transfer their outlines to the 2x4 before cutting.

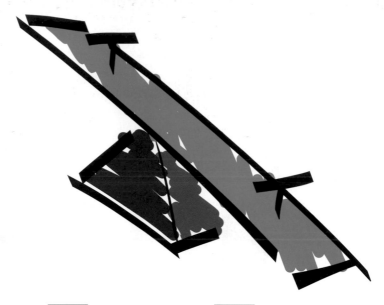

Teeter-Totter

Not long ago the teeter-totter, or seesaw, was as common on public playgrounds as swings and slides. Many adults have tales of perilous joyriding on the teeter-totters of their youth, as well as the scars from resulting accidents.

Because of potentially hazardous misuse, teeter-totters are seen less often, and seldom on new playgrounds. The design shown here is for younger children, before they reach an age when daredevil antics become common. This teeter-totter is small and relatively short, so that a child on the high end is never at a dangerous height. It is also portable and easily moved, or removed, from the play area.

Before they are allowed to use the teeter-totter, all children should be instructed in these basic rules:

▲ Only two children are allowed on the teeter-totter at a time.

▲ Only children of comparable weights should pair up.

▲ All other children should stay well away from the users.

Building the Seat Assembly

Cut the seat assembly from 4x4s to the following lengths: one 9 feet, seven 12 inches, two 7 inches, and two 6 inches. If you use a table saw, radial arm saw, or power miter saw, you can make cuts in one pass. The smaller blade of a circular saw will require two careful passes, one in front and one in back. Also cut two 13½-inch lengths of 1-inch hardwood dowel for the handles.

1 Make the Seat Blocks and Bumpers. The four seat blocks are made exactly the same. Lay out and drill ⁷⁄₁₆-inch-diameter holes in each block, but wait until Step 5 to drill them. Miter the ends of the seat blocks and bumpers as shown.

2 Make the Handle Blocks. The two sets of handle blocks are identical. Lay out and drill the 1-inch-diameter dowel hole in the center of the upper block. Miter both ends of each block.

3 Attach the Handles. Cut and insert the dowels into the holes on upper handle blocks. You may need to hammer the dowels lightly, centering them with a 5-inch exposure on each side. Then drive two 2½-inch decking screws through the bottom of the block into each dowel.

4 Make the Pivot Block. The pivot block is identical to the handle blocks except that it requires a larger hole. The 1⅛-inch-diameter hole shown here assumes that you are making the pivot with galvanized steel pipe that has a 1¹⁄₁₆-inch outside diameter. This is the typical outside diameter of ¾-inch galvanized pipe, but measure first. Be sure to drill the hole slightly larger than the pipe.

Teeter-Totter

Difficulty Level:

Tools
Applicator for Wood Sealer
Bolting Tools
Clamps
Measuring, Marking & Squaring Tools
Metal-Cutting Saw
Mill File
Safety Equipment
Sanding Tools
Sawhorses (2)
Utility Knife
Wood Cutting, Drilling & Edge-Forming Tools

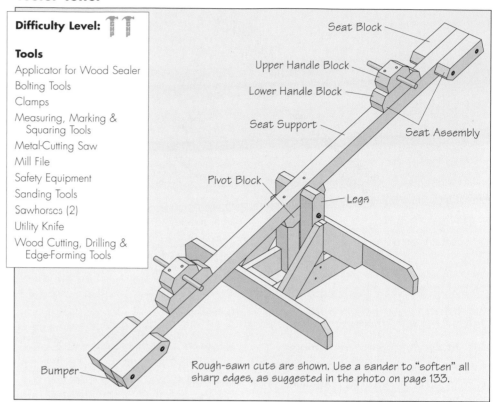

Rough-sawn cuts are shown. Use a sander to "soften" all sharp edges, as suggested in the photo on page 133.

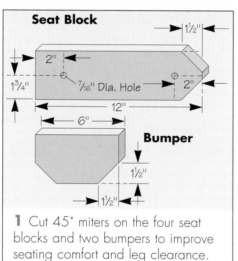

1 Cut 45° miters on the four seat blocks and two bumpers to improve seating comfort and leg clearance.

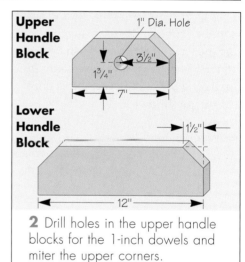

2 Drill holes in the upper handle blocks for the 1-inch dowels and miter the upper corners.

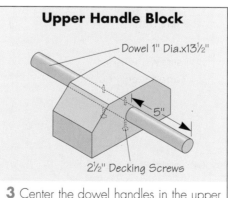

3 Center the dowel handles in the upper blocks, and fasten them from the bottom.

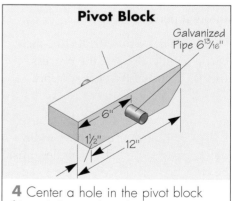

4 Center a hole in the pivot block ¹⁄₁₆ inch larger than the pivot pipe.

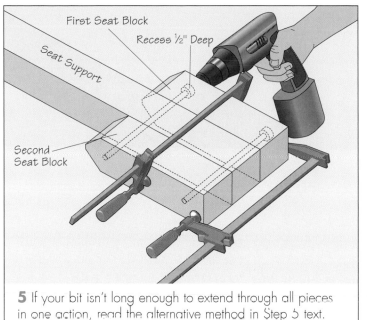

Seat Support

First Seat Block

Recess ½" Deep

Second Seat Block

5 If your bit isn't long enough to extend through all pieces in one action, read the alternative method in Step 5 text.

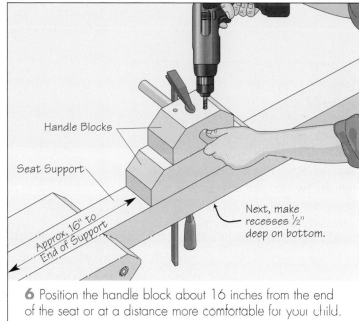

Handle Blocks

Seat Support

Approx. 16" to End of Support

Next, make recesses ½" deep on bottom.

6 Position the handle block about 16 inches from the end of the seat or at a distance more comfortable for your child.

5 Attach the Seat Blocks. Unless you have a drill press or a bit long enough to extend through all pieces in one action, as shown, you'll need to bore through the seat blocks and seat support in three stages. When clamping, be sure all sides are flush and square. The drawing shows clamping for a long drill bit. If your bit is only long enough to pass through one piece of wood, clamp just one block to the seat support; drill a recess; and then drill through to mark a starter hole in the seat support. Next, clamp the other seat block to the far side of the support, and drill through the support to mark a starter hole in the second block. Then drill through the second block. This will ensure that your hole is continuous, even if it doesn't pass through perfectly square.

Assemble the seat with ⅜x10½-inch carriage bolts. Repeat the process on the other end of the seat support.

6 Attach the Handle Blocks. The exact positioning of the handle blocks is up to you. The handles must be close enough so young users can grasp them comfortably, yet far enough away to allow for knee

clearance as that end of the teeter-totter descends to the ground. The 16-inch dimension is a good approximation. Because the handle blocks can be installed last, you can make adjustments for your own children.

After positioning the handle bars for your children, drill offsetting holes through the handle blocks and seat support. Drill a ½-inch-deep recess on the bottom. Then fasten with ⅜x10½-inch carriage bolts.

Lumber and Materials Order

Lumber	Quantity	Size
4x4	2	12'
2x6	3	8'
Hardwood dowel	1	1x36"

Hardware	Quantity	Size
Carriage bolts, washers, nuts	8	⅜x10½"
	2	⅜x7"
	4	⅜x4"
Lag screws, washers	4	⅜x5½"
Threaded steel rod	1	⅜x13"
Locking nuts, washers	2	⅜"
Galvanized steel pipe	1	¾" (nominal) x8"
Washers	2	3"
Deck screws	4	2½"
	44	3"

Finish

Cutting List

	Quantity	Size
Seat support	1	4x4x9'
Seat blocks	4	4x4x12"
Lower handle blocks	2	4x4x12"
Pivot block	1	4x4x12"
Upper handle blocks	2	4x4x7"
Bumpers	2	4x4x6"
Legs	2	4x4x23¼"
Lateral ground supports	2	2x6x43"
Leg supports	2	2x6x24"
Spacers	2	2x6x7¹³⁄₁₆"
Cross braces	4	2x6x22½"
Hardwood dowels	2	1x13½"

³⁄₈x10¹⁄₂" Carriage Bolts (Recessed)

³⁄₈x7" Carriage Bolts (Recessed)

Align center marks.

Seat Support

Pivot Block

Bumper

Bumper

³⁄₈x5¹⁄₂" Lag Screws (Recessed)

7 Bolt the pivot block to the bottom of the seat support, and attach the bumpers with recessed lag screws.

7 Attach the Pivot Block and Bumpers. The pivot block is attached to the bottom of the seat support, centered exactly between the ends. To center the block, measure and mark the center of the pivot block and the seat support. Then align the marks. Drill two bolt holes with recesses on the bottom. Fasten with ³⁄₈x7-inch carriage bolts. Attach the bumpers with ³⁄₈x5¹⁄₂" recessed lag screws.

Building the Legs

The two legs brace the teeter-totter and support the pivot pipe, which ties the legs to the seat support. The legs and spacers are prepared individually, but are assembled a bit later.

1 Prepare the Posts. The two 23¹⁄₄-inch 4x4 posts are identical. The bottom must be notched to fit over 2x6 supports. To cut the notches, mark a layout line 5¹⁄₂ inches from the bottom. Then, using a tablesaw or circular saw with the blade depth set for a 1¹⁄₂-inch cut, make a series of cuts (kerfs) across the post, as shown. Use a hammer to knock out most of the remaining wood before cleaning out the notch with a chisel.

Miter the top edges of each post as shown. On the notched side of the

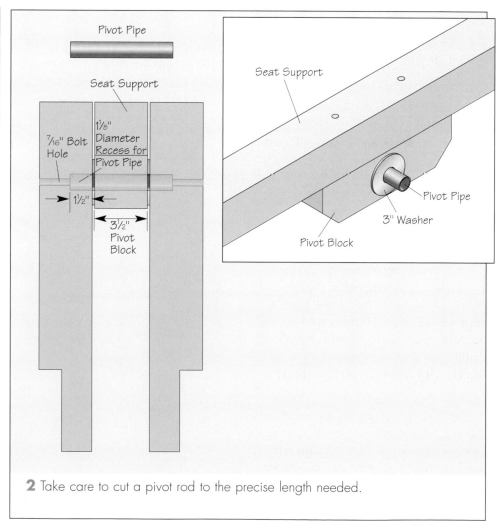

Kerfs from Saw Blade

Wood Chisel

1¹⁄₂"

5¹⁄₂"

1"

1"

5¹⁄₄"

23¹⁄₄"

⁷⁄₁₆" Bolt Hole, with 1¹⁄₈" Diameter Recess on Other Side

4x4 Post

1"

5¹⁄₂"

Notch

1 Notch the two 4x4 posts to fit over the 2x6 horizontal supports.

Pivot Pipe

Seat Support

⁷⁄₁₆" Bolt Hole

1¹⁄₈" Diameter Recess for Pivot Pipe

1¹⁄₂"

3¹⁄₂" Pivot Block

Seat Support

Pivot Pipe

3" Washer

Pivot Block

2 Take care to cut a pivot rod to the precise length needed.

post, drill a 1⅛-inch-diameter hole 1½ inches deep to support the pivot pipe. (If the pipe you are using for your pivot pipe is larger than 1¹⁄₁₆ inch, drill this hole the same diameter as the hole in the pivot block; see above.) Then drill the ⁷⁄₁₆-inch bolt hole, continuing through the post.

2 **Cut the Pivot Pipe.** First, determine the length of pivot pipe you will need. This requires several measurements, as follow: Measure the exact depth of pivot-pipe hole in each post. (If you drilled them exactly as instructed, they should each be 1½ inches deep.) Then measure the combined width of the two 3-inch washers that will be slipped over the pivot pipe; ours, in the illustrations, measure ⁵⁄₁₆-inch. Finally, add the width of the seat support; this should be 3⅓ inches, but check to be sure. Add all of these figures together, and cut the pivot pipe to length (6¹³⁄₁₆ inches in our example).

Cut the pivot pipe from a length of ¾-inch (nominal) galvanized steel pipe; its actual outside diameter will be about 1¹⁄₁₆ inch. Use a hacksaw or a saber saw with a metal-cutting blade. Use a file to smoothen the sharp edges. Slide the pivot pipe into the hole in the pivot block, and place one 3-inch washer on each side.

3 **Make the Leg Assembly.** Center a 24-inch 2x6 support in the notch of each post. Use a framing square to align the edges. Drill two offset bolt holes through each assembly, also drilling recesses on the back side. Fasten with ⅜x4-inch carriage bolts.

Cut two 2x6 spacers, each 7¹³⁄₁₆-inch long. (Note that if your 3-inch washers on the pivot pipe don't have a combined width of ⁵⁄₁₆ inch, you will need to add or subtract the difference from the length of the spacers.)

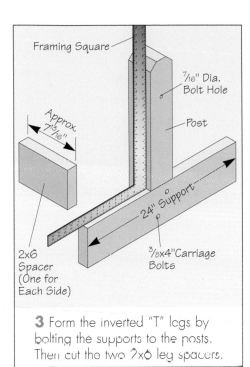

3 Form the inverted "T" legs by bolting the supports to the posts. Then cut the two 2x6 leg spacers.

Assemble the Teeter-Totter

The final steps involve attaching the legs to the seat assembly. With the addition of bracing and supports, the construction will be complete.

1 **Join Legs to Seat Assembly.** With a helper or two, stand the two legs upright. Raising one end of the seat assembly, move its pivot block into position between the legs, and then slide the pivot pipe through the legs and pivot block. Slip the ⅜x13-inch threaded rod through the pivot pipe so that it protrudes equally on both sides of the posts.

Slide washers over the threaded rod on each side. Then loosely fasten

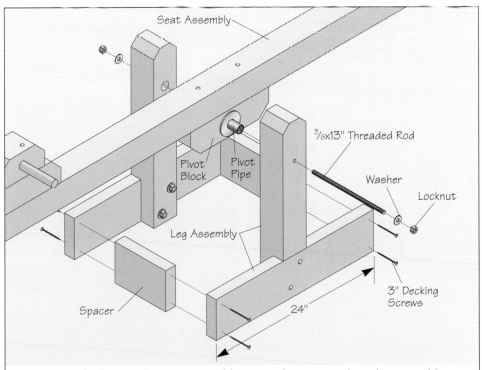

1 To join the legs to the seat assembly, insert the pivot rod on the assembly into the legs. Then secure the assembly with threaded rod and 2x6 spacers.

locknuts on each side (you may need two socket wrenches to tighten the locknuts). Attach the 2x6 spacers between the legs with 3-inch decking screws, as shown on page 137.

Finish tightening the locknuts. But avoid overtightening, which would restrict the movement of the teeter-totter. With a metal-cutting blade, cut off the protruding ends of the threaded rod. Then file off any sharp metal.

2 **Add Bracing.** Cross bracing on each side helps support the legs. Make four braces from 22½-inch 2x6s, cut with 45-degree miters as shown. Check each pair of braces for a proper fit; then trim off the sharp tips. Attach braces to the legs with 3-inch decking screws.

3 **Attach Supports.** To ensure that the teeter-totter won't tip sideways, add two lateral ground supports of 43-inch 2x6s. Miter the top corners on each, and then fasten the supports to the legs with 3-inch decking screws.

Finishing Touches. Round-over all sharp edges and sand the entire teeter-totter. Apply the finish of your choice. You may notice that the rocking motion is a bit stiff immediately after assembly. But with continued use, the stiffness vanishes. Overly tightened locknuts can also restrict the up and down motion.

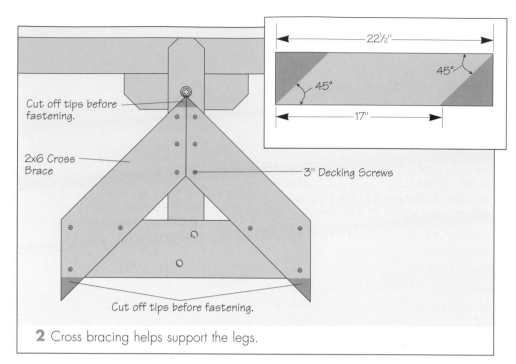

Cut off tips before fastening.

2x6 Cross Brace

3" Decking Screws

Cut off tips before fastening.

22½"

45°   45°

17"

2 Cross bracing helps support the legs.

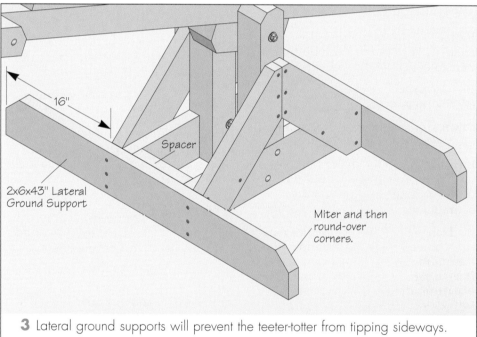

16"

Spacer

2x6x43" Lateral Ground Support

Miter and then round-over corners.

3 Lateral ground supports will prevent the teeter-totter from tipping sideways.

If the threaded rod protrudes after you tighten the locknuts, saw it off with a metal-cutting blade and file the sharp edges smooth.

Glossary

Actual dimensions The exact cross-sectional measurements of a piece of lumber after it has been cut, surfaced, and dried. For example, a 2x4s actual dimensions are 1½x3½ inches.

Air-dried lumber Wood seasoned by exposure to the air without use of artificial heat.

Architectural scale A three-sided ruler, triangular in cross section, with feet to-inch conversion scales that allow you to instantly convert measurements in feet to fractions of an inch in creating "scaled" drawings on paper. See page 13.

Baluster Vertical board or dowel installed between top and bottom rails for safety and decoration.

Bevel An angle cut along the edge or end of a board.

Bevel siding A tapered siding board used as roofing for the Playhouse.

Box nail A slender-shafted nail used when a thicker common nail would otherwise split wood, especially at board ends.

Building code Municipal rules that regulate building practices and procedures. Local building permits are almost always required for new construction or major renovations. Inspections may be required to confirm adherence to codes.

Carriage bolt A round-headed bolt used to fasten wood members face to face. In this book, the threaded part and its nut and washer are recessed in wood whenever the protruding end could otherwise cause injury.

Cleat A small wood piece that supports another wood member.

Concrete At first a semifluid mixture of portland cement, sand (fine aggregate), gravel, or crushed stone that hardens rock solid.

Curing The slow chemical action that hardens concrete. Also describes the air-drying of wood.

Decking Boards nailed to joists to form a deck surface.

Frost line The maximum depth to which soil freezes in winter. Your local building department can provide information of the frost-line depth in your area below which structural supports must be dug to prevent heaving from ice.

Galvanizing Coating a metal with a thin protective layer (e.g., zinc) to prevent rust. Connectors and fasteners should be hot-dipped for outdoor use.

Impact-reducing materials Wood mulch, wood chips, sand, or pea gravel used to soften the landing of a child falling or jumping from any part of a play structure. See page 35.

Joist One of parallel framing members that support a floor or ceiling.

Kickback The forceful backward reaction of a saw whose blade has met with unplanned resistance, such as from a pinching saw kerf.

Lag screw A large hex-head screw used to fasten framing members face to face; typically used to join horizontal framing members to a post.

Lumber grade A label that reflects the lumber's natural growth characteristics (such as knots), defects that result from milling errors, and manufacturing techniques.

Miter joint A joint in which the ends of two boards are cut at equal angles (typically 45 degrees) to form a corner.

Nominal dimensions The identifying dimensions in inches of a piece of lumber (e.g., 2x4), which are larger than the actual dimensions (1½x3½ inches) after milling.

Penny Unit of measurement (abbr. d) for nail length, such as a 10d nail, which is 3 inches long.

Permit A license issued by local building authorities granting permission to do work on your property.

Pier footing A concrete base encasing or attached to a post.

Plumb Vertically straight.

Plywood A wood panel composed of thin wood layers glued together.

Post Vertical framing member (e.g., a 4x4 or 4x6) set in the ground to support a structure.

Posthole digger A hand tool composed of two hinged, shovel-like parts that loosen soil and then grasp it for removal from postholes.

Power auger A gas-powered tool used for drilling into the ground. Often rented by homeowners to dig multiple postholes.

Premixed concrete Bagged, dry cement, sand, and aggregate that is mixed with water for small jobs, such as securing the base of a post.

Pressure-treated lumber Wood that has had preservatives forced into it under pressure to repel rot and insects.

Rail Horizontal member fastened between posts and used for support or as a barrier.

Ready-mix concrete Wet concrete that arrives by truck ready to pour.

Recess A shallow depression drilled in wood to allow the head or threaded end of a through-bolt to be flush with the wood surface.

Rim joist A joist that runs along the outside of the floor platform.

Rip cut A cut made with the grain on a piece of wood.

Shank The part of a screw or nail that is driven into wood.

Site plan A drawing that maps out your house and yard.

Slat A narrow strip of wood.

Wood preservative Liquid chemical applied to wood to prevent decay and insect attacks.

Index

Above-grade surface, 43
American Wood Preservers
    Association standard C17-88, 32
Angles, tools for squaring and
    finding, 22
Angle square, 22
Architect's rule, 13
At-grade surface, 44

Back wall post, attaching, 106
Balance beam, 123–26
    assembling, 125–26
    making supports for, 125
    permanent, 126
    portable, 125–26
Ball swings, 40
Balusters
    calculating gap, 78, 109
    installing
        for central tower, 77–79
        for playhouse, 109–10
    marking and attaching,
        109–10
    spacing, 79
Belt sanders, 26
Bevel gauge, 22
Bevel siding as roofing, 111
Bolt-cutting tools, 27
Bolting the frame, 107–8
Bolts, 37
    for playhouse frame, 107–8
    staggering holes for, 73
Bracing
    diagonal, 81
    for picnic table, 131
    for teeter-totter, 138
Building codes and permits, 18
Bumpers for teeter-totter, 134, 136

Carpenter's level, 21, 107
Carriage bolts, 37, 55–56
Cedar, 30
Central tower, 70
    basic, 82
    deluxe, 67–69
    framing, 73–75
    height of, 68
    marking reference line, 72
    preparing lumber for, 70
    setting the posts, 71–72
    site layout for, 71
    temporary frame in, 71–72
Chain, 38

Chalkline, 20
Chisels, 24
Chromated copper arsenate (CCA), 31
Circular saw, 22–23
    aligning blade to line, 51
    avoiding kickbacks, 49
    choosing blades for, 23–24, 49
    making cut, 51–52
    making square and accurate cuts,
        50–52
    setting blade depth, 50–51
    squaring the blade, 50
    using, 49
Clamps, 27
Cleats, installing, 76
Clips and hooks, 38
Clothing and grooming, 25
Collisions, minimizing chances of, 15
Combination square, 22
Concrete, 34, 47–49
    estimating needs, 48
    mixing, 49
    power mixing, 47
Concrete piers, pouring, 47
Consumer Product Safety
Commission. See also Safety
    on baluster gap, 77, 78–79, 109
    on impact-reducing material, 35
    on pressure-treated lumber, 32
    safety standards of, for public
        playgrounds, 14
    on trapeze bars and exercise
        rings, 89
Contracting for postholes, 20
Covered sandboxes, 116, 117–19
Crowning of wood, 53
Cutting plywood, 52–53
Cypress, 30

Decay-resistant woods, 30
Decking
    installing, 53–54
    for central tower, 76
    for playhouse, 108–9
Deluxe central tower, 67–69
Diagonal bracing, 81
Dowels, 38
    attach dowels, in monkey bars,
        95–96
Drill
    hand, 24
    power, 24
Drill bits, 24

Drilling tools, 24
Durability, 59
Dust masks, 25

Easement, 18
Edges, avoiding sharp, 16
Environmental factors, 10–11, 32
Exercise bars, 89, 90
Eye bolts, 37, 87–88
    drilling holes for, 87
Eye protectors, 25

Fall hazards, reducing, 14, 34–35
Finishing, 58–61
    Kids' Playland, 81
    picnic table, 131
    playhouses, 112
    play structures, 60
    sandboxes, 119
Footprint with safety zones, 11–12, 67
Foot protectors, 25
Framing square, 22

General maintenance, 61
Grass in impact-reduction, 34–35
Gravel as base for playhouse, 102
Ground-fault circuit interrupter
    (GFCI), 25
Guardrail, plywood for, 33
Gymnastic equipment, 40

Hammers, 27
Handbars, 112
Hand brace, 24
Hand drill, 24
Handle blocks for teeter-totter, 134,
    135
Hand protectors, 25
Hand sander, 26
Hand saw, 24
Hand tools, 137
Hardware, 27, 36–38
    bolts, 37
    chain, 38
    clips and hooks, 38
    nails, 36
    recessing, 73
    rungs, 38
    screws, 36–37
    swing, 40
Hardwoods, 29
Hazards, reducing, 14–17
Head entrapment, preventing, 16

Health issues, 32
Hearing protectors, 25
Heartwood, 30, 31
Hex-head bolts, 37
Hybrid grade option, 44
Hydration, 34

Impact-reducing material, 35–36, 61,
    81, 89
    general guidelines, 35–36
    pea gravel, 35
    sand, 35
    wood mulch and chips, 35

KDAT, 31
Kickback, 49
Kids' Playland, 68–82
    building and installing stair, 79
    central tower in, 70–75
    cutting and treating post tops, 80
    deluxe central tower in, 67–69
    finishing touches, 81
    installing balusters, 77–79
    installing decking, 76
    installing ladder to the upper
        level, 80
    installing lower-level rung, 79–80
    installing middle- and upper-
        level rails, 76
    installing slide, 80
    sliding pole, 81

Ladder, installing, 80
Lag bolts, 37
Lag screws, 55–56
Landscape timbers, sandbox from,
    120
Lattice roofing, 111
Launch pad, creating, for monkey bar,
    97
Leveling, tools for, 21–22
Line level, 22
Lumber, 29–30
    for balance beam, 125
    buying, 32–33
    cedar, 30
    for central tower, 70
    cypress, 30
    decay-resistant, 30
    defects in, 29
    delivery of, 34
    drying, 34
    grades, 32–33
    hardwoods, 29
    life expectancy of, 30
    nominal versus actual dimensions
        in, 32, 33
    for playhouse, 101, 103
    plywood, 33
    pressure-treated, 59, 311–32

redwood, 30
ripping, 52
softwoods, 29
storing, 34, 42
working with crooked, 53

Maintenance, 58–61
    of playhouse, 112
    of sandbox, 117
Marking tools, 20
Measuring tools, 20
Monkey bar, 67, 92–97
    assembling, 96–97
    attaching rails and dowels, 95–96
    building, 94–96
    checking post spacing, 94–95
    creating launch pad for, 97
    cutting dowels, 95
    drilling dowel holes, 95
    laying out postholes, 93–94
    preparing posts, 94
    preparing rails, 95
    sloping, 93

Nails, 36
    avoiding splitting with, 55
    driving, 54–55
Nail sets, 27

Overnailing, 54

Paints, 59
Pea gravel, 35
Pencils, 20
Phillips-head screws, 37
Picnic table, 127–31
    assembling frame, 129
    assembling seats and tops, 130
    attaching braces, 131
    smoothing and finishing, 131
Pinch points, avoiding, 16
Pivot block for teeter-totter, 134, 136
Plane, 24
Planning and design, 8–18
    building codes and permits, 18
    choosing site, 10–12
    preparing site plan, 13–14
    reducing hazards, 14–17
    utilities, 18
Play accessories, 39–40
    gymnastic equipment, 40
    slides, 39–40
    swings, 39, 40
Playhouse, 101–13
    attaching back wall post, 106
    bolting the frame, 107–8
    building side walls, 104–5
    checking plumb and square, 107
    completing roof frame, 106–7
    customizing, 113
    final touches, 112–13

framing front wall, 105
installing balusters, 109–10
installing decking, 108–9
preparing lumber, 103
raising side walls, 105
roofing, 110–12
site preparation, 102–3
trimming rafter tails, 112
Playsite layout, 44–46
    checking for square, 47
    finding rough dimensions, 45
    marking posthole locations, 45–46
    playhouse in, 102
    sandbox in, 116–17
    stringing lines, 45
    swing frame in, 84, 85
Play structures
    applying finish, 60
    construction and maintenance, 17
    durability of, 59
    paints for, 59
    preparing surface, 60
    reasons for building yourself, 14
    renovating, 61
    sealers for, 59
    stains for, 59
Plumb bob, 20
Plywood, 33
    cutting, 52–53
Plywood roofing, 111–12
Polyethylene rope, 39
Posthole digger, 20
Postholes
    adding gravel to, 47
    digging, 47
    laying out, for monkey bar, 93–94
    marking locations for, 45–46
    tools for digging, 20
Posts
    cutting and treating tops, 80
    preparing, 94
    setting, 46–47
Power auger, 20
Power drill, 24
Power miter saw, 24
Power sander, 26
Power tools, 137
Pressure-treated lumber, 31–32, 59
    avoiding splitting, 54–55
    for playhouse, 101
Protrusions, avoiding, 16

Quadrille paper, 13

Radial arm saw, 24
Rafter tails, trimming, 112
Rails
    attaching, for monkey bars, 95–96
    installing middle- and upper-
        level for central tower, 77

Rebar, 43
Recessing hardware, 73
Redwood, 30
    grades of, 30
Reference line, marking, 72
Renovating, 61
Restrictive covenants, 18
Ripping lumber, 52
Roof frame
    for covered sandbox, 117–18
    for playhouse, 106–7
Roofing, 110–12
    bevel siding as, 111
    lattice, 111
    plywood, 111–12
    slat, 111
Roof sheathing, plywood for, 33
Rope, 39
Router, 26
Routing wood edges, 56–57
Rungs, 38
    installing lower-level, 79–80

Saber saw, 24
Safety. See also Consumer Safety
    Product Commission
    avoiding edges, protusions, and
        pinch points, 16
    and baluster gap, 77, 78–79
    creating spacing for, 10
    diagonal bracing in, 81
    ensuring safer sliding, 16–17
    equipment for, 25
    and footprint with safety zones,
        11–12, 67
    handbars in, 112
    impact-reducing material in,
        35–36, 61, 81, 89
    and kickback from circular saw,
        49
    and maintenance, 17
    minimizing chances of collisions,
        15
    preventing head entrapment, 16
    reducing fall impacts, 34–35
    swing beam in, 84
Sand, 35
    choosing, for sandbox, 117
Sandboxes, 114–22
    attaching seats, 119, 121
    basic, 121
    building, 118, 121
    choosing sand for, 117
    covering, 116, 117–19
    design options, 116
    finishing roof for, 119
    joining roof frame and box, 118
    maintaining, 117
    site for, 116–17
    sunken, 122
    timber, 120

Sanding tools, 26
Sapwood, 30, 31
Saw
    circular, 22–24
    hand, 24
    larger, 24
    saber, 24
Sawhorses, 43
Screws, 36–37
    driving, 54–55
Sealers, 59
Seat blocks for teeter-totter, 134, 135
SEL STR, 33
Shock protector, 25
S-hooks, 38
Site, choosing, 10–12
Site plan, preparing, 13–14
Site preparation for playhouse, 102
Slat roofing, 111
Slides, 39–40
    ensuring safer, 16–17
    installing, 80
Sliding pole, 81
Snapping the line, 20
Softwoods, 29
Splitting, avoiding, 54–55
Spring-loaded connector clips, 38, 40
Square
    angle, 22
    combination, 22
    framing, 22
Square-head screws, 37
Stains, 59
Stairs, building and installing, 79
Stand-alone projects
    balance beam, 123–26
    picnic table, 127–31
    playhouse, 101–13
    sandboxes, 114–22
    swing frame, 90
    teeter-totter, 132–38
Sunken sandbox, 122
Surface, preparing, 60
Swing beam, 67
Swing discs, 40
Swing frame, 83–91
    basics, 84, 85
    installing beam, 88
    installing swings, 88
    preparing beam, 86–88
    preparing swing posts, 86
    safety precautions, 84
    for single swing, 91
    site layout, 84
    stand-alone, 90
    swing substitutes, 89
Swings, 39, 40
    hardware for, 40
    minimizing chances of collision
        with, 15
    seat choice for, 84

Synthetic rope, 39

Table, picnic, 127–31
Table saw, 24
Tape measure, 20
T-bevel, 22
Teeter-totter, 132–38
    assembling, 137–38
    building legs, 136–37
    building seat, 134–36
    bumpers for, 134, 136
    handle blocks for, 134, 135
    pivot blocks for, 134, 136
    seat blocks for, 134, 135
Timber sandbox, 120
Tire swings, 40, 89
Tool holders, 27
Tools, 19–40
    for digging postholes, 20
    drilling, 24
    hand, 137
    of layout, 44
    for leveling, 21–22
    measuring and marking, 20
    power, 137
    routing, 26
    safety, 25
    sanding, 26
    for squaring and finding angles,
        22
    wood-cutting, 22–24
Trapeze bars, 40, 89, 90
Trapeze rings, 40
Turn fasteners, 27

Undernailing, 54
Utilities, 18
    consideration of, in site plan, 13
Utility knife, 27
UV blockers, 59

Wall construction for playhouse,
    104–5
Walls, playhouse
    attaching back wall post, 106
    building side, 104–5
    framing front wall, 105
    raising side, 105
Water level, 21–22, 57
Water repellents, 59
Wood. See Lumber
Wood-cutting tools, 22–24
Wood edges, routing, 56–57
Wood mulch and chips, 35
Work site
    laying out, 44–46
    preparing, 43–44
    setting up, 42
Work surface, 27

Metric Conversion Tables

Lumber

Sizes: Metric cross sections are so close to their nearest U.S. sizes, as noted at right, that for most purposes they may be considered equivalents.

Lengths: Metric lengths are based on a 300mm module, which is slightly shorter in length than an U.S. foot. It will, therefore, be important to check your requirements accurately to the nearest inch and consult the table below to find the metric length required.

Areas: The metric area is a square meter. Use the following conversion factor when converting from U.S. data: 100 sq. feet = 9.29 sq. meters.

Metric Lengths

Meters	Equivalent Feet and Inches
1.8m	5' 10⅞"
2.1m	6' 10⅝"
2.4m	7' 10½"
2.7m	8' 10¼"
3.0m	9' 10⅛"
3.3m	10' 9⅞"
3.6m	11' 9¾"
3.9m	12' 9½"
4.2m	13' 9⅜"
4.5m	14' 9⅛"
4.8m	15' 9"
5.1m	16' 8¾"
5.4m	17' 8⅝"
5.7m	18' 8⅜"
6.0m	19' 8¼"
6.3m	20' 8"
6.6m	21' 7⅞"
6.9m	22' 7⅝"
7.2m	23' 7½"
7.5m	24' 7¼"
7.8m	25' 7⅛"

Dimensions are based on 1m = 3.28 feet, or 1 foot = 0.3048m

Metric Sizes (Shown before Nearest U.S. Equivalent)

Millimeters	Inches	Millimeters	Inches
16 x 75	⅝ x 3	44 x 150	1¾ x 6
16 x 100	⅝ x 4	44 x 175	1¾ x 7
16 x 125	⅝ x 5	44 x 200	1¾ x 8
16 x 150	⅝ x 6	44 x 225	1¾ x 9
19 x 75	¾ x 3	44 x 250	1¾ x 10
19 x 100	¾ x 4	44 x 300	1¾ x 12
19 x 125	¾ x 5	50 x 75	2 x 3
19 x 150	¾ x 6	50 x 100	2 x 4
22 x 75	⅞ x 3	50 x 125	2 x 5
22 x 100	⅞ x 4	50 x 150	2 x 6
22 x 125	⅞ x 5	50 x 175	2 x 7
22 x 150	⅞ x 6	50 x 200	2 x 8
25 x 75	1 x 3	50 x 225	2 x 9
25 x 100	1 x 4	50 x 250	2 x 10
25 x 125	1 x 5	50 x 300	2 x 12
25 x 150	1 x 6	63 x 100	2½ x 4
25 x 175	1 x 7	63 x 125	2½ x 5
25 x 200	1 x 8	63 x 150	2½ x 6
25 x 225	1 x 9	63 x 175	2½ x 7
25 x 250	1 x 10	63 x 200	2½ x 8
25 x 300	1 x 12	63 x 225	2½ x 9
32 x 75	1¼ x 3	75 x 100	3 x 4
32 x 100	1¼ x 4	75 x 125	3 x 5
32 x 125	1¼ x 5	75 x 150	3 x 6
32 x 150	1¼ x 6	75 x 175	3 x 7
32 x 175	1¼ x 7	75 x 200	3 x 8
32 x 200	1¼ x 8	75 x 225	3 x 9
32 x 225	1¼ x 9	75 x 250	3 x 10
32 x 250	1¼ x 10	75 x 300	3 x 12
32 x 300	1¼ x 12	100 x 100	4 x 4
38 x 75	1½ x 3	100 x 150	4 x 6
38 x 100	1½ x 4	100 x 200	4 x 8
38 x 125	1½ x 5	100 x 250	4 x 10
38 x 150	1½ x 6	100 x 300	4 x 12
38 x 175	1½ x 7	150 x 150	6 x 6
38 x 200	1½ x 8	150 x 200	6 x 8
38 x 225	1½ x 9	150 x 300	6 x 12
44 x 75	1¾ x 3	200 x 200	8 x 8
44 x 100	1¾ x 4	250 x 250	10 x 10
44 x 125	1¾ x 5	300 x 300	12 x 12

Dimensions are based on 1 inch = 25mm

Have a home improvement, decorating, or gardening project? Look for these and other fine **Creative Homeowner books** wherever books are sold.

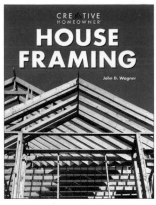

Designed to walk you through the framing basics. Over 400 illustrations. 240 pp.; 8¹/₂"×10⁷/₈"
BOOK #: 277655

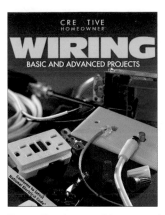

Best-selling house-wiring manual. Over 700 color photos and illustrations. 256 pp.; 8¹/₂"×10⁷/₈"
BOOK #: 277049

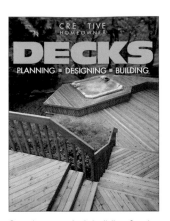

Step-by-step deck building for the novice. Over 500 color illustrations. 176 pp.; 8¹/₂"×10⁷/₈"
BOOK #: 277162

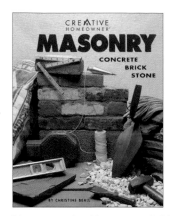

How to work with concrete brick and stone. Over 500 Illustrations. 176 pp.; 8¹/₂"×10⁷/₈"
BOOK #: 277106

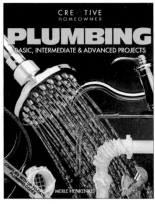

The complete manual for plumbing projects. Over 750 color photos and illustrations. 272 pp.; 8¹/₂"×10⁷/₈"
BOOK #: 278210

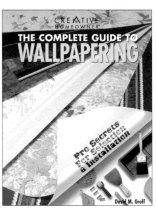

Proven tips for hanging and removing wallpaper. Over 250 illustrations. 144 pp.; 8¹/₂"×10⁷/₈"
BOOK #: 278910

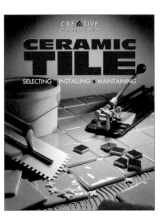

Complete DIY tile instruction. Over 150 color photos and illustrations. 160 pp.; 8¹/₂"×10⁷/₈"
BOOK #: 277524

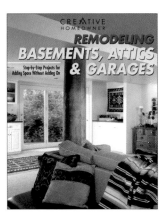

How to convert unused space into useful living area. 570 illustrations. 192 pp.; 8¹/₂"×10⁷/₈"
BOOK #: 277680

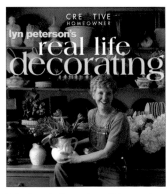

Interior designer Lyn Peterson's easy-to-live-with decorating ideas. Over 350 photos. 304 pp.; 9"×10"
BOOK #: 279382

Original ideas for decorating and organizing kid's rooms. Over 200 color photos. 176 pp.; 9"×10"
BOOK #: 279473

A comprehensive tool for the aspiring water gardener. Over 400 color photos. 208 pp.; 9"×10"
BOOK #: 274452

An impressive guide to garden design and plant selection. More than 600 color photos. 320 pp.; 9"×10"
BOOK #: 274615

For more information, and to order direct, call 800-631-7795; in New Jersey 201-934-7100.
Please visit our Web site at www.creativehomeowner.com